Finitude

Self, the United States,

the human species

by

Anton Androv

Dedicated to my 90-year old cousin Arlene who has spent her life promoting spirituality.

Acknowledgements

This work would not be possible without the typing assistance from Lynne and Dee. Cover art and production assistance was provide by Ann Marie. Review, editing and publishing was accomplished through the tireless efforts of Mark. In addition, Mark has been a trusted advisor in all matters, technical and literary. This is the " "Finitude" team; they were great and I thank them for all of their extraordinary efforts.

Content

Preface

When you reach end of life, there is a tendency to reflect on your life, on what you accomplished, your meaning. There is a similar tendency to want to pass on useful information to those who remain. When my father died, my brother and I found handwritten notes on all of the mechanical systems in his house and summer cottage. They gave details on how to deal with each. They were incredibly helpful to us in taking care of his estate. He apparently knew that he was dying. I am supposed to die by year end (It is October).

This book is my attempt at instructions on how to get the planet back to civility and sustainability. This book is my "note" on issues to readers. It is a call to action based upon my life experiences. All lives are the product of experiences and most learning and knowledge comes from the experiences of others.

I spent my life in materials engineering and my engineering training and manufacturing experience shades everything written in this book. This book is heavy on criticism of USA's government. I spent 50 years of my outside-of-work life involved with local politics. I was a county and town committee person and political committees run American politics. I have observed elected government officials at the "lawn-sign" level. I psychoanalyzed every politician that I worked with. I learned their abilities, their motivations, and their faults. The pool of candidates for all elective offices in the USA come from the political committees and that, in my opinion, is the root cause of our incontrovertible decline in democracy. We are being governed by the least of our numbers and that is the biggest problem that I bequeath to remaining Americans.

Thus, the purpose of this book is to present lifetime observations on critical life issues and to make recommendations on how to fix things.

The objective of the book is to tell readers how to deal with self, your internal sustainability, to try to prolong America's fragile democracy, and to prolong the human race which has veered from its self-preservation instincts.

This book is my legacy; it is my: "Well God, I tried to do something about the mess on Earth" statement at final judgment. I just hope that God gives partial credit for effort.

AA

Prologue

This book was intended to be an expose of about 70 years of mistreatment of USA's Great Lakes. They represent 20% of the planet's freshwater and all that water is being compromised because of what the USA and Canada governments have done to the system. In 1950 or thereabouts they built dams and canals that control the outflow of the Great Lakes to the Atlantic Ocean. They also built canal locks which allow ships from all over the world to sail into the Great Lakes. The problem that needs to be brought to the attention of the entire world is that the St. Lawrence Seaway, the name given to this misadventure, is the source of more than 150 invasive species that are attacking the viability of the water for drinking and other uses. Also, the dam built as part of the Seaway project has caused the water in the last Great Lake, Lake Ontario, to rise to the point of destroying all of the natural beaches that are supposed to cleanse the water. Flooding from the dam causes billions of dollars in damage every time that there is a high-water event. The St. Lawrence Seaway project is a threat to a significant part of the world's freshwater. This book was originally intended as calling for action to prevent further damage to what's left of the Great Lakes. However, it evolved into a book on life issues and philosophies to address these issues.

Who am I?

I am a research engineer working in the field of engineering materials and I am at end of life because of medical problems (cancer). It has been a life of business, travel, pleasure, companionship, friendships, acquaintances, and most of all, learning. I lived the Great American dream: humble beginnings and working to achieve my life goal which was to become a technical expert. I worked in manufacturing for my entire 60-year working career. Most of my career was spent at what was once the largest factory in one place in the world. At one time there were more than 30,000 employees at the site. The plant where I worked had every resource known to man for manufacturing and research. We even had entomologists that I used to use to identify unusual bugs I found around my home. I was married with two sons when I started at this company, and we settled into being a typical manufacturing family. Back then (early 60's), if you landed a job with a big manufacturing company you were set for life. Everybody made good money; we had completely free medical coverage for the family, and my company offered many fringe benefits and a generous pension: Nirvana.

As a materials engineer, if a production machine shut down because of a broken part, I would determine the cause of the failure and propose a material or treatment change to prevent recurrence. If a chemical tank corroded through, I would do research and establish corrosion rates of candidate materials and recommend a substitute material. I did the same type of analysis the parts that wore out. This latter activity became my specialty: friction, wear, lubrication, and erosion which is now called tribology. Within five years at the company, I was attending conferences, doing friction and wear research, and writing papers for presentation and publication. Eventually I became the company expert and thus achieved my life goal of becoming a technical expert in an engineering field. I became a fellow in three technical societies and in 1979 I authored a materials engineering college textbook that evolved into nine additions and is still selling well in 2020, I wrote other technical books along the way, but the product of my life's work in tribology culminated with the publication of a seminal book on "Tribomaterials" in 2021. I've completed my life's work; I have had financial success; I have had the happiest life that one could ask for: a good job, a devoted wife, three sons in engineering, good friends, and I have religious beliefs take care all mental health issues.

So why write a book on finitude?

I was lucky enough to spend my entire working life, now 64 years, in one city. I worked five years in the auto industry, 38 years in the chemical process industry, and 19 years at my son's tribotesting company. I am technical director, but I mostly work on fundamental tribology problems of my choosing. Shortly after I finished graduate school in another state, my wife's parents purchased a cottage on a bay off of Lake Ontario, which is the last of the Great Lakes as water from them flows to the ocean. For the next 15 years or so, our family spent every summer on Lake Ontario. The lake level was always stable and predictable with one high water event in 1973. This event wiped out all beaches, marinas, countless cottages, and significant municipal facilities on all 760 miles of shoreline. In 1982 we bought our own cottage on Lake Ontario, but only used it as a rental property. In 1990, the boys were long gone, and we decided to build my wife's dream house on Lake Ontario. We tore down the cottage and built a 4000 square-foot house with all the features that my wife wanted. She fought the architect tooth and nail to get her special house right. It is at this point; that I started to investigate lake levels and research the behavior to Great Lakes. It was then that I discovered what may be one of the world's greatest environmental problems; the destruction of the Great Lakes caused by the building of the dam and locks at the outlet of the Great Lakes to the ocean.

Chapter one in this book presents the details of the problem, but basically, in the 1950's New York City had a Parks Director who loved grandiose projects and he made damming of the Great Lakes one of them. He had great political power and an open checkbook full of government money. He sold the US and Canada the St. Lawrence Seaway project that dammed Lake Ontario for hydro power and built locks to allow ocean-going ships to reach the center of the USA. The US and Canadian government were glad to go along with this project since the hydro dam would supply a steady stream of money from the sale of electricity. The environmental problems that resulted were the flooding of 760 miles of shoreline from high water and environmental havoc caused by more than 150 alien aquatic species into all of the five Great Lakes from inbound ships carrying bilge water from all over the world.

Since 1990, I have been attending public hearings on Lake Ontario water levels and I have boxes of full of data on Great Lakes water level and quality issues. I intended to eventually write an expose on what has been going on with the water in the Great Lakes since the Massena dam was built in the 1950's. However, almost 10 years ago my beloved wife of 50 years died. I addressed my grief by attending a philosophy school one night a week. The school dealt with achieving inner peace, social order, dealing with others, and the

4

meaning of life. In seven years of engineering school, I only had to take one humanities course, so studying and learning these sorts of things was new to me. However, I thought that these kinds of teachings would benefit everyone. I decided to write a book about life issues and make my Lake Ontario research a chapter on environmental issues and rest of the book would be my philosophy school's teachings on critical life issues.

In my writing, I decided to take some DVD courses in philosophy as taught in various universities. One of these background courses, one on molecular biology, changed my book plans significantly. I took the course to learn more about DNA, RNA, and the genetic aspects of behavior, but to my astonishment, the professor in his final lecture stated that the human race is well on its way to extinction. I wrote this into this book, because on examining the basis of his statement, it is incontrovertible that many countries have fertility rates below replacement. Extinction of the human species appears imminent. He stated the facts regarding extinction. The human species will become extinct if they do not reproduce in sufficient numbers; this critical number is 2.1 offspring per female. It takes 2.1 children, because one may be a boy and the 0.1 percent arises because some offspring will die at birth. The world is currently under 2.4 offspring per female down from 5.5 about 50 years ago. Some very large countries like China have fertility rates of 1.4. USA, Korea, Japan, and some European countries are similarly around 1.5 offspring per female, well below replacement rate and the 2.1 extinction threshold.

I did not do significant research on extinction, but I have contacted extinction experts and they all agree with my professor's fertility numbers, and my personal observations. Most people have a smaller family size than when I was young. There is declining enrollment in schools in the USA; there are a few kids in public spaces; in my average neighborhood of 80 homes, there are far less children running around that should be.

The reasons for declining fertility are well known. Up to the 1960 or so, the world never had fool-proof birth control systems. The ones now in place are very effective. In addition, Abortion became legal in the USA in 1973 and many other countries followed suit. However, what may have had a more significant, was that the worldwide media have been denigration motherhood as a profession. Women are now encouraged to-be- astronauts, politicians, CEOs, and everything, but stay at home moms. Unfortunately, stay at home mom has become the lowest form of female life in media accounts.

Needless to say, denigration of motherhood is absurd, but this is the way that civilizations around the world have evolved in my lifetime. Some of the anti-motherhood effort is economically fueled. Couples can usually have more pleasures and possessions if both parents work. Extinction took over as more important than the life issues that I was going to address in this book. Therefore, now there are some extinction thoughts in each chapter.

Thus, the purpose of this book is to bring awareness to the issues of life including the issues of finitude of self (one's self), finitude of what is left of the USA's democracy, and finitude of the human species.

Objective of this book

This book offers up solutions to the world's most vexing problems with the hope that some of the solutions are adopted and world betterment progresses. This book is for the world, all countries, and all peoples. It is written for people of all educational backgrounds. It is not a reference work, but a decision guide that is the product of a lifetime of observation.

Many of the book suggestions for betterment must ultimately be accomplished by country and world leaders. For example, the book proposes changes to the St. Lawrence Seaway. The changes suggested can only be done by international treaty. However, leaders of the world must eventually adopt the philosophies of their citizens, or they will be voted or forced out. We hope to reach both the governors as well as the governed. We are seeking to make life more meaningful for all.

What is a meaningful life?

There is a Native American legend that when you die, the value of your life on earth can be measured by the number of people who were happier because you were born. We modify that legend not to emphasize number. You do not have to have many people glad that you were born, but rather a meaningful life is one that produces betterment, wherever, and whomever, your life touches. You made the most of what you were given, and your way of life improved the world and inspired others to do the same.

This book was about 60 percent completed when I learned about our pending extinction. I never thought about the human race becoming extinct. We have been around for possibly hundreds of thousands of years. However, I believe that my biology professor was right in his prediction. He called human extinction "finitude" and that is where the title of this book came from. It means that something has limits. There is a start and an end. It is finite.

This book has an additional objective, besides a happy life with sustainable species, people need to rethink their priorities. Why worry about global warming when there will not be any humans to burn fossil fuels? The human species must think about sustainability. All the things going on in the USA in 2020 under the "woke" philosophy are incommensurate with survival of the human species. The woke people are against marriage, family, peace, order, work, laws of nature etc. I asked a young person to define" woke" to me. She said we are "aware". This awareness seems to mean chaos in all matters. Motherhood is not high on their agenda. Thus, an added objective of this book is to counter the woke culture with truth and reason.

Format

This book is written by a practicing engineer. I am of retirement age, but I never retired because I just moved on to working at my son's business and continued working on what I spent my life working on: tribology research. Going to my son's testing lab six days a week to work on problems of my choosing is not taxing. Thus, because I am still a practicing engineer, the style of this book is somewhat like an engineering report. Sorry. Here is the format:

8

1. Problem
2. Fix related to the problem
3. Conclusions and the philosophy or basis for each conclusion
4. Suggestions for improvement

Concerns addressed

Chapter 1 discusses environmental issues, but mostly related to the Great Lakes, Chapter 2 is about the categorization of people by skin coloration; Chapter 3 is on peace and order in society, Chapter 4 on knowledge, work, and learning; Chapter 5 is on technology; Chapter 6 is on government (mostly USA's). Chapter 7 is on communication; Chapter 8 is on health; Chapter 9 is on economics, the reality of the current economic situation; Chapter 10 on Self, addresses how individuals can cope with their situation and achieve a meaningful life.

These subjects cover most of the significant issues that one will encounter in life. I have been exposed to many philosophies on these subjects, and I married them into to what I believe to be a practical philosophy of life. Life is best when lived happy. This is a personal observation, but lots of others agree. The philosophies presented here will guide you in the direction of lifetime happiness.

However, I offer this caveat, this book will make some readers angry, some may want to do the book and me harm. I'm very critical of many misguided US government activities mostly my criticisms are based upon my 50 years of activity in one of America's two political parties. Petition problems and how these political parties' function is stressing America's democracy. Hopefully this book will bring systemic problems to light so that they can be addressed.

Chapter 1
The Environment

Nothing else matters if our environment cannot sustain life

HarleyRuft

I started swimming in Lake Ontario during the war (World War II). My mother used to take my brother, sister, and me to a private beach on Lake Ontario owned by a hot-dog stand. The hot- dog stand was no more than two feet above the lake level which never changed during the ten years or so that we went there. The beach was all fine sand that sloped gently to the water. The hot-dog stand was a short run from the water – maybe 200 feet.

The beach and the hot-dog stand were always the same. Sometimes the lake had breakers, sometimes not. There were no lake problems. It was the main summer attraction for the City of Rochester. The city's official beach was called "Ontario Beach Park" and it was about two miles east of the beach that my mother took us to. She took us to the private beach because there were no crowds like those at Ontario Beach Park. On a hot summer day, it would be difficult to find a spot to lay down a blanket and stake out a "beach claim". There was plenty of room at the hot-dog stand, but you had to buy a hot-dog to use it. There were no signs stating this, but people always bought food from the stand because it was good and the right thing to do.

Lake Ontario was stable, clean, and wonderful.

In 1950 or 1951 my brother and I bought a 15-foot sailboat for $100 dollars from our paper-route money, and we decided to teach ourselves to sail on Lake Ontario. The boat needed rehab so first we learned how to caulk a wood-planked boat with caulking compound and caulking string. You rubbed the string in the putty-like compound and forced it into the 1/8- to 3/16-inch-wide gap between planks. We also learned how to recanvas a deck and what the rigging should look like. Our father lived most of his life on farms, then in the city, so he knew nothing about boats or sailing. We got our instructions on how to fix our boat from the boating store that sold us the repair materials. This store was about five miles from our house in the inner city and my brother and I would ride our bikes there. There were two early-twenty brothers who tended the store for their father, and they told us all of the countless things we needed to know to get our boat sea-worthy and ready to sail.

When the boat was fixed "good-enough", my brother and I rode our bikes to marinas on a bay off Lake Ontario to see what it would cost to rent a slip for our boat. The first marina that we asked about renting a slip was called Jim's Marina. There was a woman tending the shop (Jim's wife) and when we inquired about keeping our boat there, she said that she had a slip available, and it would cost ten dollars for the season. We of course said, "We'll take it".

We later learned that adults paid at least $100. We were fortunate that Jim's wife had a soft spot for two skinny kids from the inner city. My father knew somebody who owned a boat trailer, and he got our boat to Jim's Marina. We did not have a trailer. The people we bought the boat from delivered it to our back yard where we did the necessary repairs.

At launch, we quickly noticed that our caulking job did not make the boat leak-free. In fact, it leaked badly. The marina owner, Jim, suggested tying the boat in swampy shallows at the marina until the wood planks swelled and made the caulking tight. So, we tied up in the shallows like Jim suggested and the boat proceeded to sink. We waited several days before returning to the marina. Then we went down and pumped her out. She no longer leaked. We put her in the slip, figured out the standing rigging and sailed her. We sailed her every day during summer vacation through high school and then not so much when we started college out of state. We did not have summers free. However, for the five or six years that we sailed on Irondequoit Bay there was no perceptible fluctuation in lake level all summer. Irondequoit Bay was open to Lake Ontario, and it was at lake level. Jim never changed dock level during the summer or winter.

We used to occasionally come down to the bay in the winter to play hockey at the marina. The space between the piers formed a nice hockey rink. The ice did not seem to be much lower from the dock surface. There was no emptying of the lake in the winter.

The water level in Lake Ontario never varied more than plus or minus a foot from the mean from 1951 to 1957-based upon personal recollection

My brother and I went to college away from Lake Ontario. We sold the sailboat while in college and sailed briefly on one of the Finger Lakes. I returned to living on Lake Ontario in 1963. My wife and I and our oldest son spent two summers on Lake Superior in the early sixties, and we never noticed any seasonal change in the level of Lake Superior, but with 300 or so inches of snow in a typical winter it was not easy to discern the winter-summer variation in the level of Lake Superior.

Our return to Lake Ontario was in the form of a summer cottage on Sodus Bay which is a large bay of Lake Ontario that used to be a port for huge lake freighters. They carried coal.

The summer-time variation in lake level was not noticeable. I would put the dock in in May and take it out on Labor Day weekend. There may have been a foot of lake level change from May through September, but not enough to warrant a change in dock height. I moored my 28-foot sailboat about 300 feet from shore because it drew about three feet and that is all the water depth that we had at the end our 60 foot dock. This was the situation from 1963 to 1973 – nothing changed in lake level throughout the summer.

> Lake Ontario levels were stable
> and changed very little during the
> boating seasons from 1963 to 1973

We stayed at the "cottage" every weekend from 1963 to 1987. We sailed every day that it was possible, so we were on intimate terms with lake levels. The first departure of Lake Ontario's level from the carefree conditions occurred in 1973. Lake Ontario rose and rose and rose. That year we had scheduled a cruise to Canada with other sailboats from our yacht club. We found docks awash everyplace that we went. Canadian customs wharfs were under water, docks were under water. The lake went wild.

Government entities started to harden the south shore of Lake Ontario with large rocks, everybody on Sodus Bay had to do something. Our cottage was on the side of a hill and the cottage itself was about twenty feet higher than the water, but our forty feet of beach was under water. We were offered $10,000 by some government agency to harden our shore so my father-in-law opted for a breakwall out of pressure-treated wood and telephone poles. When the wall was built, we had many truckloads of dirt brought in to raise what used to be our natural beach, two feet. The lake level never went back to what it was. The 1973 high water event permanently (today) raised the level of Lake Ontario at least one foot, possibly two.

It may have started as a weather-related lake rise, but since the lake level could now be controlled by the dam at Massena, the people who operate the dam, kept the lake permanently higher. None of us shore-line property owners suspected foul play, but at that time we did not recognize what was going on; we did not know the meaning of "Massena". We could not imagine that our government would do anything to knowingly harm the lake or the environment and the shoreline residents. We were naïve, to say the least.

1973 – 1990
In 1982 we purchased a small cottage on the shore of Lake Ontario in Rochester (Greece). The cottage was built in 1939. It was situated about 60 feet from the water and was

protected by three-foot-high rip-rap (large stones) placed along the shore during the 1973 high-water event. We had about twenty feet of sand beach outside of the rip-rap. We rented the cottage year-round, and nothing changed in lake level from 1982 to 1990. In 1990 we tore down the cottage and built a large new home where the cottage stood. At that time, we tried to improve protection from high water by improving the existing rip-rap. After months of waiting and hundreds of hours spent negotiating with the five government organizations that control Lake Ontario building in our area (Greece) we were given permission to add ten 1000-pound rocks to the existing rip-rap. Then we got a citation from the DEC because they counted eleven rocks. They let us "go" when we proved that one of the 1000-pound rocks broke in two during crane installation. We learned that it is a waste of time to try and get permits to improve shoreline protection when no water crisis exists.

In 1990 we started to monitor the level of Lake Ontario daily using the data published in the local newspaper. In 1991, the Army Corps changed the datum. They said that the earth was changing shape and that a water level of, for example, 247 feet above sea level was now 246 feet above sea level. In 1991 the Army Corps changed the datum for sea level measurement and thus, permanently raised the level of Lake Ontario one foot.

Shoreline residents who recognized this as the environmental crime that it was questioned Army Corps officials and they produced a report in double-talk justifying their action. I personally challenged this action and the accuracy of the Corps Lake level measurements. I got to see the lake level measuring system used in a small concrete block building about a mile from my lakefront home. Inside this 8' x 8' building was a metal shelf with a pipe coming out of it. They measured down to the surface of the water in the pipe and told me that the metal pipe in the building connected to a horizontal pipe that went along the lake bottom out one mile. I asked how they established the height of this line above the pipe in the little block building above sea level. They told me that they surveyed from the sea a thousand miles to the east to the block building. I asked what the tolerance was on this reference line, and I was told there was none. Survey readings are absolute. Lake level data from USA government regulators are not audited for correctness.

Thus, not only did the Army Corps dishonestly raise the level of Lake Ontario with a "datum change", the establishment of their lake level information is questionable because there is no non-government organization in a position to question any lake level measurements. They could be completely false, and nobody has authority over the US Army to question their results. Congressional representatives could question Army Corps data, but they do not.

The 1993 high water event

In the spring of 1993, the level of Lake Ontario rose to the point of shoreline flooding and damage. Many fifty-year-old cottages were simply washed away. We were given sandbags and we had to fill them ourselves from government sand piles. I remember inventing a sandbag scooper from a plastic pipe and boat cleat. The sandbaggers came up with different devices to speed up the filling of sandbags. Tying off the bags was definitely the most time-consuming part of the process. Mostly I used the sandbags to backup my wooden sea walls. Sandbags even up to eighty pounds are thrown about by lake waves when we get an onshore wind in excess of 20 mph. The force of six-foot-high waves cresting on a shoreline structure is more than sandbags can endure. I survived the 1993 event by boarding up the windows on the lake side of the house for three months and by raising my breakwall height by two feet with rock-filled gabions. The gabions I used look like boxes with a lid made from chain link fence. I used gabions that were 2' x 4' x 8'. I brought in trucks carrying 40,000 pounds of "surge" which were football-size limestone rocks. The surge cost $7/ton and the gabions cost about $120 each. You put the gabion in place when the lake is calm. Fill it with 6000 pounds of rock then wire the lid shut with really heavy wire that was supplied with each gabion.

The gabions were wired to each other to make a continuous wall of rocks in cages. The gabions "quenched" the big waves. They worked well, but people who could not physically put them in place and fill them could not use them. There were no gabion-filling companies. My neighbors on both sides hired people to build concrete barriers, but neither got professional jobs. Both really did not keep the waves out.

After 1993

The 1993 high water event brought attention to the "Plan" that allegedly controlled the lake levels. On paper, there is a treaty with Canada that established a six-member commission called the International Joint Commission or IJC. Three commissioners are appointed by the President of the USA and three by the Governor General of Canada. The USA members have always been people who raised a lot of money for the standing president when he was running for office. They are one-hundred percent patronage jobs. The IJC commissioner job is the best job in America. You get "ambassador" status, a salary of $172,000/year and your duties are to attend two meetings a year.

The Canadians are similarly fundraisers for MP elections, and they are patronage jobs. The commissioners on paper agree to controls on bodies of water that are shared by the two countries. When the dam was built in Massena, NY, a plan was established by the IJC called plan 1954 or something like that and it gave the IJC the control of the level of Lake Ontario. This is the only Great Lake where the outflow can be significantly controlled. There is a dam at Massena, NY that stretches across the Saint Lawrence River to stop outflow and direct flow to hydroelectric turbines. The first IJC plan for Lake Ontario set triggers for opening and closing the dam. When the lake got close to flooding shoreline structures the plan called for opening the dam. The Massena Dam is not owned by the IJC. It is jointly owned by the NYS Power Authority (NYSPA) and their Canadian equivalent. They sell the power and decide what to do with the profits. The governor of NY appoints members to the NYS Power Authority and thus really controls actions of the Power Authority.

Thus, the IJC supposedly controls the lake level, but they do not have access to the "valve", only the NYSPA can control the valve. I have tried unsuccessfully for years to identify the person who turns the valve and really controls the lake level.

Nobody but the dam operators really know who opens and closes the valve?

The Lake Ontario Problem

I have lived on the shore of Lake Ontario for more than sixty years and I have witnessed its degradation from a recreational treasure and essential source of potable water source treasure to a putrefying mill pond. It is full of pollutants and invasive species brought by making this world treasure into a ship canal and hydroelectric dam reservoir.

The Facts- In the 1950's the State of New York and the New York City Parks director/Robert Mores decided that it would be a good idea to dam Lake Ontario and produce a continuing source of revenue for New York State's leadership. New York State would get into the power generation business even though there were many private electricity generation companies in the state at the time. Of course, there were no environmental impact studies because the government does not need such things. They only apply to the private sector.

In any case, the dam was built in 1963 without approval of any citizens in the US and Canada. The dam belongs half to Canada and half to the US and is operated by the New York State Power Authority. The NYSPA consists of appointees of the Governor of NY, and he essentially controls the use of the billions of dollars that the USA gets from its half of the dam.

Part of the dam project was creation of the Saint Lawrence Seaway. This is a 370-mile series of locks and waterways intended to raise ocean-going ships from sea level to Lake Ontario's height of about 250 feet above sea level.

The Seaway is also operated by an authority type of entity and the maintenance costs/profits are shared by a treaty between the US and Canada.

A shipping conglomerate called the St. Lawrence Seaway Development Corporation (SLSDC) was created in 1954 "by statute". They lobby and promote the use of Lake Ontario as a shipping channel.

Superimposed on the NYSPA and the SLSDC is the IJC which allegedly controls the water level in US/Canada border waters. They seemed to be involved with the treaty with Canada that initiated the construction, but today they control the water levels in all of the Great Lakes, and they are the root cause of the greatest environmental crime of my lifetime: the ever-rising water level of Lake Ontario.

Another party complicit in the environmental crime is the Army Corps of Engineers (Army Corps). They are a shadow organization of the US government. Few Americans have ever seen an "Army Corps" engineer, but they are the official source of water level data. I have been to hundreds of water-level meetings at different locations around Lake Ontario and in only one did I see a person in an army uniform in attendance. Their role in the destruction of Lake Ontario may be the most significant. They "cook the books" on water level. When the dam was built in 1953 the water level was immediately raised in Lake Ontario by one foot. In 1991 when I built a new house on Lake Ontario, they raised the water level in Lake Ontario another foot and called it a change in datum. Each foot of water level increase takes away from twenty to forty feet of shoreline over the 760 miles of Lake Ontario shoreline. Where structures exist, the rising water used wave action to erode and eventually remove these structures.

A final fact about the problem is that in 2016 and 2019 all structures on the shore of Lake Ontario were significantly damaged by the high-water levels mandated by the IJC Plan 2014. The assessed value of the damaged property may be hundreds of billions of dollars and the damage was recorded as billions, but it is much more because the shoreline properties are partially washed away. The State of New York gave about $50,000 to every shoreline resident who claimed damage, but steel seawalls cost $1000 to $2000 dollars per foot of shoreline so $50,000 does not even pay for seawall repairs much less destroyed homes.

The Cause of the Problem - Building of the dam at Massena, NY should never have been permitted. Citizens of either country were not consulted. There was absolutely no consideration given to the effect of the dam and the rising water level it produced on the ecology of the Great Lakes or on the residential, industrial and municipal infrastructures on the shoreline. The dam, the seaway, the entire mess was the "cause celebre" of one person: Robert Moses. His official job was Parks Commissioner or something like that in New York City, but he was really more powerful than the governor of New York in the State of New York and in Washington D.C. There was no control on his appetite for building monuments to himself.

As an aside, he built the New York State Thruway, one of the longest superhighways in the country (NYC to Buffalo), about 350 miles. It is still a premier interstate, but it is now contaminated beyond belief by corruption. But that is another story. Robert Moses also built the Lake Ontario State Parkway. However, it is a highway to nowhere. I use a portion of it almost every day. His plan was to build a four-lane expressway (he called it a parkway) to follow the shore of Lake Ontario from Rochester to Buffalo, a distance of about 70 miles.

It was started in the 1960's and there were many environmental challenges, like Braddock's' Bay was in the way, Long Pond was in the way, many houses were in the way. No problem. Fill in the wetlands and move the houses. About forty miles of the parkway were completed before the money dried up. Today only about ten miles of the parkway is maintained (by NYS) and the other thirty miles are in progressive disrepair. A unique feature of the parkway is a height of only eleven feet for bridges that go over the parkway. Legend has it that Robert Moses put these low bridges across the road to prevent buses from using the road to bring inner-city children to the lakeside parks along the parkway. To this day this highway is closed to commercial vehicles and buses.

So, this is the nature of Robert Moses. He gets an idea to build something. He had the power and connections to do it, so he does it. He erects another self-monument like the St. Lawrence Seaway and the Dam at Massena.

Now, back to the flooding, the local newspaper publishes the Lake Ontario water level every day. I built a new house on the shoreline of Lake Ontario in 1990 and I immediately started to plot the lake level daily. My living room floor was built at 252 feet above sea level. The road that my house is situated on has an elevation of 250 feet and Lake Ontario for the past one hundred years cycled in height above sea level from 244 to 246 feet above sea level. I felt safe with my sea wall with a height of 251 feet above sea level. How naive I was. In 1991 as I previously mentioned the Army Corps raised the level of Lake Ontario another foot because they changed the datum. So when the lake was at a height of 246 feet above sea level they declared that now it was 245 feet above sea level so they can raise the water level to 246 and say this is normal.

Why "They" Want High Water - Shipping interests want ever higher water because they can bring in deeper draft ships: more depth, more cargo, more revenue. The seaway charges ships for locks by the ton, the weight of its cargo. The Moses–Saunders Dam at Massena produces more power when the lake level is higher. The governments of Ontario and New York State reap the profits of power generation. The governor of New York wants ever higher water levels: more power, more discretionary income for his or her whims.

The Army Corps is the official water- level height measurer and as evidenced by most every Army Corps water contract project that I have observed, they are insulated from the actual problem. They only work from afar. Like many government organizations, they exist as vestiges of organizations that are useful during wars and disasters, but not so useful in peacetime. They do not have to produce a success. The levees that they built on the Mississippi do not work and they continue to do these kinds of projects. They flooded New Orleans, and nothing happened. They destroyed the ecosystem in Central Florida with a 40-foot-high berm hundreds of miles long and putrefied the gulf and Atlantic beaches and nothing happened.

So, I have been dealing with lake levels for about fifty years and in all of that time I never encountered a person from the Army Corps that offered help of any sort in dealing with shoreline flooding. Also, since I started keeping daily records on Lake Ontario water levels, I had to fill countless sandbags in 1993, 2017 and 2019 to try and mitigate massive flooding. All of these floods I attributed to the dam at Massena and the IJC who allegedly control the dam outflow.

Who is the IJC? - The IJC was established in 1913 by the USA and Canada to deal with water issues on the bodies of water that are shared by the USA and Canada. There may be some shared waters out west, but the biggest shared water is the Great Lakes and the St. Lawrence River. There are six commissioners on the IJC appointed in the USA by the President and three from Canada appointed the Governor General of Canada. All are political patronage jobs. I have met a number of the IJC Commissioners at public hearings on lake levels. Some take the job seriously. Some have no ability to deal with technical issues and barely know where the Great Lakes are located. Some are from landlocked US farm states.

The latest water level plan put forth by the IJC Plan 2014 was the last nail in the coffin for Lake Ontario. It is a recipe for the destruction of the lake and all shoreline structures. It could not be any worse environmentally. Shoreline damages produced by the 2017 and 2019 floods are probably in the trillions of dollars, but so far only about two billion have been paid out by New York State. Each shoreline resident could write a book about their damage and sand bagging efforts. And the IJC continues to have no concern about the shoreline damage or the ecological damage to the Great Lakes. They cannot be sued. They do not have to produce any benefits to citizens of either country. They are not elected. The organization exists as payback for successful fund raisers for presidential or prime minister elections. The IJC caters to the wishes of the power generation and shipping interests. They have the lobbyists. Citizens and municipalities have none.

What about the environment? Incredibly, the bogus "environmental" groups the Nature Conservancy and their ilk have been hoodwinked by the bird watchers to believe that periodic flooding of the Lake Ontario watershed is good for making swamps that birds like. The bird-brained people do not have sufficient intellect to understand that erosion is forever. If you raise the level of the lake one foot, it takes away forty feet of shoreline (times 760 miles) and the land is lost forever. It does not come back when the water goes down. The lack of understanding of technical concepts is the root cause of the danger of groups like the Audubon Society and the Nature Conservancy.

Erosion Control

Tribology is my business. It is the art and science associated with interacting surfaces – friction, wear, erosion, and lubrication. The lab that I work in does erosion testing on a regular basis in specific areas of erosion such as slurry and solid-particle erosion. We also deal with droplet erosion and cavitation. There are machines such as jet engines that are very susceptible to solid particle erosion; aircraft are very susceptible to droplet erosion as in flying through a rain field at supersonic speed. We have tests to rank materials for resistance to these kinds of erosion. When I moved to the shores of Lake Ontario, I learned about wave erosion. We had a cottage on a bay off Lake Ontario for 25 years and never had a shoreline erosion problem because the bay was protected by bluffs on the sides and a sandbar at the lake entrance. Waves were small. Wave erosion was not a problem. Things are different on Lake Ontario. The lake is 173 miles long and 50 miles wide. Wave size is a function of the fetch, the open water distance that a wind can blow across to build waves. Waves routinely build to ten feet when winds are maintained at 30 to 40 mph. This happens several times a year. Waves can be no higher than the water depth. Waves ten feet high cannot exist on a beach where the water gradually gets shallower. However, since the Massena dam raised the lake level at least two feet many shoreline properties lost the beaches that kept waves small. I soon learned that I needed a four-foot-high rock wall to keep waves from knocking down my shoreline house. That was in 1990. Now that rock wall is seven feet high. You cannot see the lake.

If a Lake Ontario shoreline is not hardened with a structure or a beach, wave erosion will destroy anything that is not concrete, ledge rock, or armored with rocks that weigh at least 10,000 pounds. However, even rocks this large will be easily moved if they are not interlocked.

The 2017 and 2019 floods on Lake Ontario prompted lots of erosion control efforts on the part of municipalities and shoreline residents. Unfortunately, government at local, state and federal levels mandate permits for shoreline hardening and the only type of hardening that they allow is placement of natural rocks and interlocking steel piling and both do not work long term. Unless the rocks are fixed to each other wave action moves 10,000-pound rocks around like they were beach balls. Interlocking steel piling driven in several feet works for a decade or two, but it either rusts away or is undermined on the water side from receding waves digging a trench where the piling is driven into sand. A concrete wall works fine, but concrete is not allowed allegedly because it hurts fish even though the fish that are stocked in Lake Ontario are raised in concrete pools in hatcheries that surround the lake.

In other words, high water means certain shoreline erosion because the regulators will not permit effective protective structures that will resist wave erosion. As an example, in 2012 or so the federal government decided to harden the end of a bay near my house. Over a period of three years, they brought in truck after truck of 10,000-pound rocks and sand and built a 1300-foot barrier island at the bay, at a cost of 10 million tax dollars.

At this writing, the millions of dollars of sand that was brought in are gone as is the barrier island. The 10,000-pound rocks are still around, mostly under water. This project was initiated by the Audubon Society to bring in the black tern which kills all vegetation with toxic feces. The designers were from landlocked Midwest US states who know absolutely nothing about Lake Ontario and of course, this was also the case with the St Lawrence Seaway, the people who live on and know the lake were not consulted and have no say.

Erosion control standards - In the 1990's when I was learning about lake erosion firsthand, I joined an international technical society of soil and rock to see what kind of erosion technology was "out there". Much to my surprise there was a very large organization with hundreds of standard tests and guides pertaining to soil and rock. Many were on erosion control. For example, there are tests to determine the susceptibility of rocks to freeze/thaw cycles. This pertains to all of the "armor-stone" dictated by the Department of Environmental Conservation (DEC). Big rocks are the only erosion control methods allowed by US regulators, but only certain rocks can withstand freeze/thaw cycles. There is a standard test for this. However, when I built my lake house, I got a permit to bring in huge rocks for a breakwall, but nobody told me about disintegration of rocks in freeze/thaw and many of my ten 1,000-pound rocks split apart after several winter freeze cycles. In the 1990's the shoreline regulators were recommending gabions and driving two- or three-inch diameter pipes several inches apart and putting what is called "surge" behind the pipes. Most of these erosion control techniques are great in that they "quench" waves to prevent erosion. However, neither method works because of freeze/thaw disintegration of the rocks that come from nearby limestone quarries. When I had my big lake front house, I used to do a few miles along the shore in my kayak before going to work. Each year I witnessed the rock levels decline in gabions and behind the steel pipe walls. At the start there may have been four feet of surge behind the steel pipes. After one winter it may be only three feet of stone, then two, then next to nothing. The football-size rocks would split into smaller ones and the smaller ones would split. Eventually the rock became small enough to be washed away through the pipe of chain link fence openings. Of course, the regulators who mandated this type of erosion control did not know that these methods do not work since they know nothing about Lake Ontario and never listen to shoreline dwellers.

Sandbags for erosion control - Almost every night on the TV news somebody is sandbagging someplace to arrest flooding. Sandbags can arrest erosion on quiet waters. One of my sons lives in Alexandria, Virginia, and their waterfront routinely floods, and they try to dam the water out of the Starbucks on the shore of the Potomac, but it never works. However, the Potomac is quiet enough in this area that sandbags prevent shoreline erosion. On Lake Ontario they are simply washed away. Here is why: at most a sandbag will weigh sixty pounds. When it is submerged in water it weighs 36 pounds. The force that is needed to slide a submerged sandbag sitting on another sandbag is the submerged bag's weight times the coefficient of friction of a polypropylene plastic bag on itself. This coefficient is usually about 0.3. So, to wash away a sixty-pound sandbag it takes 36 pounds x .3 = 10.8 pounds. Of course, a four-foot-high wave collapsing can produce a lot more than ten pounds of force.

However, I also own property on a pond off of Lake Ontario and the waves never get more than about eighteen inches high. Sandbags are effective in erosion control on this body of water if they do not degrade from the ultraviolet rays of sunlight. They do. When flooding occurs in the USA,

FEMA,(the Federal Emergency Management Agency) and the Army Reserve, usually distribute sand and sandbags to residents of the flooding area.

In 1993 I filled thousands of green government-supplied sandbags to back-up my stone break wall. They are still intact. In 2017 and 2019 the government-supplied bags became white, and bags placed during the spring floods were disintegrated by the next spring. They are made from who knows what plastic and most unpigmented plastics are readily damaged by the ultraviolet radiation in sunlight. It causes chain scission. So, all the efforts in filling and placing sandbags are wasted because the USA buys these bags from some foreign country that knows nothing about ultraviolet stabilization of plastics. Today on the TV news people were shown filling these white government sandbags in Melbourne, Florida in anticipation of a hurricane. Their bags will surely fall apart like mine have.

I tried to do something in 2017 about the disintegrating sandbags. I got mine (filled) from my town's Public Works Department (some days soldiers would load my truck). I contacted the Town Supervisor and told him about the disintegration of bags and said that I need to track down the person in the US government who is buying these bags and tell him or her to find another vendor. The Town Supervisor said he gets the bags from the county. I sent a letter to the County Manager and asked where she got the bags from. She thought they came from the State. I sent a letter to the state governor as a freedom of information request. I got no answer. I sent a letter to the US General Accounting Office and received no answer. This spring the town put more white bags on top of the ones that fell apart from sunlight

31

exposure. Last year during hurricane season they were selling the white sandbags at the Home Depot store near my Florida house. I bought some to see where they were made:

Made in India, AFM 7548/2018
14x26" UV White Color
Bale No. 530

The label suggests at least recognition of ultraviolet radiation (UV) as a factor relating to these bags, but it did not say "UV–resistant". The bags appear to be made from unpigmented polypropylene (PP) and as materials engineer, I know that this material will rapidly degrade in sunlight. Pigment is used to make the plastic opaque, and this helps to protect PP from UV degradation. I buy green sandbags from a US supplier, and I have seen no deterioration after twenty years exposure on the shores of Lake Ontario.

So, the sandbag situation in the USA is: all sandbags supplied by any US government agency will rapidly disintegrate in sunlight spilling their contents.

Nothing can be done about this situation and thousands if not millions of Americans across the country are wasting their time filling and placing defective sandbags. Nothing can be done about this problem and related erosion problems because government officials do not need to respond to citizens and elected officials are insulated by staff such that citizen input never reaches the government official. Try writing to your US congressman or senator. Sometimes you will get a phone call from a staff person, but never will your petition reach the intended elected official.

I wrote to President Obama about an incredible election fraud issue. Months later I received a letter form the President promoting his Obama-care plan. No mention of the subject of my letter. I suspect that my two US senators have no idea where Lake Ontario is. I cannot count how many of my letters the senior senator has ignored. He has only one concern: election for life. Unfortunately, it appears to me that this is the goal of most members of Congress.

Erosion control measures that work - In the 2019 flood, some neighbors banded together to lease an inflatable wave barrier to protect their homes from destruction during the highest month of the 2019 flooding. The barrier is a fabric/rubber tube that fills with water from a garden hose. The erosion barriers come in different sizes, but in this case, theirs' was about thirty inches in diameter and about four hundred feet long. They were really forty-foot sections joined at joints. These barriers can be purchased or leased. In my neighbors' instance, they put the water barrier on top of their regular breakwalls and it went across their properties. In Florida I came across these tubes eight feet in diameter and thousands of feet long. They were being used to protect a high use hotel that was only about forty feet from the Gulf of Mexico.

Of course, water-filled tubes work as a temporary bandage, but cannot be considered as a long-term solution. The fabric/rubber material of construction will fail from sunlight degradation or puncture. Rubber of some type is the basis of the water-filled tubes and very few rubbers can tolerate sunlight long-term.

Natural shoreline erosion controls include all sorts of sand-loving plants that grow on ocean beach dunes. The Florida Keys are protected from extinction by a tangled mess of two-to-four-inch diameter branches that make up mangrove trees. It is an indigenous weed in Florida and regulators made it illegal to cut it down. Many people own a million-dollar beach house on the Gulf of Mexico and cannot see the ocean because the mangrove trees grow as dense as the Berlin wall and about twenty-foot high. But it works in protecting against erosion. The tangled branches quench waves.

Some shoreline municipalities use sand dunes to try to minimize erosion. Sand quickly becomes suspended in water by wave action. This sand/water slurry moves with currents and huge dunes, even islands, can disappear in a single storm event. However, governments spend millions or billions in bringing sand back to depleted beaches. In Galveston I watched scores of huge earth movers attempt to restore a beach that lost hundreds of feet of width at a sand depth of up to twenty feet and a beach length of miles.

My daily kayak paddles along the shores of Lake Ontario demonstrated to me that one of the greatest beach erosion protections is trees, the bigger the better. I witnessed lakefront lots with no beach trees lose twenty feet of shore in a year compared to zero for the houses with trees. It was dramatic. When I built my wife's lakefront dream house we dug the basement by hand. The property contained several huge poplar trees. Every shovel of dirt in the basement excavation contained thousands of tiny roots coming from the large trees. This is how trees and related vegetation prevent water erosion. Tree roots form like a "steel wool" of roots. These fine roots trap the soil particles under erosion conditions. Unfortunately, almost all of my lakefront neighbors cut down their big shoreline trees to get better views. They unwittingly lost their best erosion protection.

The Case for the Dam and Seaway

If one performs a web search on the St. Lawrence Seaway or the Massena Dam, the internet ejaculates all sorts of grandiose benefits of these projects:

"The Great Lakes/Seaway system is a key supply chain for the world's third largest economy."

According to a special report compiled by BMO Capital Markets (whoever they are), the eight states and two provinces that border the Great Lake/St Lawrence Seaway System generate an immense economic impact within North America.
- GDP of US $6 trillion (2017 est)
- Population 108 million (2017)
- 30% of Canada/US economic activity
- 52 million jobs
- More than half of Canada/US cross-border

Over 200 million tons of cargo travel on the Saint Lawrence Seaway yearly. The cargo money supports:

46 billion US
59 billion Canada
in economic activity:
18 billion US wages
23 billion Canada wages

329,000 jobs
(Source: an ad agency)

Related "facts"
- distance from ocean to Duluth, MN = 2324 miles
- 25% of seaway travel is to overseas ports
- locks can accommodate ships to 766 ft long 80 ft wide
- locking through takes 45 minutes (each one took two hours when I locked through on my brother's boat)
- each ship can carry 30,000 metric tons
- ships carry grain, dry bulk, iron ore, general cargo
- cargo tolls apply to each lock
- Major ports:
     Thunder Bay
     Duluth
     Milwaukee
     Chicago
     Detroit
     Toledo
     Cleveland
     Port Colborne
     Toronto
     Ogdensburg

The Saint Lawrence Seaway Development Corporation (SLSDC) is the claimant of the preceding. They are a wholly owned government corporation within the US Department of Transportation created in 1954. They are responsible for operations and maintenance of the US portion of the seaway between Montreal and Lake Erie with headquarters in Washington, D.C. and have 144 full-time employees: 2019 income 18 million US, expenses 20 Million US.

The Dam at Massena - The Saint Lawrence River has many islands in the area by the city of Massena, New York. The river had rapids in this area and building locks for the seaway quelled the rapids and also created the opportunity to dam the remaining portion of the river. All water from the Great Lakes would have to flow through the lock and dam spillways. The dam was built. It cost about 400 million dollars and about two- thirds of the cost was paid by Canada. The dam was filled with thirty-two turbines to generate electricity. One half of the turbines were owned by Canada, the other half by the USA.

The part of the dam owned by the USA was taken over by the New York State Power Authority (NYSPA) which is a "public benefit corporation" that existed since 1932 in New York State. It was created by then governor, Franklin Roosevelt. A "public benefit corporation" can be created by any government entity for most any purpose. In the city where I live in New York State an authority was established to build a baseball stadium. Another was created to build a soccer stadium. An authority is a legal entity with a board of directors. They issue bonds to build the project and pay the bond debt from proceeds from the project. When the projects do not work out, like our soccer stadium, the related authority becomes silent and the general public is never informed of the remedy, but it is usually taxpayers who are on the hook for repaying the bonds.

One underlying purpose of authorities is to provide employment for politicians who are voted from office and need a job. Authority board members or director jobs normally pay about $150,000 and the work is to go to some meetings and discuss activities.

On paper, the NYSPA operates three or four hydro projects, a few other power plants and a power transmission system. Since about 2015, or so, the NYSPA also acquired the 150 year and 300-mile-long Erie Canal. New York State authorities are controlled by the governor of New York. He appoints people from his or her party as directors so essentially the governor has complete control over authorities. The NYSPA makes money from the sale of power. In 2018 they had about one billion in profits that can be used for any purpose at the discretion of the governor. The Erie Canal was a burden to whatever government entity that it belonged to so the Power Authority "bought it". One year they bought the State of New York prisons to resolve some financial matter.

Thus, the dam built to harness the flow of water from the Great Lakes provided substantial continuing source of discretionary income for the governor of the State of New York.

The Dam Water Problem - To the average person, dams with hydro plants seems like a good idea- free electricity. Similarly, the Saint Lawrence Seaway sounded like a good idea. Ocean ships can reach the middle of the United States. So, what's the problem? We'll do the seaway first.

38

The negative feature that is number one and why it should never have been built is it has allowed over a 150 invasive species to enter what was twenty percent of the world's fresh water. The sea lamprey destroyed commercial fishing. The giant Asian carp have completely destroyed even recreation boating in some areas of the middle of the USA. The fish are huge and get annoyed by boat motors and jump into boats injuring occupants. They eat vegetation intended for useful fish. However, the zebra mussel is the master of physical damage. The mussels are only a few centimeters in diameter, but they grow on any and all things submerged in the water. They plug municipal water intakes. They cover boat bottoms. They cover rocks. Then they die and get washed up on beaches and get broken up. The shells are razor sharp. What were once sand beaches are now "shards of glass" beaches. And they smell.

Several times a year my Lake Ontario house used to get inundated with huge piles of zebra mussel shells. The mound was typically one meter high, two meters wide and the width of my lot was twenty meters. One year I tried to use them for mulch around plants and they killed the plants. In my opinion, these invasive species brought in by foreign ships have already dealt a death blow to the Great Lakes and these ships are bringing new alien species with each ship.

All environmental groups in the USA have tried to do something about this problem to no avail. The invasive species are in the bilge water taken in in foreign ports and pumped out in the Great Lakes. Of course, there is a no-discharge law, but that is absurd. Nobody on the ship knows how infected their bilge water is with bad creatures and the USA and Canada have no way of enforcing no-discharge and no way of inspecting bilge water.

The SLSW annual report of 2019 said that their staff inspected 238 "tanks" on ships in 2019. Mongolian perch vampires from Liberian ships do not live-in ship tanks, they live in bilge water and head flush water which is not inspected. The SLSW annual report did not say how many ships they inspected. It could have been only three. Each ship had 77 tanks. The report curiously neglected to say how many ships used the seaway in 2019. It did say that 25% of the ships were from foreign ports.

I tried unsuccessfully (using the Freedom of Information Act) to get the number of ships that locked through Eisenhower lock which all in-bound ships must use. Nobody will spill the beans. There is an app for smart phones that lets a person track all ships in transit at any time on the Great Lakes. I did it one day and counted twenty for the entire Great Lakes. It takes about two hours to lock through a big lock (based upon the time I locked through – (out-bound) on my brother's sailboat. So, on a good day maybe five ships can transit into the seaway. The Seaway is open eight months a year. So the number of ships coming into the seaway from the outside world could be 8/day x 7 x 32 weeks equals about 2000 ships/year.

What are the economics? I could not get any information from seaway government entities on fees received per year, but one website showed fees to be about $1/ton and the ships can carry thousands of tons. One SLSDC report stated that the seaway carries over 200 million tons per year. So, if they charge $1 per ton, they bring in $200 million per year. Then why did the seaway SLSDC lose two million dollars as shown in their 2019 annual report?

I believe that the SLSDC loses money each year on shipping and the maintenance costs are largely born by US and Canada's governments. There are fifteen locks in the Seaway; thirteen locks are Canadian and two belong to the USA.

However, the economics of the Seaway is meaningless compared to the environmental damage produced by the invasive species. Bringing in invasive species makes allowing foreign ships into the seaway or returning US/Canadian ships an absurdity. As I write this, I am not allowed to fly from my home in New York to my winter home in Florida. I will get arrested and quarantined since I am from a state with currently high pandemic infection rate. But a 760-foot ship full of water toxins of every sort can travel to the center of the country. There is no factor on earth that can justify ships from outside the Great Lakes entering the Great Lakes. Millions of people depend on the Great Lakes for life-giving water and a single ship can render twenty percent of the planet's fresh water undrinkable.

As another comment on the ecological impact of the Seaway: in 1995 or thereabouts I received a phone call from my brother who lives on Lake Huron north of Detroit. He wanted me to help him "lock-through" the Welland Canal, the part of the Seaway that bypasses Niagara Falls (six locks 210 feet of height). He was bringing his 37-foot sailboat to the ocean and needed help locking-through. I drove seventy miles to meet him at the canal entrance. You need help handling the lines and fending off the jagged rock walls that are the sides of the locks. Pleasure boats usually carry bales of straw to use as fenders since the lock wall will destroy conventional rubber fenders. The way that locking-through works is you receive orders for the lockmaster on your ship phone. He or she tells you what to do. Pleasure boats cannot go through alone. We had a lockmate of a 600-foot Polish freighter. The locks are 760 feet long, so we did not have much room. At the first lock we were told to lie up behind the freighter and the water went down about two feet. I wondered why my brother needed me. While we sat waiting after the drop, I learned why I was needed. Out of nowhere a 700-foot long 50-foot-high ship rose up. The next lock was a 40-foot drop. I was on the bow with a line to a lock tether; my brother was on the stern and his wife fended us off as we lowered forty feet in about ten minutes. I learned why he needed me. There were six locks, and it took us eight hours. The locks are engineering marvels. However, I observed another environmental negative of these wonders. The deck of our Polish lockmate was piled thirty feet high with garbage from the ships crew. Foreign ships are not allowed to offload any garbage. Of course, once they are back on the open ocean, there is nobody watching to make sure that they bring their garbage back to their home port.

Hydro - Shipping needs high water, but it is hydro that is causing the unconscionable destruction of the last of the Great Lakes: Lake Ontario. Lake Ontario is the lowest Great Lake, currently at 246.5 feet above sea level. The next upstream lake is Lake Erie and because of rapid rise at Niagara Falls, it is about one hundred feet higher than Lake Erie. High water on Lake Ontario only affects Lake Ontario shoreline, all 760 miles of it. I say that the NYSPA is the root cause of the flooding of Lake Ontario shoreline because they physically control the Massena dam. The dam is off limits to all but operators because of terrorist concerns. Nobody but the crew of twenty or so employees who control the dam have access to control of the gates. The IJC may issue "orders" on control levels, but nobody but dam operators can open or close the gates of the dam. Nobody but the dam operators know what the outflow is and there are no third parties to audit dam outflow. The dam operators want ever rising water and we riparians are the witnesses. My estimate of properties affected by dam-produced flooding is as follows:

Number of properties = 760 miles of shore x a house every 100 feet = 402,864
Estimate of the value of flooded shoreline houses = 402,864 x 200,000 =
2.1 billion dollars.

In 2019 New York State offered $50,000 to every flooded house on the south shore of Lake Ontario:

402,864 x 50,000 = 10 billion dollars

They actually only gave out maybe 500 million dollars, but the costs of these floods to property owners is probably in the ten-billion-dollar range.

In 2019, the New York State Power Authority made about a billion dollars based upon their annual report. The dam at Massena has sixteen generators (US made) that generate about 900,000 Kwh. Assuming electricity is selling for ten cents per Kwh, gross income from Massena could produce about 800 million dollars in income per year.

However, about sixty percent of the electricity output from the Massena Dam is relegated to a private aluminum smelter at a charged rate known only to the governor of NY. He is currently bartering low-cost electricity to the smelter as an incentive to keep the smelter open and keep hundreds of smelter jobs. The smelter is losing money and the owner wants to shut the facility down. So, the governor of New York State is part of destroying Lake Ontario and its shoreline structures to garner votes from Massena smelter employees.

In summary, the Saint Lawrence Seaway and its related power dam have destroyed Lake Ontario from many ecological aspects; what can the world do about it? Some suggestions:

1. The IJC should immediately ban ships that visited non-USA, non-Canadian ports from entering the seaway.
2. The IJC needs to mandate that all hydro projects on in the Great Lakes operate such that they never raise or lower lake levels outside of the one-hundred-year average.
3. The New York State Power Authority should be sold to a private entity and the political aspects of the authority, like municipal electric companies, buying troubled government authorities, and the like, need to be relegated back to the State of New York legislature.

4. The members of the IJC should all be licensed professional engineers with appropriate credentials in environmental sustainability, not political fund raisers. They should be the best of the best technically and ethically.

Conclusions- the environment

This account of the worst environmental disaster of my lifetime should serve as an example of how a good sounding "infrastructure project" can produce cataclysmic environmental results. People and governments should ponder the long-term environmental effects of every major and every minor action. There are risks to every project, both ways. There are risks in not doing them and risks in doing them. When unintended consequences start to occur, projects need to sunset.

As I write this, we are in a global pandemic that is likely to not end until eighty percent of the world gets the virus and herd immunity occurs. From one to ten percent of the world's population will die from it. It is analogous to the Saint Lawrence Seaway project. Having a global economy sounded like a good idea. Move production of goods to the current low-cost producer and use shipping to distribute the goods. As it turned out shipping also transmits the virus to 140 countries within six months. People will needlessly die in most of the countries of the world because of an errant environmental philosophy.

We have presented our number one parochial environment issue, but we all know environmental issues do not stop with a single dam and water pollution issue. The "environment" comprises all of the things needed to sustain life: air to breath, water to drink and a climate that is commensurate with life. A livable environment must also be sustainable. Certain ranges of air, water and temperature must be maintainable.

One internet site (Environmental Protection) proposed the following as the top five environmental issues in 2020:

1. Deforestation
2. Air pollution
3. Global warming
4. Water pollution
5. Depletion of critical resources

Our example of a waterway and dam problem had negative consequences in all five of the areas. However, we conclude this chapter with conclusions and discussions in these five areas.

1. Deforestation is removing the forests that supply our oxygen at an unsustainable rate; global action is needed.

Discussion-Anybody who travels has seen unbelievable examples of environmental damage done by deforestation. There are essentially no trees in Ireland, China, and many countries. Ireland allegedly was deforested to supply lumber for British ships. China lost all of its forests to people using the forest for fuel and furniture without replacing it. My first trip to China in 1983 was a part of a scientific mission sponsored jointly by the USA's National Science Foundation and the Chinese Academy of Science. Our delegation of six were guests of the Chinese government and we were shown things that outsiders normally never see. At that time, trees were planted about twenty feet apart along rural highways to serve as guardrails and as a future source of "lumber." Our Chinese host told us the entire country shuts down for the day and everybody plants tree seedlings in their designated place. Our hosts at the Metal's Research Institute in Shenyang took us to their tree planting site. Their trees were doing well, and they were proud of their environmental contribution.

On another trip, I explored the State of Washington by auto. We encountered mountain after mountain clear cut to create forever useless land. That is what clear cutting does. I went to graduate school in a university in the Upper Peninsula of Michigan (UP). The UP is vast, about one hundred miles wide and three hundred miles long. It was clear cut in the 1850's or so to supply lumber to build Chicago and Detroit and today it contains no timber, only scrub: small skinny trees and brush. It appears forested at first glance, but it contains no usable timber. My school had a forest products research facility that had been working for about sixty years to find a use for the UP-scrub growth. They even tried making bowling pins from it.

Every year in the USA millions of acres of usable forest is burned by careless residents. This happens because nobody maintains the forests. Overall, the planet is on a course for extinction and deforestation is a contributor. In the USA at any given time, we are paying healthy young people to do nothing for their daily bread when they could be asked to maintain our forests in payment for their daily bread.

Maybe if the entire planet followed China's lead and every person stopped what they were doing and spent a day planting vegetation we could sensitize the planet's citizens to this world crisis. Everybody needs to plant something that gives off oxygen.

2. Air pollution - Air quality is below accepted health standards in most large cities worldwide. Immediate action is needed.

Discussion: The global pandemic produced incontrovertible evidence that vehicles clogging city streets is the source of the gray smelly air in big cities. Cities where lockdowns were in place had clean air for the first time in decades. As mentioned in the preceding section I first visited China in 1983. I was there three weeks and the skies were always cloudless but gray. I never saw a blue sky anywhere from Shenyang in the north to Shanghai in the south. I traveled for three days on a train, looking out the window the whole time except for meals. I saw only gray skies and people, people everywhere. At that time there were no cars, only a handful belonging to institutes. However, people cooked on coal-fired stoves and heated their homes with open coal fires. In some cities there were large piles of powdered coal on street corners for people to use for cooking and heat. Coal is a fuel that produces lots of particulate on the air.

The house that I grew up in was a residential area peppered with factories, some large enough for hundreds of employees. Our backyard abutted the clothing factory where my mother worked as a button-hole maker. The factory made very expensive suits and these suits required hand-sewn buttonholes. The power plant for the two-story block-long factory was only about one hundred feet from our house. Black smoke was emitted 24/7 from the powerhouse smokestack. All houses in the neighborhood were gray from the soot. My father shingled our house with charcoal gray shingles.

Thirty years later I owned a rental house across from an industrial incinerator. It was about one thousand feet south of my property, but the area has two predominating wind directions: from the north and from the south. The aluminum screen door that faced the incinerator turned to perforated matt material not unlike the dross found on pots of molten aluminum. The chemical fumes corroded all aluminum on the building in areas that faced the incinerator.

Thus, in the past, air quality was threatened by coal and chemical emissions and now it is predominantly automobile and trucks that are taking away the world's breathable air. It does not have to be. We had the technology in the USA in the 1950's to manufacture automobiles that got fifty-five miles per gallon. Now in the US cars have been replaced by pickup trucks and utility vehicles that get about ten miles per gallon. Each year these vehicles get bigger and less fuel efficient. If governments were serious about the health of their citizens, they would immediately put a significant fee on vehicles that get less than fifty miles per gallon. If you want to drive a gas-guzzler it will cost, you $5000 per year in pollution tax.

Electric vehicles are not the answer since they require a power generation facility that burns fossil fuels. On average, eclectic cars use energy equivalent to having a gasoline mileage of fifty-three miles per gallon. Electricity from nuclear would produce no air pollution, but nobody knows what to do with spent fuel that is dangerous to humans for thousands of years. If I were in charge, I would put research dollars into exploring the feasibility of geothermal heat for driving conventional turbine generators of electricity. It is free and clean.

Wind energy is a fraud. According to my back of the envelope calculations, it takes more energy to make a wind turbine than it can produce in its design life. In addition, we have about four hundred years of data showing that such devices are not workable in the long term. The Dutch tried windmills and now only use them to delight tourists. Wind energy is inconsistent, and we lack the technology for energy storage and coupling the propeller to the turbine. Life of the gear boxes is less than ten years when the economics require a thirty-year life.

Hydro as presently practiced is not reliable; it depends on rainfall in the watershed of the dam; also it often destroys too much to make it worth doing. The Three Gorges dam in China displaced millions of people and has done yet to be accessed environmental damage. In my decades of fighting the Massena dam I learned from power generation experts that you do not need to build a dam and destroy cities and farms with flooding. We have turbine technology that can harness moving water for energy without building a dam and making a deep lake. Why isn't the technology used? Governments do not look for it.

What can the average planet resident do to reduce his or her share of air pollution? Buy a fifty-mpg car, heat with natural gas and don't smoke.

3. Global warming – The world is in a warming cycle, and nobody is taking remedial action.

Discussion: In 2010, or thereabouts, I gave a technical paper at a conference in Kyoto, Japan. It was held in the same hall that was used for the Worldwide Summit on Climate Change. Delegates left fired up about changing things to reduce global warming from carbon dioxide (CO_2) emissions. Since then, nothing has happened. Many believe it is another of planet earth's normal temperature cycles. Researchers show data on how the temperature of the planet varied over millions of years. We are currently in a hot surge.

The incontrovertible evidence of warming is the loss of polar ice. Ice melting cannot lie. We are getting warmer

Each year the world manufactures about thirty million vehicles. The world already has a billion vehicles that on average burn about 2000 gallons of fuel a year at six pounds per gallon and we end up with $30 \times 10^6 \times 12 \times 10^3$ lb/auto $= 360 \times 10^9$ pounds of organic matter converted to vapor with a lot of CO_2. As mentioned in the previous section this can be drastically reduced by taxing gas-guzzlers.

Heating and cooling houses has got to produce similar significant amounts of CO_2. These can also be significantly reduced. Ten years ago, when my wife died I sold our 4400 square-feet house with fourteen rooms that required heat and air conditioning. I built what was called a zero-heat house in the 1970's when they were conceived. It is a regular house with super insulation. The inside walls do not touch the outside walls. I had to modify the double wall plan because the town would not permit the double-wall construction. However, I ended up with an 800 square foot one-room house with no central heat or air. I use a gas fireplace in a corner to keep the room at 72° and the super insulation precludes use of air conditioning. I cool with air from the 60° sealed crawl space under the house. In any case, I have been through three or four winters with temperatures as low as ten below zero and I easily maintain my 72° F. My utility bill is one fifth of my utility bill with the big house. The moral is: every individual can reduce his or her percent of our greenhouse gas problem.

What can the world do as a whole about global warming? Every government can establish a greenhouse gas reduction program crafted to meet their country's situation. I saw one study that showed that cows farting produced a very significant amount of greenhouse gas. A cow etiquette program could help there.

What really would help would be the fifty mpg cars and improved insulation technology. The latter could be a huge help. Current insulation practices are no less than absurd. Windows are everywhere and a window provides a heat transmission rate of 100 compared to one for an inch of polyurethane foam. A window is a hole in your wall at outside temperature.

I am in the process of converting my pied-a-terre in Florida to no windows. Windows will be replaced with TV cameras and screens that resemble windows. From the inside you will see windows where they were, but it will be a framed TV screen with an image from a camera pointing in the view of the "TV window". Simply getting rid of windows could reduce energy use fifty percent planet wide. Window and doors are energy thieves that can easily be arrested to reduce global warming.

4. Water pollution – Our oceans are full of plastic and oil spills; our rivers are full of feces and chemicals and our lakes are threatened by mismanagement. Help is needed on all fronts.

Lake Ontario's invasive species is the most blatant example of avoidable water pollution. The last time that I heard from the invasive species people the list in the Great Lakes was up to one hundred fifty and these are all caused by the Seaway allowing ships in from foreign ports. There is no way to remove bilge water from ships. All ships take on seawater and moving seawater from the Black Sea and dumping it into the Great Lakes is going to have repercussions. There are creatures and biological elements in all water and mixing them will create an unknown result – like zebra mussels. Allowing foreign ships into the Great Lakes is an act of insanity on the part of governments of the USA and Canada.

I have a gnawing concern for the effect of untreated pet excrements on water pollution. Wherever you go in the USA you will find dogs everyplace at all times. The last time that I heard an estimate of the number of dogs in the USA it was ninety million. It is probably twice that now. What this means is at least one hundred million pounds of dog feces go into our ground water every day. We drink this water. Most dog owners in my neighborhood pick up their dog's excrement in a plastic bag. This goes in the garbage and in a landfill. It is not treated.

Of course, a huge component of water pollution is chemical spills. As I write this there is a Japanese oil tanker containing millions of gallons of bunker crude oil breaking up on a coral reef on a pristine island beach complex in the Pacific Ocean. Before that it was a runaway oil well that destroyed the shrimp and fish in the Gulf of Mexico. Then there was the Alaskan disaster that twenty years later still has an effect.

Chemical spills from offshore oil wells probably pose the largest environmental risks. If there weren't a billion cars and trucks on the planet's higways, we would not need oil taken from the bottom of the sea.

5. Depletion of critical materials

As a metallurgist by degree, I have been aware of our current crisis of critical metals. For example, everybody loves their electronic devices, but not everybody is aware that predictions show that by 2050 the world will be out of copper. Electronics cannot currently exist without copper for conductors and connectors. Electric vehicles and all sorts of power tools use lithium-ion batteries. Lithium is plentiful in the earth's crust, but the easy-to-reach compounds are being rapidly depleted.

Everybody in the machine tool industry knows that manufacturing equipment cannot be made without cemented carbide cutting tools. Cemented carbide, in my opinion, is the most critical engineering material on the planet. Chemically it is a very hard metal-like material made by liquid metal bonding of particles of tungsten carbide. Cobalt is usually the metal binder. The depletion problem is currently man-made. China has bought up all of the mines in the world that produce the metal tungsten. Cobalt is also not easy to get. Canada has cobalt, but it is hard rock mined in deep mines.

Rare-earth elements like Europium, Samarium, Praseodymium etc. are necessary for high performance magnets for motors as well as for many electronic applications. China has also cornered the world supply of these critical materials.

What to do? Enemies of China may not be able to have manufacturing. Germany is researching the use of other metals to replace tungsten for cemented carbide, but worldwide research on depletion of critical materials is almost non-existent outside of China. This needs to change.

Summary

Overall, this chapter sort of sets a hopeless tone. "Woe are we as a planet". The Seaway is a money-loser for both countries and it caused one hundred fifty invasive species to enter the Great Lakes threatening twenty percent of the world's fresh water. The dam that is part of the seaway is continually raising the water level on Lake Ontario and within the past three years has caused tens of billions of dollars in flooding damage. And the International Joint Commission that oversees this crime against the planet is comprised of appointed political fund raisers who may not even know where Lake Ontario is.

What can be done to save the Great Lakes? Pray for enlightenment of the President of the United States and the Prime Minister of Canada.

What can be done about the top five environmental issues of 2020? The answer to deforestation that I would like to see in the USA is a return to CCC camps comprised of out-of-work individuals. There are currently twenty-five million young healthy individuals who elect not to work, make them tend our public and private forests to reduce forest fires and to plant seedlings. During the pandemic, employ social distancing by giving each person their own three acres to maintain- working alone with hand tools. Every country should have such a program.

Water pollution can be addressed by application of what we already know about water treatment. Much of the world has less than desired access to municipal wastewater treatment. The World Health Organization and others need to publish guidelines to help all people in all countries have proper waste treatment – to keep drinking water clean. We also need a plan to clean the oceans of plastic. A good start would be worldwide banning of disposal of any waste from ships and from shorelines. A significant reward from an international fund can be given to individuals who report ocean discharges of anything that doesn't belong in the oceans.

Depletion of critical elements can be addressed by research funding from every country. Somebody needs to study the situation that we know to be critical and develop recommendations. For example, German researchers are studying niobium as a replacement for tungsten in cemented carbide. China currently does not own worldwide production of niobium. Also, the world needs a replacement for lithium in batteries. Every country should designate research dollars to the effort.

Are we environmentally doomed? Probably, but every person on the planet should be educated on the meaning of sustainability. This must start in kindergarten. If any action creates an unsustainable situation, don't do it. Building thirty million vehicles worldwide per year is not sustainable. Clear cutting forests in not sustainable. Disposing of trash and waste in the ocean is not sustainable.

Chapter 2
Birth Circumstance

The second commandment is love thy neighbor as thyself.

USA's 2020 protests, rioting and looting

As I write this, there is a presidential election in the USA about seventeen weeks away and the national media has made race, ethnicity, and gender the center of all "reporting". Most long-time members of our federal legislatures, as well as our President, have been branded racist by all media: social, TV, radio, newspapers, and anybody with an audience.

I do not even know what the word "racist" really means. What it means in the media is: not liking people with a different color skin than theirs. The dictionary definitions is (yes I had to look it up): hatred or intolerance of another race. Okay, I understand intolerance and hatred but not race. What does "race" mean? I Googled the biography of an infamous congressional representative (AOC) and under race, it said: American. That is exactly what I would write on a similar questionnaire.

The dictionary has fifteen definitions for race, but the one that appeared related to this discussion is: a group of persons related by common descent or heredity. To me, common descent means same parents, and heredity means I do not know what. (I look up both descent and heredity): descent – derivation from an ancestor; lineage heredity – the characteristics of an individual that are deemed passed on by parents/ancestors.

In summary, I do not know what race or racist really means, but I know that America's media essentially calls any newsworthy person a racist if he or she says anything negative about a person designated by the media as "black".

This is another miss-used term. It is used in the media to describe any person whose skin is darker than skin that is incorrectly termed white. Some people on the planet have skin that is almost as white as this piece of paper, but the majority of the planet's people have skin hues that go from the white of a Japanese geisha to the black of some indigenous people in Australia.

There really is no such thing as a "black" person. America has citizens with skin colors that follow the Gaussian distribution that applies to all physical attributes. We will talk about Gaussian distribution repeatedly in this book, so it is probably appropriate to define it and discuss it here. I believe that it should be the basis of all matters.

I do not know who Gauss was, but what this person established as a mathematical rule is that if you have a "normal" distribution of properties or measurements of something and you plot for example the height of 100 people on a graph where the measured property is the abscissa and the ordinate is the number of people with a particular height you will get a graph with the shape of a bell. The center is the median of the measurements, and the curve will decline on both sides of the median. Half have less than the median height, and half will be taller. The reason why this concept is so important in philosophy is that millennia ago the Greeks learned that you have to govern to the mean of a Gaussian distribution. You cannot design doorways to accommodate the tallest in the distribution or the shortest in the distribution. To be economically practical, you must design doorways to the median height. And this applies to all matters. Unfortunately, some countries and the USA in particular have ignored what the Greeks learned the hard way: You cannot run a country to please all of its citizens in all matters.

What has this to do with birth circumstance and "black" people? First, it is dead wrong to categorize citizens of a country in any way. All categorizations are wrong. There are no black Americans or Asian Americans or Irish Americans, there are only Americans. Americans have a Gaussian distribution of skin hues from snow white to towards black. America is comprised of citizens from all over the planet and that is why there is a Gaussian distribution of skin coloration. It is like this more in the USA than in many other countries because the country from the start was an amalgamation of people from many different countries.

Getting back to the 2020 riots, looting and the Black Lives Matter Movement, these riots were initiated by media who inflamed the country with videos of a police officer miss-treating a person with darker skin. They implied that all people with darker skin than the median skin tone will be similarly miss-treated. Protests, rioting and looting ensued. The entire mess, which is still going on as I write this, is a product of news media run amok. The United States and many other countries have lost unbiased reporting of news events.

Participation in Government

Just as disconcerting as the absurdity of black and white citizens (there are only citizens, period) is the absurdity of what is happening in politics to promote "diversity". Diversity is a euphemism for discrimination – granting something based upon birth circumstance. The premise for diversity is if you have a company of ten people, you will have better success if those ten people have very different birth circumstances, particularly darker than median skin coloration and half should be male and half should be female. Such a composite company will be successful because this diversity produces better products, better sales, and overall business success. There is no consideration about employees bringing needed skills.

When I was in a management position with a large company and we needed to add an engineer, the HR department gave me a list of accepted races/ethnicities. I could not hire anybody not on the" minority" list. I ended up hiring a person whose father was born in Mexico, but he was born in the USA and had never even visited Mexico, but he had a name that granted him "minority" status. Such practices are absurd and are a leading cause for business failures. Successful companies and organizations staff based upon qualification only.

Every time that I run into so called minority or diversity issues, I ask proponents of this concept to look at the makeup of sports teams. Sport teams hire based entirely on game skills and physical attributes. Entire basketball teams are comprised of people with darker than medium skin hue.

They are exempt from diversity initiatives because they must win to keep fan support. Companies that want to beat their competitors also need to staff based on skills and not birth circumstance (skin color etc.).

Many elections in the USA have candidates running for office just to achieve some perceived benefit obtained by having a person with a particular birth circumstance win. Again, this makes no sense. Women can have the same managerial skills as a man. There is no need to force fit women or people with darker than normal skin color into government. All citizens have the right to seek elected office and any birth circumstance is acceptable. All that is needed is the will to serve and commensurate skills and personal traits. Women and darker-skinned people have run countries since the start of recorded history. There is no need to force fit. A woman with darker than median skin hue ran one of the greatest civilizations that the world has known in pharaohtic Egypt over 2000 years ago. Her name was Cleopatra.

Housing issues

The government in the USA mandates that all large condo and apartment projects must have a certain percentage of the units that they build designated for "low income" residents. In US government terms, this means that they must be from a sanctioned "minority". The net effect of these laws is to prevent building of projects that have such government mandates. For example, the prettiest site in my city, on a hill overlooking Lake Ontario, has been for sale by the city for at least ten years without a nibble from developers. Because the property is city-owned they will for certain have a cadre of lawyers and government inspectors enforce housing designated minorities for $400/month rent in condo units that will sell for $400,000 to $600,000. Needless to say, having low budget housing as part of an upscale community will endanger the value of the upscale units. Nobody will buy them, and nobody has developed the best property in the city.

In my city, the US government did this same sort of thing in every nice section of the city. "Nice" means better built homes on bigger lots. The federal government (HUD) built ten to fifteen story high rises in every nice neighborhood and these buildings are rented to designated minorities.

The intention of all of this government intervention is to eliminate clustering by birth circumstance. They do not want neighborhoods where residents mostly have black skin or brown skin or other hues. However, for all of my lifetime it has been my observation that people with similar country or cultural origins tend to live together. Many American cities have a "'Chinatown" or Italian area or an Irish area. When I was growing up in an upstate New York medium-size city, we had neighborhoods for immigrants from many countries: we had a Polish section, Italian section, Ukrainian, German, Irish, African, Greek, Russian, Middle East, Jewish , Chinese, etc. They had their own social clubs, restaurants that specialized in foods from their native countries and we were a happy family composed of differing birth circumstances. It was a wonderful thing. It was a natural thing. Nationality clusters formed as one would expect. My family immigrated to the city from Poland. If immigrant families liked their new situation, they wrote to friends and family in the Poland about this and some of them immigrated to the USA. The Polish family that was established located living arrangements nearby for newcomer immigrants from Poland and eventually a Polish "neighborhood" was established.

Clustering of people with common backgrounds, traditions and origins is a natural thing that should not be altered by governments. In fact, in some areas of the USA the federal government is ceding entire cities to people from a single birth circumstance. I attended a conference in a northern state with rather harsh winters and was surprised that the birth circumstance of a significant part of the city was Somalian.

President Obama allegedly was bringing in tens of thousands of immigrants from certain African countries and placing them together in cities that he perceived to be declining in size. The absurd part of this is having the immigrants come from the same country. There are probably millions of people from more than one hundred countries that would like to immigrate to the USA but have been on waiting lists for years.

Government housing mandates do nothing but destroy neighborhoods and cities. This has been my observation. Most American cities with a population of more than one million are uninhabitable. City centers are devoid of shopping, safe streets, good schools, restaurants, and livable neighborhoods. Why? - Because of government housing mandates and the infamous "housing projects". These "projects" force like people to move into these monstrosities and they became centers for crime and all sorts of situations that negatively affect livability. Cities that allow natural clustering of people with like ethnicities seem to thrive. The largest city in Canada is still highly livable and it is a composite of ethnic clusters of every sort.

One time a coworker who was born in England, arranged for me and my wife to stay at his friend's bed and breakfast in London. It turned out to be in the Kuwaiti section of London. They had a Kuwait bank as well as Kuwaiti restaurants and tea houses where men smoked hookahs on rugs on the floor. Who knew that London had a concentration of people from Kuwait? It was a lovely neighborhood and these areas of people with like birth circumstance and traditions should continue. Government housing mandates of any sort are incommensurate with democratic principles and the Constitution of the USA.

Gender

Today I received a pandemic travel form from the New York State Health department to be filled out on returning to New York from any out of state trip. I had to make a trip for business. The form asked for date of birth and gender: male, female, non-binary. I had to Google non-binary. The definition was: not male or female. The State of New York in the USA believes that there is gender-less residents. They recently enacted a law that a public restaurant and the like have to install a gender-less bathroom.

In the USA, a significant part of the young girl, teenage girl population have decided to transition to the male gender. Some want to stay non-binary, girl today, and man tomorrow.

What is causing this bizarre situation? We all know the answer: mobile devices. Kids in the USA have to have one by no later than eight years of age because of peer pressure. You are an outcast without one. Then they have on their person from then on, a source of evil in all areas. First, the device steals the child's childhood, spending an average of 4 to 7 hours, or some such number, a day staring, texting, and swiping when they should be running and playing in the great outdoors.

Adolescents are susceptible to any sort of distraction that provides a new experience. I once watched a documentary on a cheetah. A photographer spent one year in the wild filming the daily life of a female cheetah that just gave birth to five baby cheetahs. She had only one year to prepare them for life on their own, because she knew that she would have another litter in a year. She constantly had to steer the babies from dangers. Some were eaten by lions, one just disappeared, and one was eaten by a large bird. She had only two left at year's end. Young cheetahs and children do not have the life experiences to recognize danger.

Of course, the world would be better today if Facebook and the like were never conceived, but these brain-eating cancers have morphed into some of the largest companies in the world because people pay to advertise in these basest of mediums. The internet and phones and related gadgets provide young people with pornography, terrorism, hate of every sort, stealing by endless methods, how to murder your parents, every conceivable and inconceivable wrong. In fact, these devices imbue young people with the idea that nothing is wrong.

In the USA, the schools assist the evil called social media by developing education curriculums that teach that nothing is wrong. Wasting a life on a mobile device is not wrong; sexual activity even before puberty is not wrong, sex in your teens is not wrong, having a baby in the eighth grade is not wrong, hallucinogenic drugs are not wrong, vaping is not wrong, nor is smoking, but must be done off campus; ditto with alcoholic beverages. Nothing is wrong and Adam and Eve and the Ten Commandments cannot be discussed. People have evolved from yet to be identified amphibious creatures.

Last year I learned that my nineteen-year-old college sophomore granddaughter became a man. Upon investigation, I learned that this transition was compliments of the internet, mobile device, and her public high school. All schools in the US are required to teach gender dysphoria in kindergarten. If you do not like you're male or female body the government will build you a new one. All schools have a homosexual/gender dysphoria after-school club with a taxpayer-paid moderator who is an LBGTQ person and all LBGTQ persons promote their particular LBGTQ proclivities to the young students. This must be where she got hooked. I was with her every Saturday since birth and I never as much as mentioned LBGTQ to her. She did not have many friends and the LGBTQ groups on the internet and phone offer up friends if you join a specific type of LGBTQ. Misery loves company. They have ceded their lives to abnormal behavior and if they convert many others to their abnormal ways they become less abnormal.

And so, my granddaughter went down the path to destruction. I had an outing with her every Saturday, even in her freshman year at college. Her school was only thirty miles away and I would make the trip for lunch with her on Saturdays. I did notice that she started to wear boy clothes after she broke up with her boyfriend in her senior year in high school. I did not pay much attention since I read lots of women's magazines and slim women wearing boy-like clothes is very popular. I did not know about the transition to male until Thanksgiving. I was at my sister-in-law's and one of her daughters came up to me and said that she admired my granddaughter's (she was in Europe for the term) coming out on Facebook. Of course, I had no idea what she was talking about, but she went on about how she changed her name to something that does not denote gender and that she is officially a man.

I was shocked beyond belief. The next day I called her college and asked about my granddaughter. They said that they did not have a student by her name, but they had a student with a no-gender name. She came home from Europe two days before Christmas. We had Christmas Eve dinner at my house with my two sons, my daughter-in-law, and my granddaughter. She had boy clothes on, but still looked girlish as always. I said nothing to her about what she was doing, and we exchanged presents and it was like every other Christmas at my house since my wife died.

Christmas was on a Friday and our normal weekend outing consisted of me calling my granddaughter on Friday night. I would ask: do you want to do something tomorrow? I always had something planned. She would reply: what do you have I mind? I would tell her my plan. I decided to just stop calling her on Saturdays. My plan was to just ghost her as they say in mobile device language. However, she called me at work on Saturday and said: it's Saturday. I was outside with a power tool and could not hear well, but I went on to tell her that I learned about her absurd plans to become a man and that I will not enable her transition in any way and that includes lunch on Saturdays. Call me back when you go back to being my granddaughter and hung up.

It has been eight months since that phone call, and I have had no contact with her or her parents for that time. A day or two after the phone call it was warm, and the ground was not frozen. I took the photos of our twenty years of Saturday outings and some mementos and went to my wife's grave and buried my granddaughter with her. She was dead to me.

I bought two books on gender dysphoria, and I learned from one that in the USA there is an epidemic of young girls, even before their teens, transitioning to male gender. According to one book this is all the product of the internet and LGBTQ clubs in public schools. Any medical person knows that changing from female to usable male is impossible, but "doctors for the buck" will do operations and counseling telling these pathetic girls that they will be fine. They will lead a successful life as a man. This is how depraved these "affirmation people" are. They belong in the hottest place in hell. Schools with LGBTQ programs should close. They are destroying lives, not educating.

Medical professionals mostly agree that about two or three percent of most countries' population is gay and only about 0.01 percent are prone to becoming hermaphrodites. Advertising on the part of the affected percentages is increasing the loss of life.

Gay people have been around for thousands of years and normally they do not create a societal problem. However, the "pride" movements have changed sexual proclivity into a circus freak show. All over the US, these people have parades and do all kinds of inane things to display their societal deficiencies. For example, one time I booked a hotel in a residential area near a city center where my conference was being held. It was much cheaper. The hotel and neighborhood were nice, but I learned that it was a "gay" neighborhood. On Saturday morning, hundreds of men in women's dresses gathered for a road race in dresses. It was fun to watch and fun for them, but the real reason that they do these things is because they know that what they are doing is wrong, immoral, and likely to earn them eternal damnation and these negatives are overridden by the party atmosphere.

I have often crewed on sailboat trips with a gay man and rented a house to lesbians for ten years. They were fine people and never said they were gay, but it was obvious. What is not acceptable by any society that wants to remain a normal functioning civilization is for LGBTQ people to go about advertising their sexual proclivities. **I, and most other people, do not want to know that a person prefers masturbation to normal sexual relations between a man and a woman. And that is what is one wrong of such organizations.** It is abnormal to advertise your sexual proclivities to strangers. However, the irreversible harm done by people with gender dysphoria is they are contributing significantly to the extinction of the human race. The human species in 2020 is well on its way to extinction and same-sex relations do not produce offspring to continue a species.

Education issues

As I write this, one of the daily newspapers that I read contained an article on race discrimination at Yale University, a prestigious American school. The article was about a lawsuit against the school alleging that race was a discrimination factor. People with "black" skin are admitted in deference to "whites" and "Asians" - again, the issue of skin hue/birth circumstance.

Of course, every American knows that all of our universities offer racial discrimination. If there was a scale for skin hue from one to ten, with one being reasonably dark, like Shaquille O'Neal, and ten being white as snow like Bill Clinton; Kamala Harris would be five, all people with one to six skins would be admitted without regard to academic credentials. This is because the United States government at every level employ people to enforce this policy. They are called chief diversity officers or some similar term. The government mandates them in all large companies as well.

This discrimination system has been in place for decades. In the 1970's I was teaching an engineering course in night school at a local community college. I had about twenty students and I was quite rigorous about quizzes and exams: a ten-minute quiz each night on the last lecture, a midterm, and a final. I had a few students trending towards failure, but one stood out. He missed probably half of the classes (and quizzes) and the mid-term. I offered makeup exams for all that he missed. He did not accept my offer. Then, near the time for the final exam I got a letter from the dean telling me to pass the worst failing student. Apparently, he was considered by school administrators to be a racial minority. His skin hue was darker than the medium skin coloration; he was possibly from a Spanish-speaking country. Of course, I could not pass somebody who did not even take the quizzes, midterm, or final exam. But this is what is happening in many American schools. Students are fraudulently passed and graduate because of their birth circumstance. They did not learn the material; they did not do the work. This is all being done to achieve favorable statistics for "diversity", (discrimination) annual reports. How wrong this is; how sad this is; how harmful this is to the individual; how unfair it is to honest students. There are no words to describe the absurdity of these American government mandates.

The net result of a diversity-destroyed education system is that the USA has lost to its competition. Our number one competitor, China, has a rigorous education system that starts at birth. When my wife and I visited China in 1983 on a government sponsored scientific mission, our Chinese hosts took us to a childcare facility for pre-K's. The children in the facility that we visited ranged in age from maybe six months to five years old. Some were not old enough to walk. Parents delivered their children to school on their bicycles in the morning on their way to work. They picked them up after work. Children started their education almost at birth and there was no preferential treatment based upon birth circumstance. Students compete for the best schools based upon their academic success, not skin hue or where they were born. My last visit to China was in 2017 or thereabouts. The international conference that I came to attend was on tribology, my field of interest (the art and science of interacting surfaces) and university students were everywhere in the conference hall to help foreign attendees. All spoke fluent English. English is taught in all schools and signage in Beijing was in Chinese and English. I toured one of their most prestigious universities, Tshinghua in Beijing. They had 170 PhD candidates in my field of tribology. The USA has only one university that I know of that even has a tribology degree and there may be three PhD candidates.

This is our global competition. The USA is forfeiting their world leadership role by catering to special interest groups mostly based upon birth circumstance (skin hue). They are sought-after voting blocks and America's elected officials care only about one thing: reelection. I believe that many American politicians will sell their children to pedophiles for votes.

Another incidence where education and birth circumstance play a role is in intellectual capability. Unfortunately, some people are born with brain issues such that they may never have an intellectual capability greater than an eight-year-old. Of course, all people, even those with no health issues, have intellectual capability that follows the Gaussian distribution (bell-shaped curve) that controls all "people properties": weight at birth, height at age five, IQ at age thirteen, age at death. This is called a normal distribution and it is a fundamental law of nature that applies to all living creatures. Heredity (genes/DNA) plays a significant role in determining intellectual capability. Some people are on both ends of the bell-shaped curve; some are very smart, and some have limited intellectual capability.

A problem in the United States public education system is that all schools are mandated to teach to the whole distribution of intellectual capabilities. This is absurd. It is not fair to those on the low end of intellectual capability because teachers cannot afford to spend the time on them, and it is not fair to the gifted because they are bored and not challenged. Schools must teach to the median and accommodate those well outside of the median in special, smaller classes.

When I was in grade school and high school, we had such a system in my birth city. We had a large private school system that taught to the median and a public school system that taught to the whims of the current political establishment. However, the public schools did have an effective system to accommodate "unteachables". After grade eight the unteachables were identified and they were sent to work in a brass and bronze foundry. They learned a trade and life skills. There was a technical high school that taught trades to those who were teachable but did not like academics. This system functioned well and accommodated a Gaussian distribution of intellectual capabilities. Gradually this workable education system morphed into the present USA mess that produces nothing but wealth for countless school administrators. The kids are dumber than rocks, as shown by global comparison. USA's students rank below most other countries in math, reading, writing, science – everything. The root cause in my opinion is the USA's refusal to fund private and charter schools. A related cause is having public schools controlled by teacher labor unions. The unions fear that school competition will yield some under-performing schools that will be burdensome to union teachers in those schools. However, this never happened when USA had parochial Catholic schools in most cities. All schools produced successful student outcomes.

The path to resurrection of a workable education system is government legislation to fund all schools, not just government-controlled schools. Also, all schools must teach to the median, except for those specified for children with special needs.

Work issues

Birth circumstance is now the most important qualification for a job in the USA. There are federal, state, and local mandates to hire to match the prevailing distribution of skin hues and perceived ancestry. First, if you have a company with more than one employee, fifty percent must be female (if you are male) and fifty percent must be male (if you are female). Some of the laws will be thirty-three percent male, thirty-three percent female and thirty-three percent non-binary. This is now the current gender selection, but USA lawmakers are busy creating several more gender options.

Gender is just the first business mandate; on top of the gender mandates, fifteen percent must be African American, ten percent Hispanic, five percent Asian, three percent Native American minimum. People with skin hues from 6 to 10 need not apply.

Of course, small businesses cannot afford to hire workers based upon birth circumstance. What to do? Most Americans who want to be entrepreneurs have to do so as sole proprietors. It is simply impossible to meet America's governmental regulations on hiring. Why does the USA have these absurd regulations? The answer is the same as always: politicians are trying to stay in office by offering special-interest groups jobs. USA governments are forcing private-sector companies to observe absurd diversity quotas. All public sector organizations have a chief diversity officer and under government pressure all companies with more than one hundred employees probably have one. A diversity officer is typically a person with a 1 to 5 skin hue and typically advocates hiring only people with a 1 to 5 skin hue.

American cities with a majority of people with a 1 to 5 skin hue usually have similar city councils and similar workforces except for police and firefighters. In the city that I live in, the mayor attributes the lack of diversity in police and fire personnel to a scarcity of candidates.

The typical American city has a diminishing city center devoid of shopping surrounded by sprawling suburbs full of every sort of store and business. People with 1 to 5 skin hues can live in the city center or any suburb, but they tend to live in the city center and people born with 6 to 10 skin hues live in the suburbs. This is changing, but ever so slowly. In my youth, the city where I was born was about eighty-five percent 6 to 10 skin hue and fifteen percent 1 to 5 skin hue. The suburbs were one hundred percent 6 to 10. Now my city is seventy percent 1 to 5 skin hue, and the suburbs are about ninety percent 6 to 10 skin hue and the percent in 1 to 5 hue is rising.

Skin hue (birth circumstance) seems to be the most important factor on the planet to politicians and executives of large companies. I worked for two very large companies in my early working career. The company where I worked when birth circumstance became the prime selection factor seemed paranoid about having people with 1 to 5 skin hue in every department. I worked at a very large division, about 33,000 employees. Normally the manager of this division would be a "lifer" – somebody who had been with the company since college and worked "his" way up to the top – yes, "his". There were not many women managers, but in the 1990's or so when diversity initiatives started, the company tried to get women managers in as many departments as possible.

I was working as a development engineer in an R & D department and the big boss (hundreds of people) job was given to a woman PhD researcher in the department. She had many academic credentials, but all of us workers could see her as a "force fit". She was ill at ease in the job. One of the first things that she did have a one-on-one discussion with all of the engineers and researchers that worked for her. I will never forget her coming to my office and talking with me. She seemed scared of me. She could fire me on the spot, but she was as nervous as a first-time job applicant. She did not last long. She went back to research. Apparently even her bosses sensed she was in a role not suited to her. About that time the company even got a woman CEO. Again, for one hundred plus years CEO's came from within. They worked their way up. This woman was a CEO of another company and took the job because my company was bigger. CEO's like to CEO as big a company as possible.
She was not scared to be CEO. In fact, she seemed to thrive on the attention paid to her. I did not get to know the woman, but I observed at big employee meetings that she called to give us pep-talks, she seemed to be on the nasty

side based upon her answers to questions and how she treated her immediate underlings. She too did not last – only about two years she went off to get another CEO job.

Thus, my experiences with women in management have been on the negative side. However, the county where I live had a woman as the highest elected official in the county. She held the job for about eight years but lost an election after some bad press over giving her husband a county job with significant pay and little work.

Lots of women claim that there is a glass ceiling limiting their attainment of important positions. Of course, this is sheer nonsense. If anything, women in the workplace have an edge over men in male dominated environments because they stand out in such instances. Gaussian distribution also attests to their potential for any position. The bell-shaped curve of attributes that apply to a position looks the same for men and women. In the USA, many more women graduate from college than men. There is no birth-circumstance problem concerning jobs and gender. All genders have equal access.

The problem of diversity quotas and skin hue was something that I had to deal with in my last job at a large US manufacturer. In the 1990's or thereabouts we had to hug co-workers and every department needed to have as many women and 1 to 5 skin hue workers as possible. We had teams for everything. We had mandatory diversity sessions where in we did the mandatory hugging. A leader would go around the room of thirty or so people and we would have to tell the group what we liked about Sally or Raymond. I'll never forget one session where one of the number 3 skin hue employees stated to the group: "I like working with Sally because sometimes I get tired and need a nap and Sally covers for me."

The diversity officer in charge of the hugging event cringed a bit but went on with the hugging. Of course, this was the pre-pandemic nineties. The sales pitch for diversity had always been your business will be better and more prosperous with a diverse workforce.

My long-term employer who won all sorts of diversity awards is now bankrupt. When I left in 2002, they still had about 100,000 employees. In 2020, the shell of my former company after bankruptcy had less than 5000 employees worldwide.

The US Postal service is America's premier model for diversity. All government minority quotas are observed. Fifty percent of the workforce must be female, forty percent male and ten percent non-binary with future plans for more genders. On the news last night, the US Postal Service will be out of money by the end of September and the US Congress is scheduled to convene and authorize a twenty billion dollar" loan" to hold them over. They supposedly are not part of the federal government. They were "spun off" as we say in America as a separate business to make a profit and support itself. I have yet to see a US company succeed based upon their diversity initiatives.

Conclusions

1. People everywhere are categorized by their birth circumstance: skin hue, ancestry,   social status, gender, etc., for purposes of discrimination.
    Basis: Almost every country has discrimination issues.

2. Birth circumstance cannot be selected.
    Basis: I tried and failed (wanted to be born tall and to a wealthy family, I got the opposite).

3. All people are the same in basic needs (food, clothing, and shelter) and common behavior and appearances serve to produce a nationality or race.
    Basis: Bounded geographic areas of the world are commonly the basis for "racial" identities. Indians come for Asian countries and the land mass identified as India. Chinese come from Asian countries and the land mass identified as China.

4. Race is a subset of a species with common characteristics. Skin hue does not make a race. Black is a meaningless adjective when used to describe a human person. To use the term "black" to describe a person is racist. It serves no purpose other than to discriminate against that person.
    Basis: people with a skin hue between 1 and 5 can be native to many countries: Australia (aborigines), India, Brazil, Africa, Indonesia, etc. Some paleontologists claim that all humans evolved from equatorial climes, where our skin would have been 1 to 6 in hue. Skin colors lightened (to 6 to 10) as humans migrated to

colder climes. This was an evolution to allow more absorption of vitamin D in the reduced sunlight.

5. All government efforts to apply quotas for different birth circumstances are done to garner political support from that group in deference to equality between the citizens.
Basis: Quotas are blatantly discriminating and unconstitutional and politicians ignore the constitution and laws against discrimination.

6. Gaussian distribution is ignored by USA government entities. This distribution covers birth circumstance, intellectual capability, physical strength – everything. Many American institutions, like public schools, have failed because the median is ignored as government concentrates on the ends of the distributions (usually the lower end).
Basis: USA schools are in failure mode. Trades are completely ignored by USA's government. Special attention is given to LGBTQ etc. interests and the mean is ignored. Perceived minorities get special government funding and programs, and the median gets nothing.

7. Meddling, (government housing, restrictions on building), on the part of the USA government organizations has destroyed the livability of most cities in the USA.
Basis: LA, NYC, Chicago, Atlanta, Houston, Dallas, Philadelphia, Cleveland, Buffalo, Detroit; and many others are unlivable from the standpoint of crime and the necessities of life (no stores, no churches, bad schools, etc.).

Recommended philosophy regarding birth circumstance

God created man and woman and they exist to perpetuate the species through marriage and procreation of offspring. The parents and the offspring form the basic unit of society. Families tend to live together in communities and countries all over the world. They have many different skin hues, appearances, and proclivities. Together they tend to create an ethnicity that people take with them as they travel the world. These become traditions and should be treasured and passed on to heirs.

Governments need to supply education and infrastructure for families to thrive, but they should not dictate where people should live, where their children go to school, what jobs they can have, what they say, what they write, what they do that is lawful. Governments should have the motto: how may I help? Government should not categorize their citizens by birth circumstance. There should be no hyphenated Americans (African, Italian, Polish, etc.), only American citizens. All categorization of Americans for any purpose should be unlawful.

I sent in an application for an absentee ballot today for the USA presidential election in ten weeks. It asked me to supply my age and gender. This should not be permitted since it will be used to establish trends to sway elections.

Overall, citizens of the world need to work to end birth circumstance as the basis of anything other than where you were born and which of two genders you were at birth: name – John Doe

born – 6/29/20
gender – male
Nothing else should be recorded and the USA has only two
categories of citizens- male and female. The other thing that
is absurd and counterproductive is inter-gender and inter-
racial competition: the first woman in space, the first African
American president, and the first woman to do whatever.
Women do not need to compete with men. In marriage we
become one. Is it right to compete with yourself? This
practice of having birth circumstance a competition
encourages young people to do stupid things just for the
publicity. U-tube and TikTok videos show hundreds of
thousands of people doing stupid things to get "likes".

Gaussian distribution shows that there are women strong
enough to do a hand-stand on a balance beam, press down
and touch her nose on the beam and press back up to a
hand-stand (my Olympic gymnast girlfriend used to do this).
Similarly, there are women who can tolerate the confinement
of being buried alive (as in space travel). Gaussian
distribution determines that women can do anything that
men can do (except for the absolute biological difference)
and the same is true for men. There is no need to have
women compete with men for political offices, for
management jobs, for anything. Men like women and
women like men. Why fight?

The same situation exists with the skin hue aspect of birth
circumstance. As I write this, the media in the USA is touting
the Democratic Party vice president candidate as the first
"black" woman to hold this office. She is not "black". Her
skin hue is a 6 which makes her "color" to be like most
people with designated "white" color. It is current practice to

call all people in the USA with a 1 to 5 skin hue African Americans. This VP candidate alleges to be one. Her father comes from Jamaica, her mother from India. There is no association of her parents with Africa. It is sheer lunacy to encourage competition between skin hues. Of course, a person with a 1 skin hue can do any job. Gaussian distribution mandates this to be true.

The United States of America is an amalgam of immigrants from various time periods and from every country in the world. Over the past two hundred years, the USA had developed many geographic concentrations of people with similar birth circumstances. Some cities developed significant percentages of residents from Germany; some cities had lots of people from Italy and so on for probably one hundred countries. I lived in a city during graduate school where most residents (except for school staff) were Finnish. More recently I stayed at a college where most city residents were from Somalia.

Whenever there are concentrations of similar people, often ill will develops between the similar people and the other area residents; discrimination can occur. When I lived in the Finnish city, the locals would not allow us students into "their" bars. When I lived on Detroit, I asked a pretty girl for a date, and she said that her father would not let her date me because I have a Polish name. Polish people were not liked in Detroit because the city had a Polish enclave called Hamtramck.

I found out after I got married that her Irish father was upset that she brought home a Polish boy. My wife's family came from a small coal mining town in Pennsylvania that was settled by Irish to work in the mines. Then Polish people started to settle there, and they competed for mine jobs. The Irish did not like the Poles. Somehow my in-laws got over my "wrong" birth circumstance. We were married fifty years when she died.

Discrimination based upon birth circumstance is wrong to both parties. The party that is discriminated against may lose a date with a pretty girl, but the discriminator (her father) suffers because ill will and hatred prevents rational thought and behavior. He was not at peace. He was not happy.

The global economy of this millennia is merging all the countries in the world and there are many differences in people's appearance and traditions that must be accommodated where they live. Lewiston, Maine was settled by people who immigrated to the USA from France. When thousands of people from Somalia were settled in Lewiston by President Obama, the long-term residents acclimated and a city that was declining was saved. There are young people, there are babies, and there is activity. Birth circumstance was not an issue. This is the way it must be to keep civilization growing on this planet.

Lastly, birth circumstance is in a way the most important issue on our planet. We have such a declining birth rate that extinction can come as early as 2300 by one published estimate if people do not go back to larger families. People need to think about procreation requirements (extinction occurs when every female produces less than 2.1 offspring) and the negative effects of lifestyles that discourage or preclude a birth rate that can sustain the human species.

Chapter 3
Peace, Order, and Freedom

"All who listen to Me will live in peace and safety"

on a sales slip from an Amish bakery

The problem

Happiness is not possible without peace and order. I learned this in philosophy school. I never thought much about peace and order since I only lived under marshal law and curfew once in my life. That was in 1964 when we had riots in my city and a significant part of the city was destroyed by rioting, looting, mobs. The riot occurred because police attempted to break-up a large street party on a very hot night. The riots lasted a week or so and the net result was many businesses moved out of the city center. We had repeat riots and looting about two months ago and again many businesses were destroyed, almost everything in the city center was vandalized. Like the 1964 riots and looting the impetus was the looting portion. Also, the initiation was novel. The two highest elected officials in the metropolitan area, the county executive and our congressional representative led the rioting group. They claim that they left before the looting and arson started.

The problem as I see it is that many politicians condone and participate in mob behaviors that jeopardize the peace and order of all Americans. They do anything to get votes to stay in office. The planet is rife with so called democracies ruled by corrupt people who have no marketable skills. Elected office in the USA has no job requirements. One of my state's most prominent congressional representatives has work as bartender as her "curriculum vitae". She has the intellect of a gnat, but she garners votes by offering free things to her constituents.

In 2020, the USA is well on its way to functional breakdown because of isolated civic incidents sensationalized by our mindless media. And failed media is not something that can easily be corrected. The common thread is "education" at colleges that specialize in teaching the personal proclivities of professors instead of facts. College professors at liberal arts colleges in the USA, are what we term in the USA: "liberals". Our definition of a liberal is: a person who promotes delusional concepts. Liberals are neutralized by "conservatives" who are working people imbued with reason, self-control, and practical knowledge. The United States is governed by a two-party system; all citizens have to be a member of one of these two parties to participate in the "democracy", but neither party will tell citizens their basic principles and beliefs. Party leaders are so concerned about keeping their lucrative government jobs that their beliefs and platform is whatever a group of listeners or readers wants to hear. Neither party will proclaim their beliefs: this is what the xxx Party stands for. I spent fifty years as a committee person in one of our two major parties and I never heard a statement of party principles. This undoubtedly is a root cause of an unworkable congress and many statewide chaotic situations.

Thus, the problem is that the USA has a political system that is broken, and this is currently leading to nationwide rioting and looting by groups taking advantage of our leadership void. The USA is not alone in civic malaise. As I write this, the people of Belarus are protesting (no looting or vandalism like in the USA) their inept leadership. In 1993 I was invited to participate in a scientific mission from the USA to Belarus sponsored jointly by the USA National Science Foundation (NSF) and the Belarus Academy of Sciences. This trip started different from the many other trips that I made around the world. We were a group of six tribology researchers who would visit various universities in Belarus and give talks on our specialty in tribology. Mine was material selection for wear applications.

We came from various parts of the USA. We flew individually to Frankfurt, Germany and proceeded as a group to Belarus. I was the last of our group as we proceeded through an armed customs inspector. I gave him my passport and visa. He said "nyet "and pointed me back to the plane which had already left for who knows where. What to do? Nobody in the airport spoke a word of English and my colleagues were in another part of the airport out of my sight. I just stood there waiting for further instructions, none came. After an hour or so our Belarus host found me and said that my visa was no good and he went to the city to get special permission from a high official to let me in, but I would need to buy a new visa for four hundred dollars. I had $1800 in US dollars on my person. Apparently, the visa said that it was denied, but it was in Russian which I do not read. My employer had a professional visa service obtain the visa. Okay, after the loss of four hundred dollars my host put me in his car to drive to our hotel. About a mile down the road a uniformed person jumped out of a woods along the highway holding what looked like a red ping pong paddle. My host was guilty of speeding. He had to give that person a cash "fine" on the spot.

The next part of the trip was settling into Minsk. My Russian friends advised me not to go on this trip. Valentina said that it is the ugliest city in the world. All buildings are made from non-descript concrete. Apparently, Napoleon totally destroyed Minsk in the 1850's or so. It was rebuilt and again totally destroyed on World War II bombing. The WWII rebuild was with ugly concrete structures.

Our hotel was 1960 era, about twenty stories high. Its appearance was fine, but I soon learned that there was an odor problem. The room smelled. I traced the smell to a drain in the middle of the tiled bathroom floor. It was sewer gas. Apparently, the trap must have run dry. The only fix was to seal the drain with a wet towel. My room on the tenth or so floor overlooked a weeded-over building site. They started to build something and stopped, probably years ago based on the weeding over.

The talks went well. The Belarus scientists were very friendly and very smart. They also loved their vodka. At one formal dinner they toasted this and that maybe twenty times and we all were expected to match their swigs of vodka. I just put the glass to my lips for each toast. A young woman in our group secretly substituted Sprite for the vodka. Unfortunately, a young professor in our group had to be "assisted" back to his room. He tried to honestly participate in each toast.

The Belarus people that we encountered were as nice to us as people can be. The meals were mostly comprised of fatty meat, and I ended up living on their brown bread which was the best bread that I ever tasted.

One day, our Belarus hosts took us to a "World Heritage Historic Site". It was a falling-down castle that was being rebuilt one block at a time by a staff of one. From a rampart on the castle wall, I saw a horse-drawn wagon. There were local villagers burying their dead. It was something from another century. In fact, on our trip through farm country we saw people cutting grain with scythes and bundling it like it was done before farm machinery. We saw no farm machinery, only hand labor. In cities, people were pushing hand carts to move things around.

The technical capabilities of Belarus in arms manufacture however was incredible. I learned that Belarus' main product is arms. They supply Russia with their tanks, trucks, guns, etc. In fact, they supply Russia with soldiers for foreign wars. I learned that most of the "Russians" who died fighting in the war between Russia and Afghanistan (prior to USA's Afghanistan War) were Belarusians. In fact, out hosts took us to a special cemetery for Belarus soldiers who died in Afghanistan. Our hosts implied that Russia has always used Belarus for a supply of mercenaries.

After talks at several universities in Belarus we boarded a bus for Poland. The plan was to give two more talks in Poland. Belarus and Poland have a common border and when our bus arrived there, we were greeted with miles of cars parked on both sides of the road waiting to exit to Poland. Our Belarus hosts told us that we have a letter from the President of Belarus telling the border guards to let us cross into Poland. Our hosts were talking with the border guards for about two hours with no progress. Then one of our Belarus hosts went to his seat on the bus (he was sitting across from me) and I saw him pull a handful of US bills from a gym bag, put them in his pocket and go back to the border guards. This worked. At the time one US dollar equaled 26,000 Belarus rubles. Our hosts had to bribe our bus across the border. Our bus went on to Warsaw and we gave talks in two Polish universities. Our group disbanded in Warsaw with each of us going our separate ways.

Belarus was at peace, but this is not the kind of peace that brings happiness. Belarus is Communist with a dictator. The current dictator had been an "elected" leader for twenty-six years, but people are protesting because they have nothing. Their only product is arms and that makes the country beholden to their biggest customer, Russia. Belarus is losing its peace to protests.

Communism is an unnatural form of government. Their credo:
> From each, according to his abilities,
> to each, according to his needs.

This sounds magnanimous, but what it produces is all working for the government with party members and leaders taking most proceeds of the worker's efforts.

Communism is against human nature. If you work your butt off, you get the same as somebody who spent the day surfing on his or her phone. Not being able to own property is another hallmark of communism. China's economy is booming. Everybody is investing in "real estate". They buy and sell condos in high rise apartments. This is a key component of their economy. Nobody can own land under communism, the "people" own all of the land. The government (the Party) leases land to developers to build condos to "sell" to Chinese citizens. However, the party can take back the land or the building at any time. It is a fake property ownership. The state owns everything.

When we crossed the border from Belarus to Poland it was like going from the 1850's farming to present day mega farming in the Midwest USA. Poland was busy, modern. And people seemed to have all that they needed or wanted. It was like the USA with better buildings and history.

Cuba is the poster child of communism. After fifty years they have only 1950 Chevrolets that they keep alive as remembrances of what life was like when they had freedom.

In summary, the problem addressed in this chapter is that happiness requires peace, order and freedom and the USA and many other countries do not seem to be providing these "life essentials" during these tumultuous times. The other sections in this chapter discuss specific items that challenge peace, order, and freedom.

Right and wrong

We are greatly divided in the USA because many elected officials do not believe in peace, order, and freedom. They believe that nothing is wrong. Things can be different, but nothing is wrong. They do not believe in the Ten Commandments, that certain behaviors are anti-social to civilized living and that secularism is mandatory.

Humans have always lived together. Animals live together by design. The species ends without mating. Some animals live in solitude and only seek like at mating time. To live together requires observance of right and wrong. We define "right" as an act that does not have negative consequences on oneself or on others - wrong does. It will have now or in the future, negative consequences on oneself or on others. As we are in the middle of a pandemic, it is "right" to follow agreed-upon guidelines to control transmission of the disease: do not congregate, wear a mask, wash hands, disinfect, quarantine when sick. Wrong would be to do none of these. The most wrong thing in the world would be for a person who was infected, but asymptomatic to mingle with other people and knowingly spread the infecting virus.

Since the start of humans living together, the groups that they formed established rights and wrongs to govern group life. Without rights and wrongs there can be no living together. There can be no life. Most animals that eat other animals to survive do not eat each other (I recently learned that Florida's alligators eat each other, so I had to add "most" to it). Most humans do not eat each other. Humans do not kill other humans that they live with (only sometimes).

For the last 3000 years or so, planet Earth has been lucky enough to have religions and spiritual beliefs that regulated the right versus wrong issue. The Jewish people had Mosaic Law which had about six hundred rules concerning human behavior. Doing "right" meant following the Mosaic Law. Christians have the New Testament, the Ten Commandments and Jesus' teachings for definition of right versus wrong and most regions of the world have something akin to some written law, some not. Indigenous people like the Aborigines in Australia have traditions to govern life going back thousands of years. These people lived off the land, so they cherished and cared for the land: they had rights and wrongs relating to the environment where they lived. Native Americans similarly believed that nature was to be respected like a god. Certain things are right with nature, others were wrong.

The difference between right and wrong in 2020 USA is blurred. A significant percentage of elected officials believe that nothing is wrong. It is okay to kill unwanted babies; it is okay to not work for a living; it is okay to claim to be a gender of your choice; it is okay to not fund schools that spiritually do not go along with mandated subjects; it is okay to cohabitate unmarried; it is okay to not have family as the basis of a civilized society.

Many western societies in the world have laws that govern behaviors, what is right and what is wrong, based upon the Ten Commandments. The USA was likewise governed by laws sort of based on the Ten Commandments before the "trouble" started. I believe that the USA's societal failure was produced by violation of the fundamental law that should be the basis of all governments: govern to the medium of a Gaussian distribution in all matters. For example, transgender people comprise less than 0.01 percent of the population, but the USA mandated in 2020 that all public buildings have a special restroom for these people. A population of 320 million people has to change their lives at great expense to accommodate a small special-interest group. Right versus wrong needs to be pondered deeply by all in all matters. Flippant decisions on what is right or wrong for a society should really be determined by referendums. Let the American people decide if it is okay to require transgender bathrooms in every public building. Anything less on such matters is tyranny and leads to complete breakdown of a society. We need a referendum on allowing rioting and looting as well.

Wars

Peace is the opposite of "War" and the planet has not been at peace in my lifetime. I was a child during World War II. I did not know what it was other than my aunts and uncles were all involved. I'll never forget my Uncle Bernie bringing home poison arrows used by natives in some island in the Pacific. We made a "group" swing in my backyard by replacing a swing with the aluminum skeleton dome from a B-29 bomber. We got it from the scrap pile of a nearby auto factory that was converted to making airplane parts for the war effort. My Aunt Helen lost her fiancé to the War. My Aunt Fran became a WAC. My father was too old to fight, but he worked at a factory converted over to the war effort. Everybody had a "victory garden" in their yard. Everyone grew their own vegetables. I used to take cans of bacon grease to the corner store. Each brought me ten cents. The grease was used to make scarce soap for the military.

As far as I knew the planet was peaceful from about 1945 to 1950, but some wars were starting up again. I got involved with war again in 1957 in some country called "Korea". It was someplace west of California. I had to register for the draft before I started college and when I finished, I was in line to be whisked away a month after graduation like my older brother. The US Army put his engineering skills to use as a cook.

However, I was accepted into graduate school and America's policy at that time gave me a draft exemption for grad school. They would get me when I finished. I got married on my way to graduate school and while there we had our first (of three) sons and there was a deferment for married men with children. So, I did not have to fight in the Korean War. My two deferments meant that I was still eligible to be drafted up to age 35, but they left me alone for the next war in Viet Nam (no idea where that place is or why we needed to fight there.)

The next USA elective war that I recall was Grenada – we quickly defeated them. Then there was Kuwait, then there was Iraq, then Afghanistan. Oh, I forgot our 3- or 4-day war with Cuba. I call these elective wars because these countries did not invade the USA, but they did something to irritate USA leaders, and the US government elected retribution, even if it kills many USA citizens.

My war experience probably connotes that I do not think kindly of wars. I admit this. If one steps back and ponders the very concept of war, it is a very strange concept. The old people of a country give their healthy, enthusiastic young people weapons and direct them to kill the healthy young people directed by the old people of another country. How is this right? World War II required USA response because the USA was invaded (bombed). The elective wars were unnecessary as well as "unwinnable". Nobody in American government even thought about winning. [We are in Afghanistan to fight the Taliban, not to "own' 30 million people.]

I started to read a book on the history of war. The book contained war details going back to when humans started to live in groups. That is when wars started, and wars got bigger, and better as new weapons were developed. Pointed sticks became spears; the discovery of metals lead to swords; herding people discovered that horses can be weapons; then came chariots, and bows and arrows, ships, cannons and on and on and on. Leonardo De Vinci had weapon development for a duke as his day job. He invented what we now know as the tank.

How do reasonable people deal with wars? The short answer is avoid them. Maybe if politicians who start elective wars would ponder "what happens when you win?" we would not get involved in wars. Many wars are internal. As I write this, many cities in the USA have been significantly damaged by riots, vandalism and looting associated with perceived injustice in isolated police/people events. First, media through the video magic of cell phones sensationalize these events and whip people into frenzies. For example, this week's riot and looting impetus was over the shooting of a person in the back by police officers. Of course, this does not seem right, but I do not know the details. The world convicted the police officer on trial by cell phone video. Thus, the root cause of the destruction of USA city centers in 2020 is media incompetence in distributing cell phone videos to the world. They knew that rioting and looting would follow.

These are the kinds of incidents that produce wars. People are incited and angered by an event, and it escalates into war. The cost of war is so high that very few incidents warrant a war. All elective wars are wrong.

Public safety

Public safety means the ability to travel in any public space and do anything legal without unwanted contact by public or private sector people. Twice recently I was advised not to walk several blocks from my hotel to the nearest Catholic Church. It was "unsafe". One of those times was by the concierge of a fancy Miami hotel; the other was by the registration person at the best hotel in Florianopolis, Brazil.

However, in my own hometown, the oldest and most beautiful church in town is now located in a drug epicenter and Masses are held only in daylight and there is a guard in the parking lot. Just two months ago the city center in the city I live in was destroyed by riots and looting associated with "Black Lives Matter" which evolved from the "wrongful" killing of a convicted felon by a police officer.

Public safety is more important than any other factor in establishing peace and order. A person cannot be happy without peace and order and public safety is a necessary part of peace and order. Based upon my personal experience of visiting almost all significant cities in the USA, I can say that our public safety was below most of the world, but better than our neighbor to the south – Mexico.

What determines public safety? I live in a small compound of houses (about 80) bordering a state park. I believe that we have acceptable public safety because I am not aware of any crime in the neighborhood. People of all ages walk the streets from sunup to sundown. I have only lived here three years, but I owned the lot that I built the house on for sixteen years. In that time, I have never had anything stolen (except one year's corn crop by some animals that ate the kernels of every single cob and left the cobs – deer I suspect). I do not lock my doors when I am at home, and I do not feel threatened in any way walking or riding by bike about the neighborhood. I believe that this is public safety.

My pied-a-terre 1200 miles away in Florida is in a city center. I lock the doors at all times and the house is completely fenced with locks on all gates. I have only owned the house for two years and I have been robbed once. They removed everything from my garage – all tools, my bike, my garden equipment. They neatly cut the padlock, took the contents, and put the cut lock back with the doors closed. Public safety is not so good in this city.

Does my Florida house have poorer public safety than my northern USA house? The answer is probably the prevailing philosophy on right and wrong. In my little enclave up north, the people who live in the eighty or so houses in the neighborhood tend to believe that stealing, fighting, ill-will towards others is wrong and should be discouraged. In Florida the prevailing philosophy is that such things are a normal part of life. I do not know a neighbor in either city. What about skin hue? Both neighborhoods have residents with various skin hues. The Florida neighborhood is likely more 1 to 5 skin hue than 5 to 10 skin hue. What has skin hue have to do with stealing? It likely has nothing to do with stealing except that economic wellbeing may be lower and this is the root cause for most stealing. Stealing is a way to improve one's income or state of possessions.

I would hope that the concept of sin would control stealing and other related crimes. Christians believe that stealing is a sin and sin is undesirable. Do my neighbors in the north avoid sinning more than my neighbors in Florida? I suspect that avoidance of sin is not a factor in either neighborhood. Secular USA has seemed to have dropped sin as a consideration in anything. The law permits murder of unborn babies and punishes people and organizations that think that abortion is a sin and should be avoided.

In some countries that I visited, stealing/burglary is so common that all houses and multi-family units are gated with windows barred. I noticed in Brazil, which has many multi-story buildings, that the doors and windows are barred up four stories from the ground and at least three stories down from the roof top.

In Miami, all ordinary houses have all windows and doors barred. Everything in China is walled with barbwire or similar on the top and all windows and doors to everything are locked. Mexico is the worst country for absence of public safety. They have organized crime controlling the government in cities and at the national level. Law and order do not really exist.

In most of the world, acceptable public safety is achieved by having a viable police presence, appropriate laws to immediately deal with offenders, and a police force that cannot be bribed. In the USA, police are paid extremely well and their benefits are better than any private sector job. Allegedly, this prevents situations such as Mexico's, where drug dealers pay police more than their municipality. This puts criminals in charge of the country. The best public safety situation that I encountered in my worldwide travels was in Japan. This country has a culture of respect for others, respect for elders, and respect for government. I witnessed cute young girls (less than ten years old) in pristine school uniforms ride the subway to school. It looked like kindergarten kids also rode the subway by themselves. In the USA suburbs, school buses pick up students at every house. They do not even walk a block by themselves. In some cities you can get arrested for child neglect if you let your child walk two blocks to play at another's house. This prevailing culture probably plays a significant role in a country's public safety.

If your culture is one of distrust for government and police you have poor public safety. The USA has almost universal distrust of government- mostly because government jobs at every level are so lucrative from the salary and benefits standpoint that people will do anything to get elected and reelected. As I write this, rioting and looting is happening this day in many American cities because city leaders perceive a loss of votes if they effectively suppress the rioting and looting.

The obvious solution to poor public safety is elected officials who care more about their community than their next election. I do not know if we have any of these in the USA.

The role of economics

In general, wealthy countries have better peace and order than countries with economic problems. When people are starving, they will riot, loot, and steal to feed their families. The reality of the situation is that when a country is in economic distress, the residents protest or leave. As I write this, maybe five million people left Syria because of the absence of peace and order over the past ten years or so. A similar situation exists in Venezuela and many other countries. These countries have no peace and order.

On the other hand, in a bygone era, countries that were at peace and in good order, lost significant population because of a poor economy. The USA received many Irish immigrants due to a potato famine. Many Italians immigrated to the USA because it was hard to make a living and support a family in Italy. The USA exists mostly because of economic situations in other countries.

The USA's current peace and order problem allegedly is related to "income inequality". This is a euphemism for capitalism. The only way that people can have the same income is to have everybody work for the government and all government employees be paid the same. There is an overt political movement in the USA to convert over to communism. Unfortunately, there is incontrovertible evidence that proves that such ideologies do not work. The USSR dissolved because their communist economy did not work. Cuba and Belarus are still surviving, but the people have nothing. They are in subsistence mode. China claims to be communist, but they had to shut down most state-run industries because they were in failure mode. They now have a carefully controlled "faux-capitalism" system that lets people start businesses and amass wealth to a limited degree. The Communist Party still controls everything; private citizens cannot own land. They can "buy" condos, but because the government owns the land on which they are built, they can be taken away at any time. Faux capitalism and authoritarian suppression of freedoms is producing peace and order in China, and it will probably continue to work as long as China remains the world's source of manufactured goods.

On my first visit to China in 1983, peace and order was well established, but Mao Zedong's communism meant people had nothing. As a guest of the Chinese government, I visited the Chinese Academy of Sciences. We were treated like royalty. We got to sit in the "soft seat lounges" at train stations. At that time, Beijing was receiving on average two flights a day from outside countries. We landed at night in pitch black. No runway lights were lighted until we were about fifty feet off the ground. The lights were off in the terminal, but they turned them on as we approached the terminal. The Chinese put them on for us and put us in a van for the trip into the city. It was really dark, and vehicles were not allowed to use their lights at night for fear of blinding bicyclists. The only way that the driver could see the road was moonlight on roadside trees. They planted fast-growing trees every ten meters or so along both sides of the roadway and painted the trunks white to guide vehicles at night. We were given rooms in a "Friendship Hotel" which was a walled compound built for soviet "advisors" when the USSR was an ally of China in one of our elective wars. The rooms were clean, but furnished with the original USSR furniture from the 1950's.

Everybody rode a bicycle; everybody worked; everybody wore a Mao-type uniform- blue for civilians, kaki for military. As guests of the government, we could shop in "Friendship Stores" which contained all of the country's nice stuff. The people could not shop in them, only escorted visitors.

Shanghai had department stores left over from British-rule years. One time I bought three hats in one store; they were only one dollar. Our interpreter told us they were only allowed to buy one per year. My wife tried on a coat that cost maybe fifty dollars. A crowd of about twenty people formed to watch her try on this very expensive coat. She did not buy it.

My last visit to China was in 2017 or thereabouts and the Chinese faux capitalism had totally changed the country from a sleepy backward sheltered, dirt-poor people to a thriving nation full of every imaginable consumer good and luxury. People lived in high-rise condos; the streets are crammed with cars, and nobody owned a bike. Ride sharing bikes were available with a phone tap on every block in Beijing. Everything was new, everything was electronic, and I ate in MacDonald's and Burger King's. China took over manufacturing for the world and it created wealth and peace and order (for them).

Role of education

Everything that happens in a country is affected by the prevailing education of its residents. The Greeks invented democracy and civilization as we know it today; at least so we are told. The Romans had a great civilization going until politics got out of hand. History suggests that there was a gap in Greek-like civilized living from about 200 A.D to 1300 A.D. This gap could be due to lack of education for all during that time. The societies that accepted a religion or organized spiritual practices as their basis of laws tended to have peace and order, that is, until one theocracy impinged on another. I guess that we are still in that situation.

Iran is a theocracy, and they have internal peace and order, but do not get along with their neighbors because their neighbor's theocracy is a bit different. And of course, they want all other countries in the world to adopt their theocracy. All theocracies are wrong.

Thus, education systems that differ can present challenges for having peace and order in a society. If all societies taught their young to observe the Ten Commandments in their schools, there would always be peace.

In the USA, grammar and high schools teach what the particular state of residence mandates. And parents are not told what that is. In my city the high school graduation rate is only about 40% and 80% of the students do not perform at grade level? What they are taught is anybody's guess. If public school students are allowed to bring their cell phones to school, they will be taught nothing.

When I had a granddaughter, I used to have her and her boyfriend help me with my home building projects. They went to different schools. His school used to make the students check their cell phone at the school entrance. He used to put his up his sleeve. His account of a typical class of forty-five minutes was that the first thirty minutes were spent in the teacher trying to establish order. That left a mere fifteen minutes per hour for instruction. The emphasis in his school was on sports. He participated in school sports; bowling, golf, and he played on weekends in the school's steel band. He had gigs most weekends. And yes, he was failing.

With schools allowing disorder to reign and dysfunction to be taught, it is no wonder that the USA is currently (2020) plagued with riots and looting in many of our cities. Young minds are overwhelmed with anti-peace and order teachings. Masturbation is taught (in third grade), but ethics is not taught at all. LBGTQ is taught, but not family as the foundation of society; history is taught to please the political party in power in a particular school district; sports reign supreme in all public schools. Scholarship on the part of serious students results in discrimination and bullying.

And thus, education plays a role in peace and order and the countries that do it right teach the basics of science, history, literature, communication, debate, languages, ethics and principles of peace and order. None of the above seem to interest school superintendents in the USA.

Conclusions

1. The United States is deficient in both peace and order.
   Basis:
   > In 2020, riots and looting are rampant in many cities and elected officials refuse to rein it in.

2. In the USA, aberrant behaviors are condoned, even encouraged. There is a general ethical malaise.
   Basis:
   > Most cities experience daily murders, most will never identify a suspect. TV is rife with mindless denigrating game shows. Elected leaders bicker like children in a school yard.

3. Public safety no longer exists in USA cities.

Basis:
> In 2020, many cities in the USA allowed riots and looting to destroy their city centers. Riot and looting are happening as I write this.

4. The economics of a country controls peace and order in that if people have jobs, they have no need (or time) to protest, riot and loot.
Basis:
> Wealthy countries with work for all contain satisfied citizens. Poor countries with work for all contain satisfied citizens. Countries with no work have citizens not at peace and disorder. For example, Iraq in 2020 had a 70% unemployment rate before the pandemic. There is citizen unrest.

5. Partisan politics are subverting peace and order in the USA.
Basis:
> Congress is unable to pass any legislation because each political party views the members of the opposing party as enemies, not as fellow Americans with a different opinion.

A model for peace and order

As individuals we can do little to prevent the wars brokered by our leaders. However, we can do our part for peace and order by our individual behaviors. And that is what this book is about: helping people make their lives more meaningful and happier.

Wars destroy everything and thoughtful citizens should speak out against all wars. It is curious that the USA's largest budget item is its military – almost a trillion dollars annually. Is all of that spending necessary? Apparently, it is. In 2018 or thereabouts Russia took over a significant part of the Ukraine because they had an infinitely stronger military. In 2020, China took over Hong Kong. Thus, a strong military will discourage these kinds of acquisitions of countries.

A proper democracy can produce peace and order. What does a proper democracy look like? There will be a whole chapter on the subject of government, but a fundamental basis of any democracy is to have an educated citizenry that understands how the system works and does their part in making it operational. By definition, a democracy involves citizen participation (as opposed to a dictatorship that allows no citizen participation). America's democracy has a firm basis, its constitution; its failure is due to lack of citizen participation. It had been taken over by politicians for life. The US government was supposed to be run by citizens who took time off from their farms and businesses to do their part, then they returned to their day jobs. Current politicians in the USA have no day jobs. Most have nothing put politics for support, so they never stop working for reelection.

What is the solution? Term limits for all, published curriculum vitae (CV's) for all candidates, a lottery for government jobs, and voter referendums for all critical issues like building dams, tax rates, licensing requirements, etc.). We will expand on these items in the chapter on government, but suffice it to say at this point, career politicians are the root cause of America's failing government. They have to be voted out, one by one.

If the United States is to try to continue to have a democratic form of government, its citizens must start to participate. I believe my city to be typical of most American cities: medium size, in a livable area, once a manufacturing powerhouse, still a home to major colleges and universities. At every level of government, the elected officials are career politicians. Most have no marketable skill or training, so government is their only source of income. This is why they make all decisions based upon perceptions that they will garner votes in the next election. There is no interest in running an efficient minimal government. Ever-expanding government means more patronage jobs for people who help with elections. Term limits on all elected offices can help solve this problem.

Peace needs ordinary people, not people with secondary causes participating in government. Peace requires elected leaders who understand that nobody wins wars that wars are the product of anger, and an angry mind is an irrational mind.

Order means a society with a designated place for every human need. A real government will start by taking care of relations with other governments, then established branches of government to unite the country's people and address their needs. In the USA, state governments address local issues, and village government address issues in the smallest groups of citizens. In the USA, we have uniformed police at every government level to enforce order. We have a national army and investigation capability (like the FBI); we have states with militias and police to enforce laws. In 2020, the US government entities responsible for maintaining order failed at every level per my observation. In my city, top government officials participated in the riots that destroyed our city center for the second time in my lifetime.

What can ordinary citizens do to bring order to their situations? In the USA we can vote out candidates for office that espouse disrespect for law and order. Deep thought is the tool that we propose to counter bad elected officials and bad media. Think about the ramifications of people not obeying laws. There can be no private property, everybody can steal each other's property. There can be no safety; people can kill each other with no ramifications. There cannot even be moving about. Highways are useless without laws to regulate flow of traffic. To allow riots and uncontrolled street protests is to cede civilization to those who profit from chaos and lawlessness.

Overall, in 2020, the USA is in finitude with regard to peace order and freedom. It is very hard to conceive survival of the USA while it is controlled by elected officials who insist on governing to appease special interests and factions, to the detriment of the majority. USA citizens who want peace, order and freedom need to vote accordingly.

Chapter 4 – Learning, Knowledge and Work

A young man must work very hard.
Prof. Taro Takeyama

I was working late one day in my office in the Metallurgy building where I was attending graduate school and one of my professors opened the door and looked at me at my desk and he said, "Very good, a young man must work very hard." This was a man in mid-career on sabbatical from the University of Hakkaido in Japan. He left his wife and young son (under ten) for two years to do research and learn things that would help him in his career as a college professor. He was in his office at school probably twelve hours a day and he spent most of his time trying to obtain proof that stacking faults occur in pure iron, a theoretical atomic phenomenon that was thought by most at that time to be impossible. He found one and wrote a paper on it. To me his greater contribution was to us students who took his course in electron microscopy and saw his incredible work ethic. He epitomized everything that this chapter is about. He trained himself to work with pure iron (that cost $10,000/lb. in 1962) and gained the necessary knowledge from the literature to plot a research path. Of course, he had the necessary education. His PhD and his work ethic inspired all of us students whom he taught. And besides that, he was the nicest, kindest person.

This chapter is about aspiring to be like Dr. Takeyama. Most mortals need to work to survive. Work is holy and sacrosanct. For most it is one's life. I started at seven years old with a 300 paper one-day-per-week paper route at sixty-five cents a week and I still go into the lab six days a week after sixty years of post-college work.

I do not know what I would do without work. I do not do social media; I do not do games; I do not like to waste a minute of the infinitesimal time that I have on planet Earth. Our solar system was allegedly formed 4.6 billion years ago, and each person lives for no more than 0.0000002% of that time. So we have to make every second count to make our mark in the human contribution to the cosmos.

The purpose of this chapter is to discuss education, training and acquired knowledge as they pertain to one's life's work. The objective of this chapter is fervor for learning as much as possible in one's lifetime and then sharing this knowledge with others to help them in their work.

I had the best training and education in the world to date and the new ideas that I am currently learning are a continued blessing. In fact, learning new things when you are very old is especially nice because at end of life you do not have to use the new knowledge to make more money. In the philosophy school that I currently attend at night I was recently asked," What are your three most valuable possessions?" Without thinking I responded: "My bicycle, my down comforter, and my grandfather's mason trowel." I use the comforter every day to sleep warm. I use my bicycle daily to keep my legs in shape for skiing and I use my grandfather's trowel as often as possible in my avocation of stone mason. If my wife of fifty years was alive, I may have had a different list. I am surprised that my list had nothing to do with acquiring more wealth or expensive possessions.

This chapter will discuss early life training, education, knowledge and establishing a career. These are all necessary for living a happy life – we think.

Childhood training

We all now know what kind of life training starts first: words, potty training, sentences, walking etc. I have no recollections before second grade. So, I do not have anything to share on my formation training and education other than what my three sons got from my wife and myself. My mother showed me a photo of me getting buried in snow by my brother and sister. My mother had her three children out for a winter walk. I was in what was then called a baby buggy and while my mother was chatting with a neighbor my brother and sister were shoveling snow on the bundled baby in the buggy – me. Apparently, I survived.

My wife trained our three sons out of infancy using a paperback edition of the Dr. Spock book on children. We had no help from my mother or her mother at the start. We left our hometown for graduate school one thousand miles away when our first son was only months old. Dr. Spock's book helped her identify potential diseases and to determine if our first born was normal in growth and behaviors. For example, Dr. Spock said to let them cry at bedtime and eventually they will fall asleep. They did. What we both did with regard to training the boys in pre-school years was to let them know in no uncertain terms that they were always to do what we asked them to do, not what they wanted to do. This essential part of training for life is ignored by many these days. Last week in the newspaper there was a report that a woman and her three-year old child were led off an airplane at the gate when her child refused to wear a face mask as required by the airline for virus control. Such instances of small children controlling their parents are now common. Of course, this is contrary to common sense. You do not let a two or three-year old make life decisions.

The United States somehow made corporal punishment of children a crime about as severe as bank robbery. I do not know how it happened, but it did. So, if you spank your child and one of the "child abuse police" are alerted, you will likely lose your child and end up in jail. For example, my niece took her one-year-old daughter to a department store photo shop to get her one-year-old portrait. The baby was sleeping in her arms by the time that the photographer was ready for them, so she took off the baby's shoes and started tapping her feet with her hand to wake her. The next day the child abuse people showed up at her house and she was summoned to "take your child away" court. Apparently, somebody in the photographer's waiting room reported her.

This is the kind of absurdity that keeps people from asserting parental control over their children. Parents must at all times have absolute control over their children's civil behavior. The basis of a family depends on it. Children should never be asked what they want to eat or wear or do. They are told what to do until they leave home to support themselves. Children must never be allowed to talk back to parents or elders. Children need to be taught to respect elders in all situations.

I never had to hit my three sons, but I had to talk assertively. Of course, my wife and I let many things slide so that they could have some satisfaction on putting something over on the old man. For example, when they were teenagers, dirt bike motorcycles would show up now and then in a shed out back. I would quiz them on the bikes (they were not allowed to own a motorcycle- too dangerous) and they would always say that it belonged to so-and-so, and they were fixing it for him. The boys had their own money from their paper routes, so they bought their own "toys" ever since they started working.

They used to buy and sell motorcycles (dirt bikes) and ride them (against our wishes) in nearby woods.

Another key part of character training of young people is to never give them an allowance. As a member of the family, they must contribute to maintaining the family and the family home. I never paid the boys for any work that I assigned to them. They had to cut grass, pull weeds, dig ditches, carry things, clean things etc. when asked and expect no remuneration other than their room and board.

Incredibly, one of the things that my sons are most proud of and brag about to others is that I gave them no money, no allowance. If they wanted to buy something (that was optional) they had to earn the money for it. They all had bank accounts and when they approached college age, I told them to save as much as they could for college, and I would pay the rest.

One son had good summer jobs and paid for his own six years of college. Another son did very well working summers and I paid for his five years of college. One son saved nothing for college, and I made him take a loan for his tuition. He had to pay back the loan. After college my wife took his paycheck and gave him an allowance. When he got married my wife gave him his enforced savings for his house down payment.

Thus, children have to be trained in behaviors and life skills throughout their life under the family roof. If they live at home, they obey parental rules and regulations and that has to be the way things are.

All I remember about my youth at home was working at every job I could so that I always had spending money and money in the bank. When it came time for a college decision, my father told my brother and me that we were to go to a particular cooperative engineering college and become engineers. We did. My sister got herself a scholarship to college. We did as our parents told us to do.

Parental control of children is achieved by proper attitude. Parents have to be in control at all times. Never play with children. This can cause the loss of parental control. They do not want to play with you anyways. I tempered this a bit. When our sons were teens, we sailed together in the summer and skied together in the winter – sort of. The boys would crew on the big sailboat, but they also had their own sailing dinghies that they spent most of their time with. When we went skiing together, I skied with a friend and the boys went off by themselves. So, we recreated as a family, but I never really played with them, nor did my wife. Children need to play with other children, not their parents.

Training in life skills and work skills should start as early as possible. I built a workbench for each boy at age three and gave them a set of tools and lumber and nails and let them start to build things. When they were six, seven, and eight, I gave them a section of our backyard where they could build tree houses and whatever else they wanted. And they did. There were so many nails in those trees it's a wonder that they did not die of rust.

I had a large metal-working lathe in the basement, and I noticed that my supply of metal round-stock kept getting smaller. I mentioned this to my wife, and she said that one of the boys goes down to the basement after school and cuts steel bars on my lathe. She advised me to say nothing about the depleting stock of metal bars. Today that son is a tool maker specializing in precision lathe work. He has been doing this for thirty years. It is good to look the other way at times, and of course listen to mothers. They know everything about everything. That is a mother's job.

Schooling

There has been an education crisis in the USA since about 1985. The same people who initiated the child abuse police-initiated dumbing-down of what is taught in public schools. Only school insiders know who is responsible, but it is public knowledge that it has occurred. Students from the USA fall below fifty other countries in worldwide reading, math, science etc. testing. In 2021, a magazine reported that 37 million kids in the USA cannot read at grade level. In my

119

home state, we spend more than $30,000 per student on teacher salaries and graduation rates in cities are often less than fifty percent. Most students graduating from city schools are functionally illiterate.

In my home city, the school board members have their school board job as their primary source of income ($30,000/year for 1 meeting a month) and there are countless administrators also doing this and that, such that most of the money allocated for educating children goes to paying for exorbitant salaries and benefits of the people who run the public-school systems.

For decades in the USA public schools have been in failure mode. A root cause of this is probably that the people who are paying for the school system and the parents who are the "customers" of the school system have no access to what is being taught or not taught. Teacher unions control how much time teachers spend in a classroom and some state entity that is who knows where, dictates what is taught. In my state, the governor's chief of staff was just appointed as the head of the state's public school system. He is not an educator, but a political crony of the governor. Thus, I suspect this is how the United States of America has failed its young people.

Public schools were mediocre when I was young, but the USA had a thriving private school system to produce its needed leaders, technical people and trades people. I attended parochial grammar school (K to 8), then Catholic high school. The nuns who taught me in grammar school were saints in black robes. They devoted their entire lives to educating children and shaping our ethics and morals.

Catholic schools went the way of the nuns. I often ponder where the nuns went. There were about thirty at my school and they taught about five hundred children. They always had perfect order in class; they taught us everything about everything and tested us until we knew our stuff. They were wonderful. I spent the seventh grade in the hallway because I was disruptive. My eighth-grade nun got me a scholarship to art school on the other side of town, so I was out of her "hair" for a day or two a week. They knew how to keep the order needed to teach.

I was taught by priests in high school. They also knew how to maintain the order necessary to effectively teach. They gave out "jugs" to disruptive students. A jug was a one hour after school detention period enforced by the director of discipline. Father Riley was an ex-boxer with a pointing-finger made from high-grade structural steel. When Father Riley poked you, it left a bruise. We had to learn; we loved the school; we loved the teachers. All did well.

Catholic and other private schools could have saved the USA's primary education system, but the same type of people as the child abuse police passed laws outlawing competition to union-controlled dumbed-down public schools. Religious-based schools were lost by the costs of operating their schools with paid staff. The nuns worked free. The five hundred- student school I attended was entirely funded by church collections plus a few fund-raising plays and the like throughout the year. When the nuns disappeared, parishes could no longer support their schools out of Sunday collections and today tuitions at the few Catholic schools left in my city are about $10,000 per student. Not many working families can afford this.

Where did the nuns go? That is another story, but I suspect that they succumbed to the feminist movement of the 60's and 70's. The premise of the feminist movement is that it is wrong for a woman to act feminine and attractive to men. Men are the enemy. Men are evil. They only want to subjugate women. Women must compete with men. Women "win" when all of the men are gone.

I believe that the women who would have given up their lives to become teaching nuns are now angry people doing what they can to punish men in any way possible. For example, the women in congress seem to all be angry and hateful.

USA schools compare unfavorably with other countries not because USA students are dumber than worldwide students, but because the curriculum has been dumbed down by the politicians who run the schools. Most USA schools have a board of directors/school board. They are supposed to be the watchdogs for each school system and each USA city, town, or village has their own school system and their own school board and their own superintendent of schools. The schools teach what the state mandates and the superintendent have the responsibility to see that the schools are adequately staffed, and within budget; they must strive to make graduation rate acceptable as well as student performance on standardized tests. Students in suburban schools in the USA generally meet worldwide performance standards. Students in cities do not.

One significant reason for their underperformance in my city is attendance. They do not go to school. Parents are not making their children to school. A second significant issue is disorderly conduct of students. My late granddaughter's boyfriend went to a city school, and he told me that it typically takes the teacher in every class one half hour of the fifty-minute class to get the students to "settle down" and listen. This only leaves twenty minutes to address the day's topic. Thirdly, sports are more important than anything else, especially in high school. The in-crowd participates in sports and those that do not qualify for teams are looked down upon.

I do not know how it works, but students with learning and physical limitations are put in with the others. I have no idea how young people with an eight-year-old intellect graduate from high school. But they do in the USA. Also, many of these students are disruptive because of their situation problems. Of course, the parents of special needs students want them to go to school with the normal children, but I have no idea how calculus can be taught to a non-verbal special-needs student with the intellectual capacity of an eight-year-old.

Thus, USA schools are failing at least for the reasons just enumerated. When I went to primary and secondary school, everybody received the same instruction. There were no special need students. There was absolute order in class, and I was taught by nuns and priests who my parents trusted completely to teach me what I needed to know to go on to college and to live a productive life.

Putting special-need students in classes with normal students is an absurdity. Allowing chaos in the classroom is an absurdity. Allowing politicians to decide what students are taught is an absurdity. Busing students within a two-mile radius of a school is an absurdity. Allowing sports to be the focus of learning is an absurdity.

Vouchers that allow parents to send their children to a school of their choice is the near-term solution in the USA. Municipalities pay for public schools through real estate taxes and parents are told by the school district where they live where their children will go to school. If the designated school is "bad" you have no recourse. If parents were given a tuition voucher for each school age child, they could have their children go to schools, public or private, that they deem suitable for their children.

The failing city schools would receive very few students and go out of business as they should. I live near a former parochial school that was closed due to religious persecution of the Catholic Church (no government money for a faith-based school). The building was sold to a charter school. I go by the building daily and I have never seen any students. I go by a city school on my same daily commute, and I see scores of students milling about outside and large groups walking to school behaving badly. What makes the charter school orderly and the city school disorderly when they draw upon the same student population? I opine that it is the same defective leadership that is causing public schools to fail. The students are in charge, and they are not interested in learning.

Because of the current pandemic, my weekly philosophy class had to be discontinued in person and they have gone over to Zoom classes. However, I started taking commercial philosophy courses that one purchases on DVD. I have done four to date and I like them. However, it occurs to me that this may be the way for America to address its failed education system. These commercial courses allegedly use world famous, award-winning college professors so they have the best teachers. There are hundreds of course options; some are twelve one-half hour lectures; some are twenty-four or thirty-six one-half hour lectures. Suppose a school district took their best teacher in every subject and recorded his or her daily lectures on DVD. These could be given to respective students for playing, replaying and study. Printed copies of the lectures and quizzes would also be provided. Students would each have a laptop and could play these lectures with headphones at their study places in a school. Aides could enforce order and study. This would be a way to greatly reduce the cost of schools (my district spends $30,000 per student per year), have excellent instruction, to teach the same things to all students and most important parents could review what is being taught to their children. In any case, action is needed to restore education in America.

Training for work life

America's colleges do not teach skilled trades. When I was in undergraduate engineering school, all students had to complete a freshman course in machine shop. The theory was that an engineer must know how to make something if he or she is going to design things. It was eight contact hours a week and we had to learn how to run lathes, mills, shapers, grinders, layout, etc. We even had a foundry and had to make and machine a casting (out of aluminum). We had to buy a kit of measuring tools that were needed to make parts. We also had to learn drafting- how to make engineering drawing of parts.

I was in cooperative engineering. I went to school for six months out of the year and worked in a factory for the other six months. The factory assignment varied each term and I had to be given a substantial project in my assigned department and then write a report on the project that was graded by the school. It was an incredible program. I worked in every department from suggestions to die casting. I did materials research and worked on the assembly line. My fifth year I worked full time on a thesis project. My thesis problem was to solve a forty-percent scrap problem in making die cast carburetors for the Corvair automobile.

Engineering students no longer have to take machine shop. Engineers are now probably taught that all parts come from Amazon. After fifty years, I still occasionally work in the machine shop where I work, and I still use the micrometers and other measuring tools from my freshman tool kit. Hands-on training must be part of every person's life. Public schools used to have programs in machine shop, foundry, sheet metal work, plumbing, electrical, carpentry, etc. In addition, all manufacturing companies used to have apprentice programs to teach skilled trades. All of these are mostly extinct in the USA. All large manufacturers are gone, only a few instances of manufacturing remain in the USA. In the city where I live and worked, there were four hundred manufacturing companies in 1939. In 2020 there are less than ten who make a product.

If the United States is to survive as a country, training in trades' apprenticeships and internships must return. Colleges do not teach machining or plumbing or carpentry, but you cannot have a society without such things. Where is the training going to come from? There are a few token programs in my state, but they are available to probably less than ten percent of the students. The training situation in the USA is beyond failure mode. It is an abomination. Kids are disruptive in school because they can be. There are no consequences. A large company that I worked for was always having programs to improve our output. One of them was taught by PhD psychologist who got famous for improving behaviors of inmates in mental institutions. His secret: the consequences for disruptive behavior must be significant, immediate, and certain. No dessert (significant), it gets written down immediately and it will always happen when he or she is again disruptive (certain). This is pretty much the way that a pet is housebroken. It works and something akin to this needs to happen to disruptive students in schools and work.

Disruptive behavior cannot be tolerated in training, education or work. Entities that tolerate disruptive behavior are bound to fail. Military organizations have known this for thousands of years. They needed order and discipline to survive in battle. And training and education are battles for one's mind.

Knowledge

The human brain is a gift from God that can be used for good or bad and with varying degrees of efficiency. Medical researchers have devised ways to identify what parts of the brain participate in activities, but they really do not know the brain's operating system. They have broken the brain down to various regions that tend to be used for certain functions, but they do not know where one's knowledge comes from. Knowledge is the usable product of training, education, and life experiences. The more knowledge a person has, the more valuable that person is if his or her knowledge is a type needed by an employer. There is valuable knowledge and knowledge of limited use. On the American TV show "Antiques Roadshow", people will bring in a dusty old porcelain bowl and ask if it had any value to others. The Roadshow will bring in an expert with incredible knowledge pertaining to the porcelain. He or she will know all of the important manufacturers in the world, when each was prominent, what they made, who their artists were and what old porcelain vases of any type will likely sell for at auction.

People tend to acquire knowledge in specific areas. Thus, part of life is deciding what type of knowledge you want to specialize in. I can scan all of my relatives and identify an area where each is knowledgeable. One cousin knows everything about Hudson automobiles, another cousin writes mystery novels, my brother knows everything about General Motors cars, my sister read every book ever written, and my wife knew every possible way to cook potatoes. My thing is engineering materials and tribology.

The best situation in life is to have acquired knowledge that others are willing to pay for. And your education, training and life experiences need to continue in your field for life. I was married for fifty years and until my wife died, she cooked the best potatoes and always looked for new ways to cook them. Constant search for new knowledge is imperative for a meaningful life. This is what the purveyors of the DVD courses that I buy, say.

However, if I ponder the most successful lives that I have encountered in my lifetime, my parents, my relatives, my friends, my colleagues, I have to agree with the Native

American saying: "when you die, the value of your life is determined by the number of people that are happier because you were born." I have gone to many funerals in my life and the largest number of attendees that I have witnessed was at the funeral for my brother-in-law's sister. The church was full – maybe seven hundred people. I did not know Barb well. I only saw her at large family gatherings. She was always smiling, cheerful, and friendly. She did not have a college education and was a stay-at-home mom all her life, but somehow, she reached a lot of people with her positive attitude and friendly demeanor. Her brother, on the other hand, was infamous at work for his authoritarian behavior. He was a big executive at one of the largest banks in America. He was known as "firing George". Firing was one of his specialties. I went to high school with him, and I like him very much, but I suspect that I am rather alone in my liking. I consider him one of the most knowledgeable people that I know. For example, he invented ATM's, so I am told. He was a computer expert when computers were in its infancy, and he was responsible in part for making banking as computerized as it currently is. Banks have been shutting down offices for years because everything really can be done by computers.

He has been retired from banking for many years and he is as rich as anybody needs to be, but he continues to learn new things. He has spent his retirement years building fancy houses for his children and himself and he has taught himself everything there is to know about home building. He acts as general contractor in building his houses. He epitomizes the ideal of seeking new knowledge.

The most knowledgeable woman that I ever knew is my Aunt Agnes. She died about five years ago at age ninety-seven. She knew everything about everything. She was a very religious person and I used to join her for daily Mass once a week. After church, we would sit for an hour or so in her car and she would tell me things about everything. She knew things about my parents that I never knew. She knew about all of the businesses in our city; she knew the birthdays of at least a hundred of her children, grandchildren, and great grandchildren. She knew about each one. She knew and cared for all of her neighbors. At ninety-six she would shovel out a neighbor lady's sidewalk. Her neighbor was not too steady on her feet at seventy-three. She would drive eighty-year-olds to their doctor appointments. She would bake me something every week when my wife died. She loved my wife, my mother, my father – everybody. Besides knowing all of the knowledge in the world, she loved everybody in the world.

Unfortunately, I never got to see how many people showed up at her funeral. Every two years for the last twenty years I attended an international research conference called the Gordon Research Conference. It is held in various New England Colleges, and it is weeklong. I was scheduled to leave for the Gordon Conference on Saturday and on Thursday Aunt Agnes called and asked if I would show her where my wife was buried. She said that she tried to visit it but could not find it. I said I would pick her up at 10:00 AM and show her the grave. I did so and she said, "while we are here let me show you, my grave. We went to another part of the cemetery, and she had a date-missing head stone next to her husband's grave. He died twenty years earlier. She said, "this is where I will be buried." I took her home and left for Maine (driving) on Saturday morning. On the second day of the conference, I got an email from my daughter-in-law: "bad news, Aunt Agnes died." The conference college was in a wooded area of Maine. I just went into the woods to grieve. I was too upset to drive eight hundred miles to her funeral. It must have been the biggest ever.

My work life in engineering and research had exposed me to many geniuses. Most of my research colleagues are college professors in engineering, physics, and chemistry. I marveled at some. They just seemed to know everything. One very dear colleague from a university in Poland used to tell me things about places in the USA where we met that I never knew. He would research a meeting venue and know everything about that venue and its location. I'll never forget a conference we attended together in Yokahama, Japan. I was paying $320 per night at the cheapest hotel. Zigmunt found a youth hostel for thirty dollars per night and arranged for a climb of Mt. Fuji over the weekend. Zigmunnt was knowledgeable about all matters, and he was the nicest person on the planet. He died three years ago.

I had a co-worker at the automotive factory who was a documented genius. It was well known that he had an IQ of 186. He knew everything. He used to study one day a week in school and spend the other nights in the local bar. Of course, he had straight A's in all courses. I worked with him on many projects, and he would say, "Let's do it this way", when I would opt to do something else. His way was always better. He was always right. He was despised by most co-workers because he was always right. I liked him as a person, and it did not bother me that he knew more than me about most everything.

I ran into him by chance many years after we left school and went our different ways. After his PhD he started a company to make automatic pin spotters for bowling alleys. He sold the company for millions to a large corporation and never worked again. He spent his time repairing antique clocks and traveling from his ski lodge in the winter to his island paradise home in the summer. Knowledge that leads to innovation can be financially rewarding.

Another genius that I worked with was the consummate polymer chemist. He knew everything about plastics and was the corporate resource on them. But his incredible knowledge over and above plastics was in details of the Civil War. He was a Civil War buff and knew every battle, every general, everything about the war. Gil retired and lived a quiet life still doing Civil War stuff. His knowledge of the Civil War did not produce any revenue or get transferred to others. This is knowledge lost, possibly meaningless knowledge.

The best knowledge is the knowledge that is converted to wisdom to produce benefits to others. This kind of knowledge was epitomized in my idol: George Eastman. Mr. Eastman's genius led to the concept of flexible film as a receptor for photosensitive chemicals. Prior to Eastman's invention photographs were made on glass plates coated on one side with photosensitive chemicals. Eastman made photography available to all by putting flexible film in a portable box. People take photos and send the box in for development of the film and printing of prints. Photography increased in popularity and George Eastman's company grew to be worldwide with as many as 130,000 employees. His knowledge created many jobs and brought immeasurable happiness to users of his technology in the form of photographs and movies.

However, George Eastman's wisdom was exemplified by what he did with the wealth that his knowledge brought him. He started a major university (the University of Rochester); he started one of the most important schools for musicians in the world (the Eastman School of Music). He started a free program that lasted for decades to clean and treat the teeth of Rochester's children (the Eastman Dental Dispensary). He gave the cities where his factories were located innumerable civic assets plus the jobs and the good done by high-paying jobs. When I was in my teens almost all Rochester youths played KPAA baseball (Kodak Park Athletic Association). The company provided resources to countess baseball leagues to keep teens out of trouble. There are not enough superlatives for the results of his wisdom. His company prevailed for more than one hundred years and died in 2010 when wisdom-deficient people invaded company management; but the legacy of George Eastman's wisdom will never diminish.

Work for pay

Nature's plan is for all creatures to work. Bees, ants, squirrels, birds, fish – all creatures work every day, all day. They work to live, to eat. Humans started doing the same as the creatures. They hunted and gathered for their subsistence. Cats are probably God's laziest creatures, but even lions wake up now and then to hunt a meal. Work in the form of a good job is the net result of a person's training, acquired knowledge and experience. At least that is the way it is supposed to be. This is what is natural; a lion who hunts every day does not go hungry. Work can be not so rewarding if a person cannot be promoted upward by nature of the job, or if the work environment is hostile. Farm laborers are often in jobs where they cannot move up the line. Many times, they speak a different language than the farmer that they work for. Thus, they will continue to be paid for what they pick with low expectations for improved work situations. If the farm laborer becomes fluent in the language of the farmer, he or she may advance to a team leader or other higher paying job. Hostile work environments are often created when the boss has a personal dislike for you. I had such a situation for a year of two at a large company. My boss retired and the person replacing him was a co-worker that I disliked because he was a fraud. He could not do his job and he knew that I knew that he could not do his job. I asked him many times for answers on what was supposed to be his job, corrosion engineer, and I quickly learned that he knew nothing about the details of corrosion and faked his way into his corrosion engineer job. He did not last that long, but he tried to do harm to me when he was my boss. This is how a hostile work environment can be created.

My wife's only "job" after marriage was "lunchroom monitor". When our three sons were in parochial school, they ate lunch at their desks and a lunchroom monitor supervised the class while the teacher got a break. My wife did this for years (as an unpaid volunteer) and she told me that the kids went "bad" in the sixth grade. This meant difficult to control. Thus, a hostile work environment can exist when the customers (students) are difficult to control. She could do it, but sixth graders do not obey as well as second graders. Teachers can have work environment problems, but most accept it as part of their work life. Farmers have poor weather to deal with. Checkout cashiers often deal with rude people. Post office clerks often have to deal with "talkers", people who want to socialize more that mail a letter. Every job had its issues, but none diminish the glory that is steady work.

Some people elect to not work; some forty percent of the USA's working- age population opts out. Physical and mental disabilities represent some of the non-working, but the USA's government assistance programs are such that they encourage not working. For example, my father-in-law was a quadriplegic. I had a job that he could do, but if he did it he would lose his government aid. USA government aid programs denigrate individuals and prevent many of the forty percent from obtaining the dignity of work. USA's welfare system is a crime, a crime committed against recipients and a crime to taxpayers who have to pay for a broken system. Many Americans have made beating the assistance system their life's work.

One of the most valuable aspects of work is acquiring friendships with co-workers. I have five best friends that I interface with frequently and all were former co-workers. My research partner and I were together in a corporate lab for about twenty years. We met every morning and reviewed the day's projects. I left that company twenty years ago and my partner left fifteen years ago. We have met every Saturday for coffee since I left in 2002. Last week I received a request from another best friend from work. He wanted some design help on a matter. He lives four hundred miles away and I have been visiting him every two years (for a sail on his yacht) for the past forty years. We worked together in the 1960's. Another best friend was my ski partner for many years. Before that we sailed together. We were co-workers in the 1970's. Six months ago, he went into a memory care facility and is not able to see outsiders because of the corona virus, but he calls me when he is lucid.

This Saturday I will be attending a funeral for a relative of another best-friend co-worker. I am in e-mail contact with her and her husband continually even though she now lives a thousand miles from me, and we have not worked together since 1968. These are the kinds of bonds with others produced by working alongside others. When the USA had a manufacturing economy there were large corporations and people had jobs often with many co-workers. In my last big-company job there were more than sixty people in the lab where I worked closely with all of them. They were like family. We had parties for milestones all the time. We went to lunch every other month on profits from the coffee fund. The corporate camaraderie of the manufacturing economy is now gone in the USA, and this is the most damaging part of the 2020 "global" economy. And it is a shame.

A consistent work life is the goal of every human. It is innate. Unfortunately, in the USA, government interference has made long-term meaningful jobs difficult to obtain. Manufacturing jobs have moved from the USA to Asia. Government interference in the form of absurd regulations made it impossible for large manufacturers to exist. For example, in the 1950's there were thousands of bronze and iron foundries in the USA. They were in almost every part of the country. In 2020 there is only a handful. Foundries melt metal; they had a smokestack. Having a smokestack became taboo. They handled molten metal, and this became unsafe even though it has been a form of work for at least five thousand years. Companies who needed castings to make things had to go to Asia where people revere work, and their governments know that a peaceful society means work for all.

In the USA, entrepreneurs and most businesses are crucified by government regulations. This will be covered more in the chapter on government, but as an example of how harmful the USA government is to business, they recently passed a national law that mandates that businesses with more than five employees provide at least three months maternity leave for every employee. On top of this the US federal government raised the minimum allowable pay to what was normally paid to experienced workers. Employers have to pay people who initially know nothing and are not making a company any profit, a lot of money. Small businesses are the start of all businesses and for governments to go after startups with devastating financial demands keeps the growth of businesses at a fraction of what they could be.

Volunteer work

People who do work for causes and not-for-profit organizations for no pay are the core of society and civilization. The nuns who taught me in parochial school epitomize the value of volunteer work. They and priests give up their personal lives to educate and inspire others. Nuns were saints in my opinion. The nuns at Holy Family School taught about thirty children in a class, 500+ in the school from grades one through eight. And the Notre Dame nuns had been doing this at that church-run school for about a hundred years when I came along. The nuns received no salary. They lived on campus in a walled house and garden about thirty strong. Their food and shelter was paid for by parishioners' church collections. These nuns were highly skilled teachers and because of their spirituality they taught not just reading, writing and arithmetic, but life values, ethics, civics – everything a youth needed They also knew each student and addressed emotional and other needs on an individual basis. I was the "badest" student in my seventh and eighth grades and they tried very hard to fix me. I successfully resisted, but they tried valiantly. It is hard to describe the value of this kind of work. Too bad they are almost gone in 2020.

A volunteer effort that I am also familiar with is what I call "church ladies". Every church that I have encountered has them. They run churches for the preaching staff. And they work for free. As I write this, we are in a pandemic so church participation is limited and the church ladies take care of observing isolation rules and disinfect the pews and other public areas after each service. Before the pandemic, they ran the clubs, the prayer groups, the fund-raising meals etc. When I was young, the church ladies even cooked for the priests. These volunteers kept churches going and churches have been essential in society in keeping family and beliefs the basis of the USA.

As a person, after my church and schools, I benefited in every way possible from participation in Boy Scouts. They are under attack in the USA by lawyers who work to destroy all organizations who do good for others. I was a very poor inner-city kid and had not an inkling as to what camping, and nature was. I got to stay in forests, climb mountains, canoe across bays, march in parades – all sorts of wonderful things with a diverse group of other scouts and leaders. It was beyond wonderful. I am certain that the lawyers who destroyed church, boy scouts, and other such organizations in the USA will reap their reward for eternity. They are the virus that never goes away. They are without souls. And they are keenly aware of their role in the destruction of society and order. Money is their god - my opinion.

The USA has countless social organizations that are run by volunteers that to date have not been destroyed as a class by lawyers – mostly because they have shallow pockets. They are the volunteer fire department, the Lions Club, the Rotary Club, The Moose, The Elk, and the VFW – all sorts of organizations dedicated to doing good for others by the action of their volunteer work. They are diminishing in number and size in 2020, but the wonderful things that these organizations do is incredible.

What makes a person volunteer time and talent for a cause? People are happiest when they are helping others. And this is a strange and wonderful part of some sections of our brains. When you do something good for somebody some neurons sense this and send a command to the feel-good node in the brain. The neurophysicists can show this with rMRI scans so they know that there is a scientific basis for feeling good about helping others.

Conclusions

1. Work is the essence of life. It determines who you are as a person and what you contributed to the continuation of humanity. You are what you did in your instant on Earth.

   Basis: - Nature. Animals hunt for food at all times. If they are not successful, they die. Humans are born with the same self-preservation instinct as animals. Every living creature must work to survive. Life is work.

2. A happy childhood and parental persuasions start your life on Earth. Parents who maintain absolute control over their offspring at all times and all circumstances establish order and respect in offspring that produces order and peace throughout life. To allow a toddler to do his or her will is to abdicate parental duty. Parental training must include teaching the role of authority.

   Basis: Lifelong observation of people, family, and acquaintances has shown me that kids that are allowed to do what they want as children end up losers in life.

3. Training and education begin at infancy. Young minds are like sponges, they can accept incredible amounts of data, good and bad. It is a parent's responsibility to make it all good.

Basis: I could have easily strayed into jail and the like as a youth. My parents kept this from happening by stressing the importance of education.

4. Schools are a determining factor in a person's life. One's life is a function of one's schooling. Parents must assess the schooling available to their offspring and do whatever it takes to make the best possible choice within one's means.

   Basis: My only granddaughter lost her life to public schools. They taught her it was OK to defy nature and biology.

5. Public schools in the USA are deficient in teaching fundamentals like reading, writing and arithmetic. They operate significantly below international norms. Private schools and home schooling in 2020 are the only possible source of complete schooling. Sports, political ideologies, and frivolous subjects are the emphasis and reason for failure in USA schools.

   Basis: Every public school in the USA has sports as the basis of school fame and students who excel in sports are aggrandized. Students who excel in academics are denigrated and called names (Geeks).

6. The incredible costs of primary and secondary education in the USA, sometimes $30,000 per student per year is wasted money in some school

systems because it is mostly spent on things other than effectively conveying knowledge from a teacher to students.

Basis: The subjects taught to my deceased granddaughter in K to 12 were mostly useless for success in work life.

7. Disorder in public schools keeps scheduled teaching times to a fraction of allotted time in USA schools. There is no way for teachers to enforce student order, so none exists.

Basis: Stories from public school students told me that this is the case in the city schools where I live. I believe that a similar situation exists in most major USA cities.

8. Parents must direct their children's secondary education. It cannot be the student's choice. Children (under eighteen) lack the life experiences necessary for proper educational choices.

Basis: I have personally witnessed bright children get college degrees in fields (like Fabric Design, Art history, International Relations, etc.) Where careers (jobs) are almost non-existant.

9. The loss of the apprenticeship concept in the USA has left training in the skilled trades wholly inadequate. Public school and community college programs in the USA are similarly wholly inadequate. They are just snippets of the trade.

Basis: As a general contractor in the building trades, I found it almost impossible to get proficient tradespeople for carpentry, plumbing, framing, masonry, and roofing. Societies need these trades, and in the USA, nobody is there to teach these trades.

10. Knowledge in the USA had descended to Google and U-tube answers. True knowledge requires individual study, experience, and research.

Basis: It has been my observation that the selfie generations rely almost entirely on social media for their "news". Where does this "news" come from? Who knows?

11. The availability of meaningful work in the USA may be the country's most significant problem. Nothing has replaced manufacturing.

Basis: I have not seen any entity/field that replaces long-term manufacturing with jobs with good pay and benefits. Public sector jobs still have these benefits, but few are available to people without political connections.

12. Volunteer work is on the wane in the USA. It is a key part of USA society and all aspects of human existence diminish without volunteers to keep organizations that do-good operating.

Basis: All of the service organizations that flourished in the manufacturing economy are diminishing in size and number. My city used to have 30 local sections of technical societies. In 2020, about 6 remained. They all used to vocational guidance programs for young people.

A proper education and job

I preached a simple mandate to my three sons: be able to call yourself something. What I meant was a plumber, an engineer, a machinist, a doctor etc. This is as opposed to just having a job. I think that all parents should tell their children this. It could be anything that requires a particular skill set. A truck driver satisfies this requirement, as does salesperson, carpenter, and mason. My three sons heeded my advice. I have two engineers and a tool maker.

My parents both had only eighth grade educations, but both acquired skills that provided lifetime employment. My father became a tool maker, my mother a seamstress. I got my parochial school education from their hard work in factories. They earned my tuition at these jobs.

Another very important part of education and training is to have children tested for their skill abilities and likes early in life and design training and education that is commensurate. A child may want to be an artist when he or she grows up, but if he or she does not have artistic ability it can never happen. Some skills like art, music, sports and writing are not acquired. You need innate ability. Parents who do their job will know their children's innate talents by the time they reach the eighth grade and parents need to nurture and support growth of their talents.

Public grammar and high schools in the USA are generally so bad that the only way to get a reasonable public education in the USA is to shop school districts and buy a house in an area that has a school district with a good achievement record. There are rankings published for all school districts. If a city has an overall graduation rate of fifty percent, do not live there. This is an absurd situation, but that is the education situation in 2020 in the USA. A potential solution is government vouchers that allow parents to select a grammar school and high school of choice.

However, teacher unions are fighting this in the courts and in political parties. They fear that public schools will get the "lesser" students under such a system. The private and charter schools will get the better students - so what. Now nobody learns. You cannot teach anything with   absent, disruptive, inattentive students .Home schooling is becoming ever more popular, but of course, this has the disadvantage of limited social interaction with others.

I envision a future school system where the fundamentals are taught by the best teachers in the USA in televised modules (PowerPoints etc.) in classrooms with a behavior monitor instead of a teacher. This can be done in many subjects and teachers can be tutors to help individual students. I take DVD courses from award-winning college professors. I love them. I learn the subject matter even without the ability to ask questions. I have the full text of the one- half hour classes and I can replay the DVD if necessary. This type of teaching will require only one-tenth the number of teachers (as tutors) and the instruction will be the best possible.

Overall, education and training of young people to acquire the knowledge required for meaningful work is the most important thing in the first thirty years of life. Work life will be thirty to forty years and retirement may be ten to twenty years. And that's your life. The first thirty years determines the rest. It needs to be your best years. And parents must make this happen.

The quest for knowledge

Knowledge is the application of learning and wisdom is the meaningful application of knowledge. Knowledge is measured in tests; wisdom is measured by results. Acquisition of knowledge should be a lifelong activity. The brain is like any body part. If you do not use it, you lose it. It does not have to be formal or complicated. Lifetime learning may be as simple as keeping up with the latest development in a sports activity, like skiing. I belong to a ski club, and they have educational programs at the monthly meetings. Becoming a good skier can be a form of lifelong learning and knowledge.

Work

As mentioned previously, work is as essential part of happiness. Something to do is a requirement for happiness. A day can be very long with nothing to do. Work makes life fulfilling; it makes life meaningful depending on the type of work that you do; you can also use it to bring financial stability throughout life. Work is best if you like to do your work. Some of us are lucky enough to get paid for what we like to do. Every person needs to find his or her work and become good at. There is also a technical reason why work is necessary. When you are working your brain is fully utilized in the task at hand. Your attention is focused on what you are doing and the electrochemistry that controls neural transmission in your brain is working like it should. An idle brain leads to an errant brain.

Summary

Knowledge is everything when it comes to sustaining a civilization. The USA is indeed in finitude mode in 2020. The elimination of school choice (by not funding private schools) has doomed the youth of the entire country to less than survival education. Some USA public school systems have even eliminated math as a required subject because it is too hard for some students. Competing civilizations teach the three R's (Reading, Riting and Rithmatic), that are the basis of learning and knowledge. The competition is not withholding learning from their young.

Media bias in the USA keeps citizens from knowledge of America's status within and with other countries. Most newspapers in the USA are owned by entities that wish to promote their opinions on every subject; and this is what they do. Objective reporting no longer exists. We are essentially back to word-of-mouth transmission of information. The public has lost faith in the media.

Work ethic in the USA is in continual decline. The government has a myriad of programs to allow healthy young people to "earn" more money by doing no work than to work. In 2020, the USA seems to be in "nobody works" mode. Every business in my city has a help wanted sign out with no takers. Government has sucked the work ethic out of its citizens with free money programs.

Most Americans are addicted to social media and electronic devices. They spend hours each day on them, and their attention is never fully on tasks or interaction with other humans. They are not in control of their own consciousness.

All of these civilization failures are fixable by attitude and behavior adjustment. Americans need to return to reason and take back cognition. They need to choose meaningful life over wasted life.

Chapter 5
Technology

*People who are addicted to Twitter are like all addicts-
on one hand miserable and on the other hand very
defensive about it and unwilling to blame Twitter.*
Jason Lanier

Most Americans think that "technology" means using
telephones for purposes other than talking to another
person. Mobile devices now do everything from measuring
the oxygen level in your blood to telling you about your
height above sea level. The companies on the US stock
exchange who make electronic gadgets are called the "tech
sector" and their stocks are "tech stocks". The common
feature of most tech companies is that they do not make
anything in the USA. Apple, the USA's biggest company in
valuation makes nothing. Chinese companies make all of
their gadgets. Facebook, Twitter, Instagram Linked-in etc.
all make nothing. They sell ads and other non-tangibles. In
2020, TikTok is a blockbuster company that hosts stupid
videos and about 80 million USA youths (one billion
worldwide users monthly) spend an average of eighty
minutes a day watching people trying to chip a golf ball into a
distant shot glass. The so-called "technology companies"
can disappear overnight because they do not make essential
products. Social media can end in the flick of a switch as
demonstrated by dictator nations like Iran and China.

Our definition of technology is:

The art and science of creating products, processes, and materials that solve existing and future problems/needs or make something better.

A new app for a cell phone is a technological advance if it offers a benefit, but so is a new pizza topping. Some technology creates significant benefits to a significant number of people; some are like my green speed gage which I thought was a wonderful invention to revolutionize golf, but to date I have not been able to sell any. I wrote a book on my proposed inventions – 176 in all- (Inventions for Entrepreneurs Lulu.com Harley Ruft). Like the green speed gage nobody bought them.

The purpose of this chapter is to discuss the technological advances that occurred in my lifetime and to suggest ways to solve current technological issues. The chapter objective is to point out to world leaders and CEOs where they should be directing their research dollars. The chapter format is to review what I think were the most important technological advances in my lifetime then discuss technology needs with my suggested solutions. The chapter ends with conclusions and suggestions on a path forward.

Important technologies since WWII

Things were quite different when I was a lad living in a center of medium-size city (#40 or so in size in the USA) after World War II. Some of the household amenities we now take for granted did not exist. I lived in a normal wood-frame house on a residential street about one and a half miles from the city center (downtown). Most houses looked the same on each street because they were probably built by the same carpenter crew. We had city-supplied drinking water, manufactured gas, electricity, paved streets and sidewalks and snow plowing in the winter by horse-drawn plows. Our house, which my family owned, was heated by a massive coal-fired furnace in the basement. Hot water came from a hot water heater with visible gas flames to heat the water. We had an electric refrigerator (not an ice box like some), a gas stove and one bathroom (upstairs) for a family of five. We had a console radio for entertainment and life was centered about our neighborhood Catholic Church and school. Most people had a land-line phone with a party line which meant that when you picked up the phone there may be somebody (one of six other families on the "party") on the line. That was not a problem because we did not have a phone (or TV) until I was thirteen years old. My brother and I worked as newsboys; my parents both worked at manufacturing plants that were within walking distance from our house. My mother's suit factory was literally in our backyard. Our yard backed up to the press-room. My mother made buttonholes on the second floor. My father was a tool maker at the auto parts manufacturer two blocks away. The first technological advance that I experienced was the TV. Some of my friends had TVs when they first came out in the late 1940's. My brother and sister and I used to walk ten blocks or so to my aunt's house to watch Ed Sullivan and wrestling on her twelve-inch diameter Zenith TV. We eventually got a ten-inch screen Air King TV that was huge and my father made a table to set it on.

I can't remember any technological advances during my high-school years, but early in my college days our state got its first "expressway", a four-lane divided highway. That was a welcome technological advance. It used to take three hours or more to drive the ninety miles to the next city to the east. Before they officially opened the expressway, we made the ninety-mile trip once in my roommate's father's Packard in less than an hour. The state police had not started patrolling the road. That Packard weighed 6000 pounds and it was slow getting up to speed but could do 100+ mph with ease.

The next technological advance that I recall occurred in the early days of my working career: computers. They were rooms-full of electrical stuff, and you inputted data in punch cards. Eventually "personal computers" entered my department. I worked in a lab with about fifty people, about twenty were engineers and the boss's favorite was to get the first Radio Shack computer. He allegedly saved the company untold thousands by using the computer to do I know not what, but he always made it sound wonderful at review meetings. By about 1972, all of the engineers in the lab had a PC on their desk. We mostly used them for internal memos. They had a messaging system called "PROFS" that you checked each morning for orders from bosses and memos from other engineers. Eventually they were used to input our expense accounts and charge numbers for jobs that we worked on.

The next major technology that I recall was the microwave oven for household kitchens. It was very expensive, about five hundred dollars, and my three sons loved experimenting with it. One son learned that it would set a sweaty sweatshirt on fire if you tried to dry it in a microwave. Another son learned that if you microwave a pinecone the insects in it get upset and run out of the pinecone and explode while running. Of course, we all learned that a whole chicken turned to caulking compound when you tried to cook it through.

TV, the microwave, and the PC were the most important technologies developed in my early years. The following are other technologies that occurred in my lifetime: the atomic bomb, natural gas to residences, numerical control of machine tools, nuclear reactors for electricity, the mobile and cell phone, voice recognition by computers, dishwashers, clothes dryers and washers, jet engine airplanes, helicopters, disk brakes on autos, auto engines with fuel injection systems, jet skis, 4-wheel drive vehicles, skateboards, frozen foods, organ transplants, the internet, artificial intelligence, additive manufacturing, hydroponic food growing, FAX, desktop copiers, seat belts on cars, LED bulbs and lights, foam insulation, backpacks, water-based paints, paint rollers, vinyl siding, aluminum siding, aluminum cans, fiberglass-based roof shingles, MRI, electron microscope, scanning probe microscopes, ion beams, electron beam welding, immunotherapy, joint replacement, cell phone apps, 3D vision, IR vision, hybrid cars, corn huskers, combines, cemented carbide, engineering ceramics, super alloys, rare-earth magnets, transistors, silicon wafers, autonomous vehicles, polyurethane, computer-aided design, digital photography, Polaroid film, fiberglass structures, plexiglass, stereo music, compact disks, DVDs, watches controlled by quartz crystals, steel-belted tires, epoxy, data transmission by fiber optics, chain saws, GPS, solar panel electricity generation, wind turbine electricity generation, carbon fiber composites, no-stick cookware, imitation stove countertops, fuel cells, etc..

Everybody probably has as list like this of technologies that developed during one's life that changed things for the better. This is what technologies are supposed to do.

Not on the above list are the military technologies that made waging war more destructive, or as some say, prevented war like the atomic bomb is supposed to be doing. It did end World War II, but the next time that it is used it may have unintended consequences.

Some of the technologies listed may have had a negative effect on the world. In my opinion, one such technology is glass-fabric as the support for asphalt roof shingles. For fifty years asphalt roof shingles had paper as the support for the asphalt and stones that stop the rain from intruding into a house. The US government in the 1970's mandated that US manufactures stop using paper for the base of roof shingles and go over to woven glass fiber in web form as the support for the asphalt and stones. All shingles made this way will fail and leak when the asphalt develops cracks from thermal cycling. These kinds of roofing shingles can fail within a few years even though they are guaranteed for twenty, thirty or over fifty years. They all will leak when cracks start. After my third tear-off on new construction, I vowed to never use fiberglass-based asphalt roof shingles. I only use steel roofing now. It does not crack from weather thermal cycling. Thus, some "new technologies" do not produce the perceived benefits. The first artificial hips made with Teflon also did not work. They wore out and had to be replaced – ouch.

An interesting technology failure during my lifetime was the turbine-powered automobile. During the halcyon years of the US auto industry, the major US auto manufacturers usually hand-crafted a new-concept car each year. One year, the Chrysler Corporation introduced a great looking car powered by a turbine engine. It took years of development to produce the turbine engine. Its advantage was greatly fewer parts than on a normal internal combustion engine. The car magazines tested the prototype, and it was universally agreed that it was a dog – no acceleration. Apparently, it took too much gearing to reduce the turbine's 300,000 rpm to the few hundred rpm needed at the rear tires.

Some of the" technical advances" in my lifetime that should never have happened. The world would be far better off without them. Here are the top five on my list of unnecessary technologies:

1. leaf blowers
2. jet skis
3. vroom mufflers
4. knobby tires
5. gasoline lawn mowers
6.

All of these things steal peace and stillness from countless people with their noise. There is no reason for the leaf blower, lawn mowers and jet skis to be so noisy and annoy so many. They have inadequate mufflers. Many motorcycles make a horrific noise, but some motorcycles make no more noise that a small automobile. People who buy these noisy tools and toys are simply inconsiderate. The noisy tires and mufflers are used by people who are intentionally inconsiderate of others. This is the only way that these people can garner the attention that they crave.

A technology that produces only harm is the so-called social media. I do not know the purpose and objective of Facebook, but I witness its damage. People who use this and others like it on their phone do not give their attention to things that need and deserve their attention: the task at hand, their job, and their children. People walk around like zombies staring at a handheld device. They hardly know where they are. The do not know that they are with other people. Whatever time is spent on mindless social media is lifetime lost. Our lives are really, really, short. In most cases our lifetime will be less than 720,000 hours on average. Spending two to four hours per day on social media will mean 30,000 "lost" hours of life over twenty years. And we already have committed about 300,000 hours of life to sleep and eating. Work life can take forty years times forty hours per week or 30,000 hours of life. Thus, non-committed life is usually only about 340,000 hours and social media may consume 30,000 hours or about ten percent of our lifetime- to what end?

Pick of the litter

There are many technologies on my lifetime list that I really like. I use them; they have made life easier, or better, or more cost effective. However, some are more valuable to me than others. These are the top ten technologies in my lifetime:
1. microwave oven
2. fuel injected automobile engines
3. down insulation (jackets, comforters)
4. computer chips
5. fiber-optic data transmission

6. GPS
7. The PC
8. search engines like Google
9. LED lights
10. cell phones

I believe that the microwave oven is the best invention of the twentieth century. I suspect that every household on the planet that has electricity has one. That number may be two or three billion. They are really cheap, and they save an incredible amount of energy. For example, cooking an ear of corn takes two minutes in the microwave oven at 750 watts. It takes twenty minutes on the stove at 3000 watts. That is four hundred times as much energy, plus cleanup costs. The energy and time savings are incredible. This technology makes life easier and better for billions of people and it makes the planet healthier. Now that is an invention.

Fuel injection and computer control of ignition has made automobiles extremely reliable compared to the automobiles powered by engines with carburetors, ignition points, and mechanical timing of ignition. I had my last carbureted vehicle in 1990. It was a horror from the reliability standpoint. In 1993 I went over to new vehicles without a carburetor. I have never had to open the hood since. I have owned about six small trucks over the past twenty-five years, and none have ever left me stranded. Fuel injection and computer ignition control have made automobiles very reliable and produces better mileage. I got six miles to the gallon on my last carbureted vehicle and all of my small trucks since have given me greater than twenty miles per gallon. Down insulation probably dates back to antiquity, but it was rediscovered in the USA in clothing and bedding in the last thirty years or so. Goose down, the fluffy feathers from the front of geese makes great insulation for ski clothing and comforters. It is not a new technology in many cultures, but its wide use in winter clothes and its availability make it a new technology.

Computers now run everything, and they have evolved from room-full of hardware in 1960 to chips the size of a dime. These computer chips are more powerful than the early room-full of equipment computers and they are used everywhere for control of just about everything. Growing large single crystals of silicon is the technology that allowed computer chips. These crystals can now be a foot in diameter and feet long. They are sliced into thin wafers and sophisticated equipment is used to put circuits on cut-up wafers. This is an amazing technology.

Fiber optic transmission of data is the basis for networking computers and sending digital data all over. Electricity requires the flow of electrons. However, light can travel faster than electrons. Fiber-optic data transmission cables are bundles of glass fibers and light is pulsed axially through the cables to move digital data from computers around faster than could be done through electric (electron) flow.

GPS is an incredible technology. Satellites sense a transmitter's location from space and relay the location of the transmitting device from space. People with smart phones can be tracked so that everyone can be located at any time. In vehicles, GPS directs drivers to locations anywhere in the "system". Maps are no longer needed. However, I never use the USA system since my experience with GPS has shown that it is programmed to always take you to your destination by expressway even if that adds hundreds of miles to a trip. GPS is also the way that surveyors now mark lot boundaries and elevations. I used to use it as my boat speedometer. It would update my location every ten seconds to yield boat speed. Current yachts and ships pinpoint their location and sail courses controlled by GPS.

The PC, personal computer, is now the basis of society. They can be as small as a wristwatch. Smart phones can be used as a PC. I paid $4300 for my first Apple PC in the 1980's and it did not even have upper and lower case. Now the same PC can be as cheap as $100. During the current pandemic our city school district is handing out a PC to every student for online classes. Personal computers have truly changed the way that our planet functions.

One of the things that make PC's useful to everyone is internet searching. You can ask a search engine any question and you will get a dozen or so answers to your question. Many "answers" are advertisements trying to sell you something, but usually one can wade through the thicket to arrive at a nugget of usable information. I love it for driving distance and finding hard to find tools, books, and restaurants. Most Americans Google daily.

Light Emitting Diode (LED) lights and bulbs are incredible energy servers. A 10-watt LED bulb may give the equivalent light of a 75-watt incandescent bulb. But the best part is the life. When I built a new house five years ago, I installed a string of fourteen 10-watt LED bulbs to allow me to see to insulate the crawl space. I left them on 24/7 because I wanted at least a little heat in the space to keep the temperature above freezing in the winter. Ten of the bulbs are still functioning after five years of continuous use. That is more than 40,000 hours. Of course, the low wattage can be a disadvantage when you are trying to use light bulbs to heat. I have an attached laundry room with no heat other than light bulbs. I use incandescent for the cold days. Chicken breeders have long used light bulbs to keep chicks warm in the winter. So, the world still needs incandescent bulbs as well.

Cell phones in the form of so-called "smart phones" are, in my opinion, the biggest enemy of civilization and world order. However, this is because of their misuse for nonsense: social media, games, selfies etc. They are the biggest distraction that the world has ever known. But the underlying technology is really quite amazing. Since their inception a hundred or so years ago, phones needed a wire connected from your headset to the recipient's headset. Now phones are wireless in much of the world. Many households no longer have a "land line", myself included.

The addiction of people to these basically good devices have put these devices in the category of the world would be far better off if they were never invented. Users have become so rude as to make all public places, airports, restaurants, churches, meeting of all sorts and all workplaces unpleasant for anyone not on the phone-users chat. Supermarkets and all stores are rife with people walking aimlessly down aisles talking loudly. They are on the phone. Last week I thought that a woman was being attacked in a dollar store. I rushed over to the aisle that was the source of the commotion and it turned out to be a young woman having a knock-down, drag-out fight with whoever was the receiving end of the call. When the woman saw my concern, she shouted obscenities at me. Of course, almost all drivers are driving while using their phones for something. It is very common to have an oncoming car veer into your lane, requiring defensive action on your part.

Proper use of this technology is possible. I carry a flip phone in by briefcase. It is always off unless I am waiting for someone to contact me. I carry it only for emergencies and client/vendor contacts. I receive no unsolicited calls, no robo calls. It is not on. In addition, only one of my sons has the number. Thus, sane use of this technology is possible.

In summary, some of the technologies developed during my lifetime are quite valuable to me and they have improved my life as well as the lives of a significant portion of our planet. If it were not for the misuse of some of these technologies many would have made the planet better.

Inventions needing reinvention

This morning, as is the case every morning, I tried shaving with one of my two battery-operated shavers. One runs okay but leaves whiskers a millimeter high. My foil shaver cuts them closer, but I have to jiggle it to get it to run. The battery connections are poor. The shaver usually quits in the hard-to-reach areas. So, I use a disposable safety razor in the shower.

Men have been cutting the hair on their face for thousands of years. One would think that a reliable technology for doing this task may have evolved. Why can't they make smart phones shave? Why has nobody applied laser oblation for home use? The world needs a facial hair cutting device that works.

There are countless inventions that have been commercialized, but do not work to expectation. They need re-invention. Besides the electric razor here are my top nine inventions that need re-invention:

Invention	Issue
1. vacuum cleaners	noise
2. tooth repair	drilling
3. dry cell batteries	life unknown
4. writing implements	short life
5. respiratory masks	nose accommodations
6. photographic prints	human intervention
7. plastic bags	lost forever
8. windows	hole in wall
9. temperature sensors	battery use

Vacuum cleaners – They are so noisy that I dread running one more than an IRS audit. My wife, a fastidious homemaker and cleaner, was equally disappointed in how uncaring manufacturers were about the noise level of these horrible devices that we all need. They do the intended job of picking up particles that escape other cleaning techniques.

In addition to the noise, I think that the bulk of these devices is excessive. They essentially require a dedicated storage area built into a house to contain the device and absurd hoses and related accessories.

From the technical standpoint both the noise and the clutter aspects of these devices are unnecessary. One time I was attending an industrial exhibit at an engineering conference and walking down an aisle of the exhibit I received a huge blast of air that startled me. A fan company was exhibiting a powerful centrifugal blower that made no more noise than a computer muffin fan. I bought one of these devices and made it into a vacuum cleaner for a wear testing apparatus in my lab. It could suck the paint off a lawn chair, but made no noise. The clutter problem can be solved by a household vacuum system. One only needs a hose and a few nozzles.

A respected magazine surveyed vacuum cleaner manufactures about the absurd noise level and the consensus reply was: They are intentionally noisy because customers equate sucking power with noise level- the bigger the noise, the more the suction. The power to fix this technology is in the hands of the consumer.

Tooth repair – I am about as old as a person can expect to be and one of my biggest physical problems is broken teeth. They keep breaking at huge fillings. For my lifetime, dentists have been drilling huge holes in most of my teeth and packing the drilled pockets with silver/mercury amalgam. Fillings are held in mechanically by making a huge hole and small opening. This mechanically locks the filling in but undermines the strength of the tooth. Dentists use the 100+ year old technology because fillings almost never fall out and the broken tooth problem occurs decades down the line. I am decades down the line with broken teeth and I implore dentists to start replacing mechanical locking of fillings with fillings that adhere to the inner and outer parts of a tooth so pocket drilling is unnecessary. I want tooth decay fixed the way we sailors fix dry rot on wood boats. We clean out the loose rot and impregnate the mushy wood with a water-viscosity resin that impregnated the mushy wood and hardens; then we cap the cleaned-out cavity with epoxy.

I spent a week in Belarus once with a dentist who did research on tooth wear and she told me that they have the materials, mostly UV-setting polymers to do tooth repair like I suggest, but dentists lack an incentive to use a new technology. Most old people go the denture route and do not bother to report broken teeth from huge fillings that compromise tooth strength. Maybe AARP needs to sue the dental association to get their attention.

Dry-cell batteries – I own two houses and a commercial building and the fate of all three rests in the hands of six double A batteries, two per building. The heat in my buildings is controlled by thermostats that are powered by dry-cell batteries. If they unexpectedly die when I am away during a cold spell the buildings can get below freezing temperature and the water pipes will freeze and break and destroy the building. How absurd is that? In 2020 we have electronic gadgets to do every imaginable thing – except reliably power a thermostat for a building.

Dry-cell batteries can fail anytime without warning and there is no way to know how long a new battery will last an application, or if the new battery is any good. I used to make lithium batteries for the company that I worked for, and I know that there are many things that can make a dry-cell battery fail.

In the winter, I change the batteries in my thermostats every two months, but is that soon enough? I have had no heat episodes due to battery failure even with my two- month life regimen. The solution may be dry-cell batteries that beep when their output voltage falls below a minimum value. Some sort of dry-cell battery help is needed. Electronic experts need to forget about cell phones that do it all and ponder prevention of broken water pipes from batteries that fail in their job of powering thermostat controls.

Writing implements – I just threw a nice-feeling nice-locking pen in the waste basket because it stopped writing. I probably throw out two ball-point pens a week because they run out of ink. I tried many fixes over the years. My eldest son tried to solve the problem by writing with $500 Mont Blanc fountain pens. I also tried the solution, but not with a $500 pen. It was a horrible hassle, and I ruined several suits with the ink mess.

Ball point pens never have enough ink and refills are almost impossible to obtain. A possible recommendation could be a ballpoint pen with a 100-cc ink cartridge – something good for 10 million medium- sized words. In any case, there needs to be a law to force pen manufacturers to state the word-life of the pens that they make and each should try to develop a "forever pen" that never runs out of ink.

Respiratory masks – This is being written during the pandemic of 2020. The world is supposed to be wearing masks over our nose and mouth, but the technology of protective masks is absurd. The USA government only approves N95 masks which prevent breathing. The medical professionals wear paper masks hooked to ears. They are loose and often allow more exposure. All of these masks fog glasses of people who wear them.

The world has been dealing with deadly contagious diseased for hundreds of years. It is well known that keeping expulsions of vapors and spit from contaminating others is the only way to prevent transmission. However, the world lacks the technology to provide the general public with an effective mask to prevent transmission of viruses.

I developed a mask to wear on airplanes that completely encapsulates my head. I've used it on ten flights, and it makes me feel safe because all air in and out of me is passed through several layers of a sheer fabric that is like an expensive window treatment. It is really a 2' wide x 8' long scarf that I bought in Lisbon, Portugal as a 360° scarf. I wear a surgical face mask; a full-face grinding shield and the scarf is put over the helmet and wrapped around the face shield opening.

I have seen TV news segments of medical people in hospitals in proper face protection: full helmets with filtered air fed into the helmet, but such hardware is unavailable to ordinary people trying to avoid infection.

One would think that USA's leaders would call together industrial talent to develop and make effective personal protective equipment. This has not happened, and startups are not going to try because of liability issues. Only government can order emergency manufacturing without liability issues. So many people will continue to needlessly die because of government inaction and incompetence.

Photographic prints – I am in an occupation that still uses photographs taken on microscopes and the like that are studied and used in reports as prints. The only way for me to make prints is to use print facilities and one of the two USA drug store monopolies. For the last eight years I have been using a Fuji thermal print maker at a drugstore chain. It was quite a usable system. The drugstore chain swapped the Fuji equipment for unnamed equipment that now requires a store employee to make prints. Something that took five minutes now takes one half hour or more and the time of a store employee. Kodak places print making kiosks is some retail outlets, but none of the store employees that I have encountered have been able to tell me how to use the kiosk. Better user interface is needed.

What an absurd situation. Photographic prints can be essential in many technical fields. Eventually the prints can be put back in digital form for reports and the like, but the USA and probably the world seem to have lost the technology of making photographic prints. There have been many attempts to make individual photo print devices, and I bought most of them, but none have created prints of usable quality. The world needs to reestablish the technology for making photographic prints. It has been lost and many applications are suffering because of it.

Plastic bags – The ubiquitous plastic bags from grocery stores are being banned from the planet because an irresponsible segment of mankind cannot store and dispose of them the way that they should. I have seen an entire country covered in plastic bags. It was not a pretty sight. The country was Aruba. It is a desert-like island in the Caribbean and the wind blows across the island between twenty to thirty miles per hour 24/7. The only vegetation in the country is desert-type cacti and short bent-over trees called Divi Divi trees. All of the vegetation on the island (mostly cacti) is covered by wind driven plastic bags. Most is unintentional. People open car doors on both sides at once and the constant wind empties the contents of the car on nearby vegetation. Messes from plastic bags are almost unavoidable.

A technological change could solve this litter problem and allow the world continued use of wonderful plastic bags: water soluble or biodegradable plastic bags. The world has the technology for both. Polyvinyl-alcohol plastic is water soluble. Plastic bags made from this material would dissolve in the rain. Litter would go away. Biodegradable plastic like cellulosics can self-destruct in landfills and go back to the wood or cotton linters from which they are made.

Why are paper bags being forced back on humanity as opposed to plastic solutions? Again, this is a question to be directed to elected officials. We can still have our plastic bags without the litter with the use of plastics that are different from the current petroleum-based polyethylene. It is also possible to eliminate all traces of plastic bag pollution worldwide by simply putting a five-cent bounty on each. This worked on beverage cans in the USA. Since they put a five-cent redemption payment on beverage cans there has never been one along a roadway for any length of time. Browsers find everyone for the nickel that they bring. This could be done with plastic bags. The person getting the bag at the store would pay the nickel. The nickels given to retailers for the bags would be collected by governments to pay for the recycling.

Windows – The United States lacks the technology to make insulating windows that can last the life of a building. USA building codes require the use of double pane windows on new construction. However, current technology employs two spaced-apart pieces of glass with silicone adhesive and the like, but these silicone adhesives fail in ten years. The windows fog and become unusable. In addition, two separate pieces of glass still has the approximate thermal conductivity of a hole in the wall.

Three clear plastic panels will do the job, but building codes only allow glass because of perceived flammability issues. Electronic windows are the real solution, but somebody had to step up and champion the technology. The window of the future will be a framed video display with a video camera placed outside to produce the appropriate view from the 'window'; there is no glass window to rob heat or fog up. There is no uninsulated hole in the building wall. (I have one on my pied-a-terre in the South).

Temperature sensors – this is a lost technology. We had it and it went away with battery operated devices that only work for weeks. This is a deeply personal lost technology. I live in a one-room adiabatic chamber in northern USA. I have no central heat so I need to open and close windows and circulation ports to keep the temperature in my living space at 72° F year round. To obtain data on how the temperature varies in the building, I have about fifteen digital temperature gages strategically placed to monitor local temperature. I average a failure a week of these devices. Mostly the batteries last only weeks, but many devices just die. Most are from the same Chinese manufacturer, and they are the only devices available in my city from the only supplier of these devices in my city: the superstore monopoly. These devices do not work, because they simply use too much energy to be successfully run-on batteries.

I have two gages taken from my old house that have been working for twenty years without a battery change. What is offered up by the retail monopolies in USA cities are devices that simply do not work long enough to do the job of long-term monitoring of temperature variations in a living space. I live in two homes, and I have the same temperature sensor problems in both homes which are 1200 miles apart. Temperature sensing is a lost technology in the USA.

What every home should have a device about the size of a cell phone that can be used to record and display the temperature in up to twenty locations in a building. It would be nice if it could record the temperature range over a set time period and offer up graphs on demand that can be printed out. We have the electronic capability to do this, and it is something that is necessary for all buildings where temperature control is needed, but nobody is offering such a device for sale through the purveyors that I am aware of.

Sustainability

This word means controlling processes in a manner that the process can be continued indefinitely with the same result. In the USA, some lumber companies changed their operational model such that the forests that supply the raw material for their lumber products are managed such that the trees that are culled to make product are all replaced. The forest will yield usable lumber forever.

Clear cutting, like I witnessed all over the State of Washington, wipes out a forest and nothing of value will ever grow there again. I witnessed this in the upper peninsula of the State of Michigan. The peninsula is about one hundred miles wide and three hundred miles long. Starting in the 1850's the entire peninsula was clear cut for timber. When I went to school up there in the 1960's the entire area was forested, but in those 30,000 square miles of forest there was no single tree usable for dimensional construction lumber. It was scrub timber. It could possibly be used for pulp for paper making, but not much else.

If trees had been selectively culled such that good species were not completely annihilated, this huge area could still be producing usable lumber. It could have been a sustainable forest.

The concept of sustainability applies to all things in nature. In my lifetime I witnessed the extinction of chestnut, butternut, and teak lumber. Both chestnut and butternut species were used for finish lumber in most of the houses in the city where I grew up. By the time that I was ready to build my first house, chestnut and butternut were no longer available for any purposes. The forests had been depleted of these two species. The teak problem was international. Teak is the ultimate material to use for decks and trim on yachts. By the time that I was on my third sailboat it was gone worldwide. The forests of Pacific islands were depleted and most countries in the world that still have some teak trees have outlawed export and local use of teak. Extinction is the opposite of sustainability.

Forests can be managed to be sustainable, as can fishing grounds, hunting grounds, flower species, mushrooms etc. If a particular product comes from a limited natural species one must be concerned about depletion of that species.

What civilization is doing currently (2020) is not sustainable. Each country has specific degrees of unsustainability. For example, the Pacific islands which were the source of teak lumber for the world had banned cutting of these trees for export lumber and anything made from teak must leave the country as a finished product such as handrails or bowls etc.

Cutting down the rain forests in the Amazon is not sustainable. Killing all the baby seals for fur is not sustainable. The most unsustainable activity of mankind at the moment is building monster motor vehicles, the bigger the better. In the USA more than ninety percent of the light trucks sold are never used for trucking. Owners cover the beds and use these huge vehicles for trips to the grocery store and other errands. Men use the size of their trucks as a measure of their manhood. Women in the USA buy enclosed trucks like the Chevy Suburban to show how they are higher than everyone else on the road. Also, they are the most protected (by the mass of the vehicle). It is my observation that American women want to ultimately drive a school bus-sized vehicle and do so.

I need a truck for my business, to haul machinery and supplies. For the past fifteen years I purchased the same model truck every three years. This same model truck is now about twice the size of the first truck that I bought. The wheels are larger in diameter the model truck that I buy is getting higher and heavier and harder to load every new model. It is sheer madness. Ever larger and ever many personal vehicles are the world's number one unsustainability problem. It does not have to be. Prudent governments can use taxes and the like to limit the things that are not sustainable. For example, in the USA, vehicle size and gas consumption can be progressively reduced by allowing only documented businesses to buy trucks, by applying surcharges to vehicles for horsepower, weight and volume.

Absurd environmental excesses like 2000 horsepower cigarette boats can be suppressed by 100 to 500% surcharges. Some things simply should not exist on the planet. Thus, if governments were considering the sustainability of life on earth, they would start to include the sustainability of everything in their purview.

The world's top technology issues

I cited a variety of technologies that have been lost to negligence and some that never really worked like ball-point or fountain pens. However, there are some technologies that are worldwide in nature and all countries on the planet need to ponder and establish a philosophy/action plan pertaining to the issue. My list of such issues is:

1. jobs
2. global warming
3. necessities for all (food, clothing, shelter)
4. supply of critical materials
5. healthcare
6. transportation

7. infrastructure
8. housing
9. education
10. engineered fertility

Jobs – Availability of jobs is a technology. When I visited China on a government-approved mission in 1983 our charge was to transfer US technology to China by technical presentations at universities and institutes throughout the country. Boy, did we do a good job. They now lead the USA in almost every technology. However, one feature of China's operating plan that caught my attention was their concern that there was a job for every person who wanted one. The "government" would assess each and every person's skills and attributes and assign him or her a job. Everybody who wanted to work could get a government assigned job. A person could opt to not take a government-assigned job, but if you take this route, you forgo government health care, pensions, and other benefits. You have to fend for yourself. Few people took this route.

Another aspect of government jobs for all that was very apparent to our group was that many jobs were made up. People had very little to do. For example, when we wanted to exchange US dollars for yuan, we told our hosts, and a group of three people would show up. All three sat at a long card-table. You told the first person how much you wanted to exchange. He or she did some paperwork and handed it to the person in the middle. He or she read it once and shuffled some papers and wrote something and passed it to the third person at the table. This person opened a metal box and gave you your yuan and took your dollars.

174

They had people in elevators that were just like the ones in the US where you push a floor button, and it takes you there. They had a person whose job was to press the floor button for you. They had "spitting police" on every block who gave out citations (fines) for public spitting. There were countless made-up jobs, but everybody could have a job. There was no unemployment.

All of that is changed now and Chinese have to search for jobs the way that we do in non-government industries. I have yet to understand the current Chinese economic system. I have read books on it and concluded that it is a secret. They seem to have private companies and state-run companies, but the private companies can be taken over at any time by the state. The "state" is preeminent in all matters. And the "state" means the "communist party". Members of the communist party get perks and the communist party runs the country. There is no opposing party.

Thus, having a government give a job to every person creates problems. The USA's system of having private and public sector jobs works when the economy is booming, and it doesn't work when it's not. The unemployment rate had been above six percent for some of the years since the last recession in 2008. In 2020, the unemployment rate was less than four percent before the virus hit. This is considered full employment. Now the unemployment rate is about eight percent in the USA, but some countries in the world (like Iraq) as high as seventy percent. Some government policies or inefficiency is curtailing jobs.

Each country is different as to the cause of lack of jobs. The situation of concern is that full employment produces a stable society. High unemployment invariably leads to civil unrest. Each and every government has to find a solution to unemployment. People need to work for peace, order, and stability to happen.

Global warming – Is it different this time than the last? Who knows? However, one does not have to be an alarmist environmentalist to know that what we are currently doing is not sustainable; it is not good for the environment that we live in without concern for the earth's atmosphere. The world cannot tolerate thirty million more vehicles on the road every year. I am an ordinary driver (about 14,000 miles/year) and this means that I burn about 3000 pounds of gasoline a year and most of those 3000 pounds of gasoline is converted to chemical compounds that are harmful to humans and for sure they are harmful in general to the atmosphere. The insanity of vehicles is that there are probably a billion vehicles in the world each producing 3000 pounds of toxins a year.

My energy use per year is in kilowatts and BTU's, but it costs me about $3000 per year. My pollution contribution for energy use is probably the same as for my vehicle – about 3000 pounds of toxins per year. Some of the toxin comes from the grid that supplies my electricity and some is the natural gas that I burn to produce my hot showers and cooking.

If one person is producing about 5000 pounds of airborne toxins per year, how much toxin does eight billion people produce? Surely, we produce enough bad stuff in the air to affect all of the air available to us on earth. Everybody needs to reduce their contribution to bad air.

Electric cars and "renewable energy" do not solve the problem. Electric vehicles simply shift the source of bad air from oneself to one's power company. Electric cars produce the same toxins as a gasoline-fueled car that gets 53 miles per gallon.

According to my back of the envelope calculations, a typical wind generator or takes more energy to manufacture than it can produce in its design lifetime of twenty years. In addition, in 2020, their life is about four years, and they only produce electricity about ten percent of the time. Wind is not a reliable source of energy and the giant wind generators have technical issues that that are limiting factors in their use. In the USA, their development was investigated by NASA, our space agency, decades ago and NASA labeled them to be impractical for use as a major source of electricity.

Solar panels are similar in practicality. They only produce electricity when the sun is out. That means twenty percent of daylight hours in my neighborhood. Nobody gets electricity at night when we could use some for reading. The cost of solar is astronomical as far as I can see. We have a local company making solar arrays. Enough panels to power a toaster may cost $30,000 installed.

What is the answer to reducing our personal pollution? I vote for 50 mpg vehicles. This is technically possible and can be easily implemented by a $3000 to $10,000 surcharge on cars getting less than 50 mpg. A five-dollar tax per gallon of gas may also do the job. They have this in many countries and those countries have lots of little cars some of which get 50 mpg.

For household electricity I vote for fuel cells run on natural gas and small nuclear reactors for all the rest of our electricity needs. Long term, geothermal energy could replace burning of fossil fuels for electricity generation. The core of our planet is very hot, as in the molten rock lava spewed by volcanos. That heat could be used to produce steam to run the conventional turbines that all the world currently uses to produce reliable electricity. Of course, there are technical challenges (like drilling holes a mile or more deep) in using this form of energy, but these problems, in my opinion, not as significant as getting rid of spent nuclear fuel, and the unreliability of solar, hydro and wind power generation.

Food, clothing, and shelter for all – This technology issue has plagued the world since its start. Nobody starves or goes naked in the US, but lots are homeless. I personally do not have compassion for the chronically homeless. Most are addicted to something and consequently are not employable. A compassionate government will round these people up and send them to a secure place for treatment, rehab in return for civic work.

The food, clothing and shelter problem that is of world concern relates to countries where war or cataclysmic events have destroyed a country's livability – like Puerto Rico after its hurricane or Syria after the wars (that are still raging in 2020). The United Nations should have a million plus multi-nation army that can go to troubled countries and set up a temporary government to reestablish peace and order and give food clothing and shelter in the interim.

Critical materials – The 2020 pandemic has produced empty shelves in all of the USA stores that I shop in. It is the first time in my life that I have seen no soup, no vitamins, no protective equipment, and no hope of ever seeing stores full of essentials. The USA no longer makes things that are essential to life. All clothing, most paper products, most spices, most prescriptions, all tools, and all measuring instruments – almost everything is made in China. These technologies cannot return because the manufacturing equipment that the USA used to make these items was scrapped and the USA no longer has the technology and machine tools to make anything.

The electronic devices that Americans are addicted to are all made outside the USA. The generations who are phone-addicted do not understand the consequences of making nothing in the USA, and they continue to buy everything on-line, which means made in China, South Korea or India for electronics and Pacific and Asian countries for clothing. Empty shelves are the consequence of this practice when supply chains are affected by disruptions like the Corona 19 virus.

However, the deeper consequence of no manufacturing in the USA is that we can no longer be innovators; we can no longer develop novel prosthetic devices, rockets, communications equipment – nothing. We cannot fight a war. All armament companies have gone bankrupt due to government gun controls, and lawsuits against armament manufacturers when somebody commits a crime with a gun that the company made.

As a materials engineer, I have been familiar with America's manufacturing capability for the past fifty years. I had witnessed the closing of all, but one integrated steel mills in the USA. All of the copper manufacturing companies have closed or were sold to foreign entities; the last time that I tried to buy titanium, I had to get it from Russia. The cobalt-based alloys needed for many critical applications are no longer made in the USA. Tungsten for critical cutting tools is owned on a worldwide basis by China. In 1985 the USA had only one manufacturer of magnesium. I doubt that any now exist. A similar situation exists for lithium. Even most aluminum production in the USA has stopped. China had flooded the world market for almost all metals thus shutting down US plants.

This situation is beyond dire. China controls the world's supply of rare earth elements needed for many electronic and motor applications. The US government had identified some thirty-nine critical materials that we need to survive as a nation, but had done nothing about obtaining them. Government actions to alleviate USA's shortage of critical materials, material that are needed to make things ourselves, have been only ceremonial.

Healthcare – The 2020 pandemic has shown that the USA had also lost the capability to deal with infectious diseases. We do not have a USA-supply of protective equipment, medical equipment, even bandages and linens. Medical "experts" in the USA do not agree on how to test for the Covid-19 virus or the validity of some tests. Vaccinations for

Covid-19 are now available, but their acceptance is insufficient to get herd immunity.

China tested everyone in a city of eight million in one week. Why can't the USA deal with infectious diseases? The root cause is our litigious society. If a medical entity tries to address a problem and one person dies in the development process the lawsuits will close the company. We use the wrong materials in hip replacements because it would take fifteen years and a billion dollars to get FDA approval on a new material. The USA has a lawyer for every eleven people. We have a doctor for every 2000 people. We have government regulators of medical devices and procedures that have no incentive to approve anything new, only risks. And they will not take any risks to jeopardize their safe, secure high-paying jobs. Regulators get paid even though nothing gets approved. If medical people and companies had protection from predatory lawyers and incentives for speedy drug approvals, medical advances would be possible.

The other incredulous problem with the USA healthcare system is that the costs of insurance are such that ordinary working people have none. "Affordable insurance" for a single working person from 24 to 52 years of age costs $400 per month for the cheapest policy which carries a $6000 deductible. A worker must spend $6000 before insurance kicks in. This is what the Obama administration saddles the American people with. Non-working people pay nothing and get free medical everything. Working people get no medical treatments unless it is something catastrophic.

Old people get Medicare, non-working people get free medical, government workers get essentially free medical and ordinary working people pay for the free insurance of others and get no access to doctors themselves. Young working people should be rioting over this crime to humanity on the part of the US government.

As I write this, the USA and the world are committing "viruscide." We have a worldwide crisis with a very contagious disease and US health officials have nothing to offer but stay in your living quarters and avoid contact with all other living beings and things. Establish a bubble and seal yourself in it. How technically astute is that? How do the "medical experts" expect life on the planet to continue? Are we to eat our bedding? The response that should have happened was to immediately convert to at-war status and voraciously build protective equipment so that we can live and work as needed and as wanted, without contact with poisonous gas in the air. I made a cocoon device for my air travel. I have other protective devices that allow me to work as usual. I have not changed my lifestyle one bit, except for wearing appropriate protective gear.

USA's elected officials at every level should be doing everything possible for arming every citizen with effective protective equipment. As an example of the absolute stupidity of some government officials, early in the pandemic the governor of the state that I live in ordered hospitals to put Covid-19 patients in nursing homes instead of hospitals. Of course, this action killed a significant percentage of the at-risk nursing home residents. This incident illustrates how governments made up of the lesser of our numbers of limits technology in all matters.

Housing – The technology of building houses gets worse each year in the USA. We went from log cabins to brick homes to stick-built houses over the past three hundred years. In 2020 in the USA, we are still building mostly stick houses except that the sticks (dimensional lumber) are now glued-together lumber scraps called oriented strand board (OSB). It does not have the stiffness of plywood or solid lumber and it will degrade with time if exposed to the elements and will be destroyed under flood conditions.

There are ever-decreasing skilled trades people to build stick or masonry houses and building codes make the process almost impossible. For example, it took me two years and a lot of time and money to get approval to build an 800 square foot house on an approved building lot that I had owned for 10 years.

Existing housing stock in most US cities has degraded in many sections and lots of houses need demolition. My city currently owns thousands of single and multi-family homes. They tear down a given number each year even though the small homes can easily be rehabilitated if it were not for the building codes that are incommensurate with financial reality. You can buy quite a nice little house for $10,000 in parts of the city but lead paint removal could cost $200,000.

Infrastructure – Some US states have eighty percent of their bridges rated as unsafe and needing replacement. Underground pipes for potable water service are sometimes one hundred years old. Critical bridges can be more than one hundred years old, and the US lacks the technology to replace bridges like the Golden Gate in San Francisco and the Brooklyn Bridge in New York City. The electrical grid is so old in places that electric power is not predictable. All Americans know that our infrastructure has been neglected to the point that a single failure of a transformer, bridge, pipeline, or rail line can shut down a quarter of the USA. New York City was shut down for days not long ago for an electrical equipment failure. I have seen my city and all activities stopped for days for a computer problem.

Americans are living off the infrastructure put in place by their grandparent's generation. The last infrastructure addition to the area of the US that I call home in my lifetime was the building of an east-west interstate highway in 1960. There is not a government entity concerned with infrastructure at any level. Where I live, we lack sidewalks and drainage of storm water. Our sewage is pumped someplace; so we are told. And this is typical of infrastructure conditions country wide. Nothing is getting fixed; nothing essential is being built at any government level.

Education – As mentioned previously, US public schools are in failure mode in most large cities. Every city resident had an opinion on why the schools are failing, but one fact that stands out in my city is that twenty percent of the students are "special needs" students. "Special needs" is a euphemism for insufficient intellect. These students should not be put with students who need an education to make a living. "Special needs" people will likely be wards of the state for life. Of course, it is wonderful that special-needs students can feel like everybody else, but it simply is not possible to teach twenty students' algebra when five of the twenty have no idea of what it is or what it is used for. I am sorry, but insufficient intellect exists. Dumbing down public schooles to accommodate intellectually-limited students ruins the education system.

Colleges only accept students with measured intellectual ability - the fancier the college, the more rigorous the test for intellectual ability. A good friend of mine is a professor of engineering at Cambridge University in the UK. He said that nobody fails any test unless he or she is sick. Everybody gets A's or B's. Students who meet the entrance requirements are smart enough to learn any subject and do well in every test. Public schools that by law must accept students of all intellectual capability are doomed to failure. A technology is needed to deal with this issue. How do you separate the unteachables when their parents insist that they be treated and educated with students with a normal distribution of intellect? Maybe every city can establish a "Helen Keller" school for special needs students. She was blind and could not speak – she had special needs but went on to become a famous intellectual.

Conclusions

1. Meaningful work (a job) for everyone is necessary for a peaceful society and most governments do not address the issue.

> Basis: USA's welfare system rewards not working. There is no US government function to create jobs, like the CCC in the 1930's. Excess government regulations stifle creation of private-sector jobs. Pandemic executive orders have shut down the jobs of tens of millions of people.

2. Global warming is ignored by USA's government.

   Basis: More internal combustion (IC) vehicles are put on the road each year and in the US they are bigger and heavier each year and consumption of petroleum products increases every year. The world made thirty million IC vehicles in 2020. Every IC vehicle converts about 2500 pounds of fuel a year into environmentally polluting combustion products (and there were 1.8 billion of them in service in 2019.)

2. The US is doing nothing to provide food, clothing, and shelter for its homeless or the world's homeless.

   Basis: Most homeless shelters are run by charities and the US government at all levels is letting homeless people live in public spaces. Nothing is done to rehabilitate homeless people.

3. Critical materials are on track for extinction in the US.

   Basis: mining and manufacture of critical materials in the US diminishes each year. In 2020, most critical materials were only available from offshore suppliers.

4. Healthcare in the US is controlled by regional monopolies, and it is unavailable to most working Americans.

   Basis: The cheapest health plan for an individual in the US is $400/month for a plan with a $6000 deductible. This means no doctor visits for most people.

5. Public education in the US is in failure mode.

   Basis: International testing shows the US to lag behind about fifty other countries.

6. Transportation in the US is a significant source of worldwide carbon emissions.

   Basis: There are 300 hundred million licensed vehicles in the US; many are behemoths that use twice the amount of fuel as vehicles that could do the same job. Americans ignore sustainability when it comes to their vehicles.

7. America's infrastructure is in shambles and needs massive rebuilding, but there is no US government agency with the technical competence to fix the situation.

   Basis: Many piping systems for potable water are over a hundred years old; fifty percent of the country's bridges need to be replaced. Some sections of interstate highway have been under construction for over twenty years. There is no professional engineering function in the US government.

8. Housing in large cities is unavailable and unaffordable and houses in general are built to codes that are outmoded, wrong, and restrict building of almost anything.

Basis: It took me two years for approvals and $10,000 in fees to build a $50,000 barn. It took me two years to get a certificate of occupancy for a commercial building I needed for a business. The local government made me to install a Chinese sprinkler system that cost two times the cost of the building.

A path forward

Energy – Our conclusions about the state of technology in the US are indeed grim. As a research engineer, I know that the situation is grim beyond what average citizens perceive. I live in the eastern part of the US and whenever I travel north to south, I always ponder how one missile strike to a bridge on the I-95 interstate highway would shut down all north/south shipping and traffic. The country only has one north – south highway serving the eastern part of the US. In fact, missile strikes to a handful of bridges would shut down all travel in the US. Our airports are essentially closed by the pandemic in 2020 and there is no indication on the horizon that air travel, domestic or international, will ever return to pre-pandemic levels. Sixty years ago, the general public did not fly. We are back there in 2020.

However, the greatest technological risk in the world is probably reliable energy. Electricity companies are now commodity companies with no R & D, possibly even no hard assets. Anybody in a strip mall can become an electric company and buy power from the "grid" and sell to households. Nobody knows who the grid is, but cyber criminals and enemies know about it. I met a person at a friend's funeral who worked in cyber security for the US electrical grid. He told me that there are two computer centers in the country that if one was knocked out it would take at least six months to restore power to most of the US. Every city needs to have a power plant nearby. Now they are few and far between and all operate in the shadows. US citizens have no access to information on their status.

Many politicians claim that the world will be running on renewable energy by 2030. Wind and solar are touted as reliable sources of clean sustainable energy. The European countries who made huge national commitments in wind farms soon realized that these devices are wholly inadequate. And that is why the people who invented those hundreds of years ago, the Dutch, no longer use them. They only run ten percent of the available time in a year and mechanically there are currently factors that limit their life to about twenty percent of intended design life.

Solar panels are only made in China, and they only work when the sun is shining. That is only twenty percent in my neighborhood. In addition, corrosion problems with the coatings and the like in panels limit their life to a few years.

Nuclear is a possible long-term answer to pollution-free energy, but the world fears accidents like Chernobyl and 3-mile Island and the Japanese tsunami. Small, self-sufficient units are proposed as the world's solution. I am only familiar with one nuclear plant near my house. It was built in 1970 with a design life of fifty years and a staff of one hundred thirty people. Because nobody knows what to do with the spent fuel the plant keeps running, only now the staff is four hundred fifty people and includes swat teams with machine guns and most staff filling out paperwork relating to government regulations. In the US, the government ruined nuclear power. It started costing three cents per kilowatt hour. Government regulations increase the cost to ten cents per kWh. In 2020. wind is 20+cents per kwh, as is solar by many estimates.

The atomic bomb was developed by top scientists collected from many companies, institutes and universities brought together with a common goal – end WWII. They succeeded. This is probably what is needed in the US and other countries to solve our woefully inadequate energy technology problems.

Global warming

The "car problem" is the "global warming" problem and it is the easiest technology problem to solve make gas $10/gallon and plant trees – make everybody in the world plant at least ten trees a year and make loggers replace all trees harvested and manage to clear the forests to stop forest fires. The world has the technology to make cars that get fifty miles per gallon compared to the current fifteen. Elimination of all gas guzzlers is doable and will positively reduce emissions that are causing climate as well as breathable air problems.

Power generation in the future could come from household fuel cells. This technology was demonstrated to me in Italy. Units the size of a refrigerator can supply a household's electricity and prevent the power outage problems that have gone from zero per year in my youth to maybe once a month now. Large electric generating facilities could be geothermal, the center of the earth is 10,000 degrees Fahrenheit or more. Pumping water into the depths of the earth can generate the steam needed to power countless electricity generators.

Burning of forests in the US is preventable. There is no forest management in most places. Forests should be maintained worldwide by young men who cannot find work. The government is supporting them anyways. They will learn additional job skills during mandated forest management work and the environment will benefit from reduced forest fires which produce air pollution, loss of wildlife, loss of timber and loss of oxygen generation from tree photosynthesis.

Device addiction – I asked a colleague what he felt was the world's greatest technology need. He replied, "Get rid of computers. Things were much better before them." As one who lived the most important years of my life before wide use of computers I have to agree. Computers do an admirable job with repetitive tasks, like controlling some machines, but wherever they are used they introduce risk. There is the risk of operational error like everyone who uses a computer at work sees on a daily basis: you ask it to do a specific function, it doesn't do it. You tweak it and finally get it working like it's supposed to. However, if the computer is flying a jet airplane with three hundred passengers, a computer glitch can kill a lot of people in seconds. What is the greater risk and more severe risk is hacking? We see this daily in the form of stealing identity and money from individuals and espionage in military system, and ransom from institutions. Are the risks of computer control of important functions worth it? I believe that computer control of important things should not be done without manual control as backup or possibly redundant systems.

The worst part of computer addictions is social media. The average addicted person in the USA spends about four hours per day on mindless scrolling and gossip. Facebook and their ilk suck the intelligence from a person's brain. An infected person cannot give his or her attention to any work or useful task. Nothing of value can come from an inattentive person. Some schools in the US make students check their devices at the door. People who work in some defense factories have to do likewise. Nobody is allowed to use a mobile device in the company that I work for. Complete government shutdown of non-essential use of the internet is necessary for future peace in the world.

One place that computers could help the world is in converting speech to writing and speech translation. This could revolutionize the world. However, in the US speech recognition has not progressed past "stupidity". Alexa and the like can order pizza and tell time but cannot be used for anything useful.

I am writing this book with a ball point pen on a spiral notebook. I have been fortunate to have people feel sorry for me and transcribe my crude handwriting to digitized printed text, but this is a job that a computer should do. I bought the best translation (speech to digital) program available in the US for books. I spent three months teaching the computer my pronunciation. I finished dictating the book and did not use the program again for a year. It did not recognize a single word. I would have to spend another three months reteaching my pronunciation. The US is totally difficient in use of computers to recognize speech. However, on my last trip to China, I could go into any restaurant or store and ask for something in English and the salesperson would pull out his or her phone, have me talk into the phone, they pressed translate and they received my request. They replied in English through their phone. This capability was available for all young Chinese. This capability should be worldwide. This is where computers could be of value. Instead, mobile devices are centers of nonsense and purveyors of inattention.

Healthcare – Healthcare in the US is an absurdity. Every US citizen is bombarded daily with advertisements on every disease known to man. These TV adds promise cures for terminal cancer - everything if you use their prescription drug that costs $4,000 to $10,000 per month for a pill that cost eight cents to manufacture. TV medical ads have made life in America not worthwhile. The absurd part of this system is that people cannot buy these $4,000/month drugs. They are only available by prescription from a doctor. The pharmaceutical companies play and replay these ads until TV viewers make themselves acquire the disease symptoms and then get a prescription to buy this drug and in most cases a government funded insurance pays for it. TV ads for prescription drugs are responsible for probably hundreds of billions of dollars of unnecessary medical treatments per year. Just today I was annoyed by the repetition of a drug ad to allow stage IV cancer patients a longer life. If you ever read the details of their claims it may be two to four weeks extra life for tens of thousands of dollars for the drug.

My congressman at one time tried to get advertising of prescription drugs banned the same as liquor ads. He did not succeed, and the US suffers horribly because of the immoral activity on the part of pharmaceutical companies. This is where government regulation should happen, but does not because of campaign contributions to politicians from pharmaceutical companies.

Helping small business - This chapter has indicted US's government for just about all of the country's technological shortfalls. This was done intentionally, and I believe rightly so. Government jobs are so lucrative in the US that the minute a person gets elected to office he or she immediately hires those who helped in his or her campaign for fabricated jobs that pay well with benefits not possible in the private sector. Often patronage jobs relate to regulations, regulations on top of regulations, regulations on everything. Most regulations are frivolous or wrong. All are debilitating to innovation and business creation.

Before the pandemic, up to forty percent of the jobs in the US were in small businesses, mostly service jobs. I work in a service job. We do tribotesting for clients, mostly large corporations. The government shut down our only advertising mechanism: exhibiting at technical conferences. Our customers are worldwide, and we would meet with and talk with potential clients at up to four international conferences a year. These meetings and our website are our only way to obtain business. It has worked well for twenty-two years. Now we lost all conferences to the pandemic, so we have only about twenty percent of our previous advertising and nothing sells without advertising.

The US government and other governments could greatly help small businesses if they offered a "Made in America" website free to small businesses in the USA. It would function like on Amazon for products and services from small businesses. It could be funded by a tax on sales.

As an example of why such a function is needed, in doing friction tests for clients, we developed a gage that could be used to assess the speed of golf putting greens. We made prototypes, tested the device and made an initial run of one hundred gages to sell. Then we investigated the cost of the smallest ad in a golf magazine. The cost was $1900 for each publication. We only would make about ten dollars on each unit sold. Thus, $1900 per ad is not cost-effective. We still have the initial one hundred gages sitting on the shelf. A free government online sales function would greatly help small businesses and could neatly fit into the USA commerce department function.

Critical materials – Solving the availability of critical engineering materials is another technology need that probably can only be done by the federal government since it may even involve treaties with other nations. For example, Canada has supplies of nickel and cobalt. The US could initiate a treaty to make these critical metals available to US industries. There are undeveloped lithium reserves in the US. The federal government could ask one of the national labs to develop a plan to utilize these reserves. The same could be done for every critical material. However, it will not get done without a champion of for the effort in congress.

Housing – The US federal government could develop technology to solve the absurd situation that we have in America: stick-built houses that blow down with the 70 mph winds that are occasionally inevitable. I built a house on the shore of Lake Ontario full well knowing that I would encounter winds up to 100 mph as a part of living in such an exposed situation. I installed an anemometer to record peak winds. We would record at least three 70-mph events almost every year. The house was built to sustain such winds.

Houses can be engineered to be super-insulated and resistant to fire, wind and flood, but not with current building codes and regulations. As an example, I currently live in a zero-heat house – no central heating system. The house self-heats. The local government refused to give me a certificate of occupancy even though I presented data that I can maintain 72° F with outside temperatures as low as -10 F. They require a central heating system. Just about any innovation in building is outlawed by decades-old codes that were forced on citizens by lobbyists selling siding, windows, and roofing.

The housing dilemma can best be solved by the initiation of a civil engineering research function in the federal government with authority to override outmoded and capricious building codes. This organization can design and approve sustainable, weather-resistant, and affordable housing designs that can conform to the regional housing needs. For example, the Housing Engineering Function may put up a factory to produce steel yurts that can be shipped anywhere in the US and cost less than $20,000. They can withstand 145 mph wind and self-heat and cool (and look nice).

Summary

 When it comes to technology, America's problem is a government that is incongruent with science and engineering. Six hundred people govern the USA. Scientists and engineers probably make up no more than six of the six hundred. Most are lawyers or professional politicians. My senators have never worked outside of government – the same with my congressman. He has no idea what manufacturing is, how a house is built, how a hospital works, how any business functions. He never worked in the private sector.

The United States was formed by people who had day jobs and the constitution was written to allow ordinary citizens to participate. Citizens did participate early on, but eventually professional politicians took over and that is why the US has a government in opposition to technology and innovation. A career politician gets paid handsomely without concerning him or herself with addressing the technology of the nation. However, life on Earth is a competition between countries. The strong countries take over and dominate the countries that lack technologies that produce citizen satisfaction and wealth.

A USA that cannot make its own armaments and weapons (as is currently the case; everything is made in China) will not survive. Survival hinges on technological progress not suppression and over-regulation.

Two places that government could help the technological status of the US is to shut down the current monopolies and to have government at every level buy only US-made products and services, including the food that is distributed daily at schools and institutions.

The monopolies in the US are so strong, so blatant, that the government does not even try to hide them. These monopolies coupled with regulation from every government entity make meaningful technology advances near impossible. The silicon-valley companies in the USA have created amazing communication capabilities, but cell phones and apps cannot make the essentials of life: food, clothing, shelter, electricity, heat, air conditioning, transportation, armaments, medicines, etc. And they cannot cook. The USA and the world's other countries need elected officials and leaders to set aside their cell phones and ponder their country's ability to subsist with their own technology

When the USA was a world leader in manufacturing, the large international corporations used to have a position called chief technical officer or CTO. It was on par with the chief financial officer, the company's bookkeeper. Governments should consider establishing such a function at a vice-president or cabinet type of level. Nobody is currently assessing the USA's technical capabilities and that is the root cause of our current technology malaise. The chief technical officer function will be a start of a critical review of the country's ability to sustain itself. Every country needs to decide their technology needs and establish an action plan for technology sustainability. In the USA, it could be a CTO cabinet position. A CTO mission statement might be:

> Continually assess America's essential science, engineering, skilled trades, manufacturing capability, access to raw materials, machine tools, fabrication technologies, research, and development, and hindering regulations, and take necessary actions to ensure that USA is competitive with all rival countries.

The CTO job description might read:

Engineer/scientist with documented successes in product development, R&D, manufacturing technologies, and the ability to convert weaknesses into strengths.

The USA is definitely in finitude mode in essential technology. The technologies associated with anything that really matters to preservation of a civilization or our species needs to be addressed. The USA's preoccupation with electronic gadgets needs to end. The United States and the world would be better off and well along on a survival path without the technology millstone termed"social media". It was started as a college prank by a troubled coder, and it has reduced the intellect of users to "three stooge" level. Productivity of companies and governments everywhere that cellphones are allowed is a fraction of what it should be. Phone addicts almost never give required attention to tasks at hand. In addition, the planet's cellphone plague has already caused revolutions, countless suicides, wars, discrimination, and other atrocities and in today's newspaper (9/18/21) they reported that students are being prompted by TikTok to vandalize their schools and post the videos to see who get the most likes. And this is the technology status of the world.

Chapter 6
Government

Whenever people live in close proximity, it is a natural instinct for these people to band together to address tasks of mutual benefit, like protection.

Anton Androv

USA's Constitution

The United States is unique in the world in that it has joint sovereignty between the country- wide federal government and the fifty states. Both have many of the same departments. Both have a military, but the states do not wage wars, only the federal government can declare war. The US citizens call our government a democracy, but it is more of a hybrid between a republic and a democracy. A democracy is a government where citizens participate in making government decisions. In a republic, citizens periodically elect representatives who make decisions for the citizens.

The American Revolution took place to protest living under a monarchy. Being on the other side of a very large ocean made it difficult for citizens of the thirteen colonies that made up the "New World" to be heard and their needs addressed. Thus, they revolted and won a war with England. They almost lost this war because there was no central government or way to finance things like a war. Each state or colony was a separate entity with its own government, a governor, a legislature, departments, militias, etc. After winning the war, a group of patriots set about designing a government for the "country" created by the colonists' victory over the previous government, the monarchy. The government in England was a king with "advisors" in the form of a house of lords, consisting of representatives of England's aristocracy and a house of commons consisting of representatives of the citizens. The authors of the US Constitution were important and learned men. Alexander Hamilton sort of initiated the project. He was Chief of Staff for General George Washington who led the revolutionary army. James Madison was a well-schooled son of a prominent Virginian businessman. He was the "intellect" behind the constitution. Thomas Jefferson the governor of the state (colony) of Virginia participated as did John Jay, a friend of Alexander Hamilton. As a group, these framers of the US constitution did not want to establish a democracy because having citizens decide on all matters is like trying to get all members of a large family to like lima beans.

After many discussions and significant number of cases of wine and spirits, the constitutional convention arrived at a prepared constitution for a government consisting of three branches, the Executive (with a president), the Legislative (with a senate with a six-year term, two senators per state) and a House of Representatives (one per every 30,000 citizens). All three branches were to be equal in power so that one could not dominate the others. Corruption was rampant in strong government as in monarchies and the framers wanted an option where each branch kept the others in control. The other government choices at the time were straight monarchy (with no legislature), dictatorship which is only nice if you are the dictator, and no government like the indigenous people in the Americas of the time. Their system was not working since they were being pushed aside and their land taken by a better arranged government, a monarchy.

The Bible recounts that the Jewish people lived for a time (many centuries) with some sort of consensus government, but their consensus at one point was that they decided that they wanted a king. And so they adopted a monarchy. Democracy, by traditional definition, means a government where citizens participate in running the government. The word "democrat" in Greek means to share with people. The framers of the constitution of the United States of America made participation of the citizens part of the government by specifying that citizens vote to elect representatives who would do the actual running of the government. Thus, citizens participate in the government in a convoluted way. Compared to monarchies, which were popular at the time (c. 1790's), this was a different "state of government". The basic features of the U.S. government as created by the constitution are:

- Establishment of a branch to make laws, (legislative) consisting of a senate with 2 elected senators per state with a six-year term of office and an elected house of representatives with one representative for every 30,000 citizens and a two-year term of office.
- States cannot enter into treaties with other countries impose tariffs or have an army.
- Election of a president by electors from each state and the number from each state shall be

equal to the number of congressmen and senators from that state.

- The President is the head of the executive branch of the government and commander-in-chief of the military.
- The President makes treaties, appoints ministers and ambassadors and judges to the Supreme Court.
- A vice-president chosen by the presidential candidate is elected to office with the president by the Electoral College.
- A Supreme Court is established that has judicial power along with its lower courts.
- Citizens of one state have the same rights as citizens from other states.
- New states can be added to the United States of America, but new states cannot be created from existing states.
- The Amendments to the Constitution require ratification of 2/3rds of both houses or 2/3 of the states.
- The Constitution is the supreme law of the United States of America

A bill of rights was added in 1789, as ten amendments to protect the rights of citizens.

Amendments:

I.   Congress shall not make laws that establish a religion, limit free speech/the press, peaceful assembly, prevent petitioning the government to redress grievances

II. All states can maintain a militia and all citizens have the right to bear arms

III. Military cannot take over a person's house in times of peace and only in a lawful manner in times of war.

IV. The government cannot search people, their houses, papers, and possessions without a proper and justifiable court warrant.

V. A grand jury is necessary for a capitol or "infamous case; a person cannot be tried twice for the same offense, a person cannot be compelled in a trial to testify against himself, nor be deprived of life, liberty, or property, without due process of law, nor shall a person's property be taken for public use without just compensation.

VI. Citizens accused of a crime shall be guaranteed a speedy and public trial by an impartial jury of the state wherein the crime was committed. The accused shall be informed of the nature of the accusation, confronted with witnesses against them, and have the right to offer his own witnesses and counsel for defense.

VII. In suits of common law, the right of trial shall be preserved, and no fact tried by a jury shall be otherwise re-examined in a U.S. court, then according to the rules of common law.

VIII. Excessive bail shall not be required, nor excessive fines imposed, nor cruel and unusual punishments inflicted.

IX. The enumeration in the Constitution, of certain rights, shall not be construed to deny or disparage others retained by the people.

X. The powers not delegated to the United States by the Constitution, nor prohibited by it to the states, are reserved to the states respectively, or to the people.

The Constitution can be amended, but it is difficult to do since it requires consensus of three-quarters of the states. In 200 years, there have only been 17 amendments. So, it is fairly well protected. It has worked well in my lifetime. In the past decade or so (2010-2020) there have been problems with the Supreme Court trying to be "supreme" over the two other branches of government by making laws instead of interpreting a law's conformance to the constitution. During the Trump administration, just about every decision that he made was sued by some faction and the Supreme Court had to say whether the President's decision on a matter can be implemented. Clearly the framers of the constitution did not anticipate this kind of situation might occur.

Overall, the United States constitution with the bill of rights seems like it is a suitable model for a country that is a blend of immigrants from every country on the planet. Much of the "free" world has parliamentary forms of government patterned after England. They do not have a president, only a leader elected by parliament. Parliamentary governments seem to me to function by bickering. Whoever in parliament "out-bickers", wins. I used to listen to Canadian radio daily and that is what I heard in broadcast of sessions in Canada's parliament. They cannot even agree on a language for the country.

I have had limited exposure to pure communism: Cuba and Belarus. I am very aware of the status of citizens in Cuba because I have had a house in Florida for 35 years and Florida has a very significant Cuban population, and it is only 90 miles from Cuba. After 50 years of communism under a dictator, the Cuban people have nothing compared to the rest of the world. They have no freedoms, no cars, limited internet, and not much fun. Certainly, there is very little investment from other countries. I only spent a week in Belarus (around 1993) as a part of a scientific mission, but we were guests of the government and they showed us what they have. Inflation was rampant. Farming was done with hand tools and animals, yet the technical people, engineers, and scientists were top-notch. The people had little because of their international isolation. The world's largest country, China, has the most thriving economy in the word. China now makes all of the necessities of life for all of the world: all of the toothbrushes, dust pans, plant containers, tee shirts, ball-point pens, etc. They have so many people and well-educated engineers that they can make everything and do so cheaper than anybody. Want a 1200-foot container ship-they too have lots of shipyards to make them; want a 100-m diameter wind turbine blade; they have many composite fabrication plants making them; want an aircraft carrier full of planes; they will make you as many as you want.

On paper, China is communist. They were in 1983 on my first visit. They had nothing but 900,000,000 people in mud huts. On my last visit to Beijing in 2017 it was a city transformed from smoky mud huts to 20-story buildings as far as the eye can see. This is a country that graduates 600,000 engineers a year compared to the United States of America's 20,000. In 1983 the government assigned people to jobs. Today you have to find your own job and people can "own" businesses and condos in high rises. However, the communist party, not the people, runs the country. They now have a dictator for life in charge and all of the possessions of the people can be taken away at any time for any reason. They have a country of "capitalistic communism" headed by a dictator with absolute power. Overall, America's form of government is okay in principle, but it is not quite working like the framers of the constitution envisioned. The true branches, executive, legislative, and judicial, are supposed to have equal power, but each one seems to want it all, and that is a problem in 2020.

Political Parties

The framers of the United States Constitution had avoidance of influence from "factions" as a primary goal in its formulation. At that time, there were farming and city factions to contend with along with factions still loyal to England. The framers anticipated political parties, but thought that they would resemble those in England at the time. There were many and most centered around parochial interests. They didn't anticipate that the United States of America would evolve into a country of two political parties. However, that is what happened right after George Washington served as the first president of the United States. James Madison, one of the primary (if not the primary) framers of the constitution seemed to develop a following that included Alexander Hamilton who had a philosophy of limited government with more powers to the states and citizens, called the Democratic-Republican Party. Alexander Hamilton, another framer of the Constitution, and the Secretary of the Treasury under George Washington developed a following who favored strong powers for the federal government. His following formed the Federalist Party. After more than two-hundred years the United States of America still only has two political parties with enough citizen participation to offer candidates in almost every election for public office at every level. The Federalist the party, advocating central government control of everything, is called the Democratic Party, and the opposing party based upon limited central government, state control of most governmental matters and following the dictate of the citizens is the Republican Party. A unique feature of America's two-party system is that they have complete control of who runs for public office. These parties have the legal status of a social club, like a country club, but through their "endorsement", they control who can run for elected office. Of almost 500 people elected to the United States of America's House of Representatives only two members are from other political parties, (Independent, etc.).

The exclusivity of the United States government is the root cause of the government's inability to deal with most problems. Elected officials at every level are lifetime politicians. As such, they have no concept of how a capitalist economy, or country works. It is like a hospital full of doctors that never attended medical school. Confounding that issue is that citizens have no recourse when an elected official or government entity messes up something. For example, the state department of transportation recently funded construction of a roundabout on a major state highway. When they started it they learned that the design did not allow tractor trailers to follow the curve. They had to redo the construction at the cost of tens of millions of dollars. Nothing happened to the party official who signed off on the design. She will still receive her above prevailing-rate pay and benefits. This happens with most career politicians. They do not have the incentive to perform that people who work in the private sector have.

As an example of a lifetime politician, just this week I observed on my mail-in ballot for the November 3, 2020 elections, a young person that I know from my 50 years as a county and town "committeeman" in one of the two major political parties. This young man is about 22- years old. He is the son of a fireman (government employee) and long-time party worker. The fireman and the son volunteered to put up lawn signs starting when the son was about 12 years old. This got him a one-year page job in Congress while still in High School. After high school he got an "assistant" job in our state senator's office. This led to another job on the town council. Now he is running for the state assembly. This person will probably get elected since the election district always votes for his party (he did get elected). He knows nothing about anything other than the mechanics of politics. It has been my observation over 50 years that this is typical of American elected officials. Most do not have the intellect, education, or functional knowledge (and wisdom) to do the job.

How does this happen? The details of the United State of America's election system are the problem. Everything in my state has to do with the petition requirements for public office. I suspect that the situation is the same in every state. Elections are run by election commissions in each state and each state has rules concerning requirements for getting one's name on a ballot for public office. Most states have petition requirements. If you want to run for mayor in a city you will have to circulate petitions to registered voters registered in your party designating, you as their candidate for mayor. You will likely have to get a minimum number of signatures to get on the ballot. In my state, 5% of the voters in an election district have to sign these petitions. They are submitted to the county election commissioner and if validated, you can get your name on the ballot. There are differing rules in the various states, but the petition requirement is the most fundamental. In a city with a population of 300,000 this means 15,000 signatures. This is a daunting task for a single person since there is a limited time over which their petitions can be certified. This is why the United States of America has only two major parties. It takes a formidable organization to meet petitioning requirements. In the United States of America, the Democratic Party and the Republican Party have significant organizations in every village, town, city, and state as well as national organizations. The party organizations at the local level are called "committees" and as previously mentioned they have the legal status of a social club and as such they can operate in any way that they want with regard to membership and operating system, and they do just that.

I was a committee member in Party A for 50 years. I attended a meeting once a month in the evening at a restaurant (later at a town hall) and the format was to discuss election issues, listen to a candidate, or vote on endorsing a candidate for office. Once a year, sometimes twice, we committee people would be assigned the task of obtaining signatures on petitions by going door-to-door in a particular election district. We carried petitions for all of the candidates that had party endorsement. Party endorsement was obtained by making presentations to the committee members and the committee members vote on who gets the endorsement. At least this was how it was supposed to work. What actually happened was the party leader presented his or her list of names for elected office and a not-counted voice vote confirmed his or her list.

I tried for 50 years to become a candidate for town council, but I was never the pick of the party leaders. In my town, all elected officials have for decades come from the ranks of government employees. I was never selected because I did not work for the public sector (town or county). Thus, in my town and particularly in the United States of America, there is an incestuous situation. Only lifetime politicians get to run for elected office. That is why the United States of America has ever-expanding government. There are no ordinary private-sector participants to bring diversity (and reason) to the system.

My career as a committee person ended after 50 years because I was ejected from the party because one year, I was unable to go door-to-door with petitions because I was in chemotherapy at the time. I appealed my ejection all the way to the President of the United States. President Obama personally answered me and said your local party can eject you because there are no U.S. laws governing political party operations. They can do anything that they please. Handicapped people who cannot go door-to-door are not permitted to be committee members of Party A and Party B. The law (Americans with Disabilities Act, or ADA) does not apply to political parties. Handicapped people, infirm people, and anybody who can't go door-to-door cannot be committee people. However, rich people like New York City ex-Mayor Michael Bloomberg can satisfy petition requirements by hiring people to circulate his petitions.

The United States of America presidential election of 2020 illustrated to the world the problem posed by only selecting candidates for elected office from the ranks of professional politicians. Twenty crackpots competed for the party A nomination. Nobody from party B dared to challenge the incumbent president. The two political party system is broken because it disallows participation from the butcher, baker, and delivery person. Only career politicians get to participate, with very few exceptions.

The Federal Government

The constitution states that there shall be a president, vice president, a supreme court, and congress shall be elected by the people and allows the president to pick helpers, like U.S. treasurer, to help him as he runs the country. What evolved is the president's cabinet. Members of the cabinet are approved by the president and confirmed by the senate.

It is called cabinet because this is what department heads were called in England's government. It comes from a French word "cabinet" meaning small room. Maybe the monarch's department heads met in a small room. Whatever the origin, it now means significant Federal government leaders who head departments with functions deemed necessary to run a government:

- Department of State –This department is headed by the Secretary of State that performs surveillance on other countries and negotiates with them to promote the interests of the United States of America. Embassies in other countries and ambassadors report to the Secretary of State. The Secretary of State is fourth in line for the presidency: Vice-President, Speaker of the House, and then Secretary of State.
- Department of Defense – The United States Secretary of Defense leads all branches of the military. Army, Navy, Marines, Air Force, Space Force. This person is usually a civilian. The reason for this is that it helps in prevention of military coups of the kind that occur in many countries.
- Department of the Treasury – In the United States of America, this department is in charge of collection the money, and the federal reserve system, which regulates banks and the department also prints the money used in cash transactions.
- Department of Justice – This department is headed by the United States Attorney General. This person is also responsible for

enforcement of federal laws and also the Federal Bureau of Investigation, the unit of the federal government that performs as a unit of police for the enforcement of federal laws and interstate crimes. This department is also supposed to prevent monopolies in business and industry that inhibit innovation and consumer choice. The office of the Solicitor General is under this department and he or she argues cases for the federal government in the Supreme Court.

- Department of Agriculture – This department was started after the Civil War to help farmers rebuild the damaged farm industry. Today this arm of the United States government oversees the USDA food inspection which is intended to ensure a safe food supply. They also administer the "food stamp" program that assists in feeding families in need.
- Department of Education – This department has existed since 1980. It's role is to ensure that every American child has access to education and that the quality of that education is the same state-to-state, rural and city. Primary and secondary schools are funded and controlled at the local level, (village, town, and city) with state oversight. This department adds federal oversight.
- Department of Urban Development – This department started in 1965 with the goal of providing shelter to all Americans. What it has done is build high-rise tenements in every city that become known as "the projects".

Typically, they are eyesores that segregate people with low incomes from other city residents. They are often magnets for crime and lawlessness. Most United States cities have been damaged by the department's actions in tearing down existing single-family houses and small retail establishments and buildings and replacing them with towers that invariably brand the people who live in them as "lesser" individuals.

- Department of Commerce – This department is supposed to promote American products on the world market. However, it is also the government department that does the census (every ten years); it houses the United State's weather service, patent office, trademark offices, copyrights, and the Library of Congress. The latter are its important functions. It does little to increase trade (and I receive monthly email on their activities to "help us small businesses"). One time we sold a machine to a university in Scotland, and they came to our lab and inspected the lumber that we used for the shipping crate. You cannot use any wood that contains American bugs. They had many other regulations that they applied to this single order for a test machine. We stopped making machines for export because of government hassles.
- Department of Health and Human Services – This department was approved by congress after World War II. It houses the Food and Drug Administration that approves the safety of

medicines and medical treatments for U. S. citizens. It also included the Center for Disease Control which provides guidance for pandemics and contagious diseases. It administers Medicare and provides medical treatment to older citizens. They have solved all issues arising from the 2020-23 Covid-19 pandemic (according to their progress reports).

- Department of Labor—this department is over 100 years old, and they compile statistics on jobs in the United States of America and make regulations on what constitutes a workday, a work week, holidays, and the like. Recently they gave government elite another paid holiday for Juneteenth. Elite government employees now get several paid days off per month, while small business owners and service workers often do not even get Sunday off.

- Department of Transportation – This department controls interstate highways. Funding of new interstate highways comes from this department, and it is home to the National Transportation Safety Board (NTSB) which investigates train, plane, ship, pipeline, and other major accidents. It makes recommendations on prevention of repeat occurrences.

- Department of Homeland Security – This is a relatively recent cabinet position. It was instituted by President George W. Bush after the 2001 attack in the United States of America by Muslim terrorists. It combines existing

United States protection agencies like border patrol, customs, and emergency preparedness into one organization with more than 150,000 employees. The Transportation Safety Administration which security screens passengers in United States Airports is part of this organization.

- Department of Veteran Affairs – Like the Department of Homeland Security this is a recent cabinet position: 2002. This organization oversees veterans' hospitals and other veteran benefits.
- Department of Energy – This cabinet position was instituted in 1971 with the purpose of surveying available energy sources and making recommendations to congress and the president on a suggested path forward for supplying energy to American homes and businesses. They fund research and development of new sources of energy and safe use of nuclear energy.

There are many more departments in the federal government that are not headed by a member of the President's cabinet. These are some of the larger departments:

- Office of Management and Budget – They help the president prepare and manage the country's budget.
- Environmental Protection Agency – They have become the regulatory body with almost cart blanch control over all matters since every action has an effect on the environment.

- United States Postal Service– This has been spun off-by the federal government on paper, but the taxpayers still are responsible for losses.
- Central Intelligence Agency –They are the United States spying agency. They monitor happenings around the world that can affect the United States of America.
- Social Security Administration – This organization controls the pensions and medical costs for Americans over the age of 65— maybe 20 million people as well as 20 million younger than 65 people who claim disability.

There are many more departments and agencies; it is estimated that a newly elected president has to approve over 4,000 department heads. Needless to say, many of these appointments are patronage jobs. They are given to people who helped the president get elected.

In spite of this, these federal agencies seem to be able to address any national issue that arises, but all government functions lack accountability to the customers: American citizens. It is not possible for a citizen with a federal issue like a social security check problem to access any department head. Each agency creates a thicket of levels to prevent citizenry from even petitioning an agency. For example, some building codes are technically wrong, but there is no way to tell this to anyone and there is no incentive for government employees to respond to citizen requests for the help that government agencies are supposed to provide. (I have written to almost all government agencies of the past 60 years or so, and my reply success is about 1 in 100 letters. One time I even wrote to all 100 senators and got the same result.)

As an example, the flooding produced by the State of New York on Lake Ontario which was covered in Chapter One has produced catastrophic flooding in 2017 and 2019 and some government agency provides us shoreline dwellers with filled sandbags (millions of them) to try and mitigate damaged to our properties. The bags that the government distributed to flood victims were made from a plastic (polypropylene) that degrades in sunlight; dams made with these bags fall apart in months. I tried to find the government agency who was responsible for buying these bags to tell them to buy UV-stabilized and pigmented polypropylene bags; it takes considerable time and effort to fill and place the bags that they are distributing and this effort goes to waste when the sandbags fall apart in a few months. I got my sandbags from some military unit at the town hall. I sent a letter to the Town Supervisor and asked where the bags came from. He responded that they got them from the county. I wrote a letter to the County Manager, and she did not know where the bags came from. I wrote to my state senator, he said he would investigate, but never did. I wrote to the Governor, General Accounting Office, and President and none replied.

So the United States of America is wasting millions of dollars buying no-good sandbags, paying somebody to fill them, paying somebody for sand, and having many millions of Americans (they are use the bags all over the United States) bring these 50,000 sand bags to flood sites to have them fall apart, and not do their intended job. In addition, they pollute the environment with foreign species of sand (sand from nobody knows where). Last week I saw them distributing these same no-good bags in New Orleans when they got 10 inches of rain in a day. I place the no-good sandbag problem well above global warming in seriousness. This type of government performance is typified in all nations, and it is the reason why government at all levels needs to be kept to the absolute minimum. There is simply no accountability, and no incentive for government agencies to solve problems under their jurisdiction. Government employees get paid even if they do not do their job. Citizen reviews are not solicited, posted, or wanted.

State Government

About two million people work for the US federal government (not counting the military) while over 15 million people work for State and Local governments. Each state has a government that mirrors the federal government. This is not dictated by the Constitution, but before there was a United States, each state operated like a sovereign nation. After the Constitution was approved and the states formed a single country, the United States, most member states evolved into structures that looked like the federal government. They established a supreme leader: a governor; most states have two legislative houses like the federal government, (for example state senate and state assembly), that enact laws. Usually, federal laws take precedence over state laws, but enforcement may be lax. All states have a military in the form of the National Guard. The National Guard are full-fledged soldiers that can be "called up" to fight the United States wars around the world, but they can be ordered into service by a state's governor to help in disasters or quelling in-state disturbances of the peace. There are state justice departments, education departments, health departments, transportation departments – practically all the same departments as the federal government.

Each state has their own constitution and election commission, but states try to have their main election of officials coincide with the annual November elections that are held for federal offices and the president. In my state, the legislature is only in session for 6 months of the year, State Senator and Assembly positions were traditionally part time. People worked their day jobs and took a leave of absence when the state legislature was in session. In 2020, most members of the senate and the assembly make their position their full-time job. In my state, the assembly term is 2 years, and the senate term is 4 years.

There is a lot of redundancy between the state and federal government, but the good effect of having state governments is to allow for differences in the common good. What is good for the citizens of New York State may not be good for the residents of Kansas, a farming state. Some states do not even want any visitors, their highways are few and far-between. Some states have very few residents and not many cities. Each state seems to have a "premier" city which is larger than the other cities. Each state has their capital in their capital city. Some state capitals have a capital building patterned after the U.S. Capital Building. For good or bad, each state seems to have a personality. For example, everything is big in Texas; everything is taxed to the hilt in New York; everybody is an immigrant to Florida (nobody has ever been born there); everything is "laid back" in California, etc.

The significance of a state personality is that moving from one state to another may require a citizen personality change that is commensurate. If you move from Massachusetts to California, you may need to learn how to wind-down. If you move from any state to Alaska, you may need to take on self-reliance characteristics.

The downside of having sovereign states with all of the trappings of federal government is the tax cost of this redundancy. With the tax cost is the regulation cost. States (and municipalities) have their own regulations on top of federal regulations. When I built my house on the shore of one of the Great Lakes, I had to get a permit to put a dock in the lake from the town, state, and federal governments, and a state government organization whose job it was to ensure consistency between state and federal regulations. Needless to say, these kinds of regulatory nightmares prevent just about any kind of business, industry, or development, from happening.

Local Government

I have 50 years' experience in participating in local government. The political party I am affiliated with has been in power in my town of about 100,000 residents for at least 60 years. As a town and county committee person I had to circulate designating petitions for every election for 50 years. All of my party's candidates for office spoke at our monthly meetings seeking our town's endorsement and I knew all of the town officials over that 50-year period. My town was governed all of that time by professional politicians. The town leader is called a "Supervisor." All town departments report to the supervisor who is elected to a four-year term. We had at least 6 different supervisors in my 50-year committee term and only one did a good job. There is a Town Council consisting of four members, one from each geographic section of town called "Wards." They are elected for a two-year term. For the last seven years, all members of the town council worked for town or government agencies. They essentially worked for the town Supervisor who was also the leader of the county's Party A. Town council members caucus before every town board meeting and all matters are decided by the town's Supervisor at the caucus meeting. The monthly public meeting is rehearsed in the caucus and there is no intention on the part of any elected town official to get even comments from the town residents who are paying for what the caucus decides. Of course, this practice is wrong, unethical, and should be a source of shame.

When our current town supervisor got elected, he also held the job of Chair of the County Party A. The Supervisor was receiving a salary of $160,000 from the town, and another salary of $250,000 as a full-time head of the county Party A. Needless to say he spent most of his time managing the 55 or so Party A races that he was responsible for each year. We had all of our Party A committee meetings at the Town Hall (Party B had to meet in a back room of a restaurant) and we even delivered our signed petitions to the Supervisor's office in Town Hall. Yes, the town taxpayers were subsidizing the political party in power. Of course, I tried to do something about this situation by reporting this conflict of interest to appropriate state and federal agencies to no avail.

In my state, there is a hierarchy of local governments. The village is the lowest form of local government. They can have a mayor and a council or board and most have some semblance of Party A and Party B. Next is the town government that works mostly like mine. City is the highest in local hierarchy. A city can do things that a town cannot, like have a wide range of courts. Their councils usually have more members than town councils. Next in hierarchy is county government. In my county, the top job is called a "County Executive." The county legislature has about 30 members and the county administrates a jail, sheriff's department, and a variety of departments that cover the entire county in matters like health, water supply, roads, airports, etc.

There are about 15 towns in my county, and they have been running with no incident during my 50 years in Party A. They all have been controlled by Party A for 50 years. The City has been in chaos for that same 50 years and they have been run by Party B for all of that time. What is the explanation? When I was thrown off the Party A Committee, I met with the head of the Party B Committee to see if they wanted me. I attended some of their committee meetings. They were all attended by bunches of crazies - shouting at each other, no order, no civility. I concluded that participation in Party B's Committee was not an option for me.

Apparently, this is indicative of that party. They thrive on continual in-fighting. The problem that runs deep in the United States of America's so-called democracy is that elected office offers a lifetime of wealth, power, and benefits that are so desirable that career politicians will do anything to get elected and stay in office. A reporter on TV stated that: in the last month Party B spent $154 per voter on campaign ads in a particular state. This is not a government built upon citizen participation. The citizens of that state each did not give the party $154 for political advertising. Some entity was trying to buy the election.

Local governments are being bought for long term party goals like gerrymandering election districts so that state offices can be guaranteed. I live in a Party A gerrymandered congressional election district. The district covers a part of the city then proceeds to follow the shoreline of one of the Great Lakes. Where I live, the district is 100 yards wide and 50 miles long, apparently the shoreline residents are predominantly Party A affiliated. Gerrymandering is not part of a democratic government, but it persists every place in the United States of America.

Judges

As just mentioned, in my 50 years as a political party committee person our monthly meeting at Town Hall almost always included a judge or two showing up at the meeting. Essentially, they were visiting us to ask us to carry their designating petitions. A petition would typically entail up to 10 names for various offices. Some of these names were for judges. Each County in the United States of America probably has a number of county judge positions: Supreme Court, county court, surrogate court, traffic courts, etc. Towns have courts as well that mostly deal with local traffic violations. As a political committee we were responsible for designating candidates for all races. Typically, a person would show up at the monthly meeting and sitting judges would all say: you know me, you carried my petition in 1997, 2002, etc. Thank you for your continued support, I am off to the committee meeting in South Fork. Goodbye.

Party nominations for county, state and federal elected positions are established in county, state, and US party "conventions". Most judges were nominated at a spring county convention of committee people. There were probably about 500 Party A committee people in my metro area of about 1 million. About 200 people would show up and vote for judges and other county candidates. This is compared with about 30 who participated at the town level. I do not know how many people typically attended a state convention (governor candidates are nominated at state conventions), however, the designating petitions showed that about 4 people from my metro area would go to the state convention. These same people may go to the US party convention. Thus, candidates at my town level were selected by about 30 people out of 100,000 residents, about 200 people voted for county candidates with about 1 million residents and maybe 100 state committee people selected state and federal candidates from about 15, million residents. Thus, candidate selection is done by a very small percentage of voting citizens.

The only time that a judge gets adequate vetting is probably the judges for the United States Supreme Court. One was approved by the President in 2020 and she received two days of questions from senators as well as private interviews with members of Congress. A fundamental problem with the United States' judicial system is that the citizens who have to elect judges have no real knowledge of the ability of the candidate to do the job. Over the years I felt satisfied when judge candidates would give our town committee a 5- or 10-minute presentation on why they wanted the job and how they were qualified to do the job. Many judge candidates did this, many did not. They were the ones that said "you know me."

Federal judges that get a lifetime appointment may or may not need congressional approval. The president appoints them usually based upon recommendations from advisors. Federal judges deal with tax issues, immigration issues, patents, copyrights, etc. Our democracy needs decision resolution of issues in these areas, but citizens are for the most part not adequately informed to make good judgement on judges that are elected by popular vote.

As I write this, a Town Court judge that I carried petitions for many times recently resigned his judgeship when confronted by an audit of court fines by state auditors. He may not be as good of a judge as he told us at committee meetings. Thus, there is a fundamental problem in the United States' system of selecting judges. We do not know them or their character.

How Political Committees Operate

A unique feature of the United States' democracy is having only two political parties. Election law in most states allows for more parties and in my state, there are about 5 parties listed on most ballots, but only the Democratic and Republican parties have the infrastructure to offer candidates for most elected offices. Individuals can run for president not on a party line, but as write-ins, but the reality of the situation is that the two major parties control the government. Many people register to vote as independents, but as such they really are not participating in the United States' democracy. Participation means doing something in addition to voting. It takes millions of volunteers to run a presidential election. Political parties have these responsibilities:

1. To ensure good government
2. Provide resources and support to elect designated candidates
3. To prepare and encourage the most qualified candidate for office
4. Fund and help raise funds for designated candidates.

I was asked to join the committee of one of the two major parties in the United States of America after I led a neighborhood fight against a proposed apartment development that was inappropriate for the neighborhood. The reason that I was registered in that party was that my employer at the time, one of the United States largest auto manufacturers, suggested this party as favorable to the company business. My boss also told me to become a member of the Chamber of Commerce. White collar workers, (I was an engineer), are supposed to be active in their community. I was even led by my boss to the blood drive in the cafeteria whenever there was a blood drive. I was forced to donate blood, even though I faint at the sight of blood. I was expected to give blood for the" company".

My mother was a union worker. She had to join the other political party. Her shop was so unionized that if a boss told her to do a particular job, she had to check with the union steward to see if it was ok to do what the boss asked her to do. She had to take the day off (and lose a day's pay) to go to the airport when a big politician was coming to town. Of course, the union took a significant part of her pay. All labor unions belong to one of the two major parties.

The differences between the two major parties are never stated by the parties. In my 50 years in Party A, I never heard a party official state the base tenants of the party. Google states that Party A stands for

- Lower taxes
- Free-market capitalism
- Immigration limits
- Gun rights
- Restricted abortions
- Protectionism
- Social values
- Deregulation
- Strong military
- Peace and order

Party B opposes these items. For the last two decades or so, Party B has had unlimited abortion as the number one issue in presidential races. They also promote forced government health insurance which typically makes health carefree to indigents and the costliest expense of working people. The cheapest government plan costs $500 a month for no health care - the cheapest plan has a $6000 deductible so to go to a doctor is not covered- while catastrophic illness is covered. What is called "Obama care", means no healthcare where there are huge deductibles.

How do political parties arrive at a platform and candidates for office? I only missed a few monthly meetings in 50 years of going to my town's Party A meetings. This is the typical format (Robert's Rules of Order applied):

1. Pledge of Allegiance
2. Call to Order
3. Minutes of the previous meeting
4. Treasurer's report
5. Old business
6. New business
7. Talks by candidates for office or a town department head
8. Raffle off a bottle of wine to raise money
9. Adjournment

In the Sixties or Seventies, we would have the meetings in the party room of a restaurant so there would be drinking to accompany the politics. Mostly petitions happened in June for November elections. If a committee person wanted to run for an elected office, he or she had to state this in writing when the party sent letters for people to announce candidacy. Candidates would have to go through a candidate screening committee. Most times the screening committee was a group of 6 or 8 senior committee people who would meet each candidate in private and vote on who they thought would be the best candidate. The members of the screening committee were approved by the committee leader, so they usually just enforced the party leader's choice. Some party leaders would do the right thing: ask candidates for office to make a presentation to the entire town committee and then the town committee would vote in secret for the candidate. The one with the most votes got the committee's endorsement. If a candidate felt that he or she should get the endorsement not the committee's choice, he or she could wage a primary election. These were almost forbidden in my town. I think that we only had two or three in my 50 years on the committee. A primary costs money and the county board of elections needed to get involved. Primaries were greatly discouraged.

Mostly, all candidates for office came from public sector employees. In fact, most candidates for town office were town or county employees. One Town Supervisor (the head of a town) banned this practice for his tenure but as soon as he moved on, they went back to their incest. I would try to run for one of four seats on the town board, but I never made it past the screening committee. They would always choose the party leader's choice.

Essentially political party committees exist to do the dirty work of the candidate for office for free. We were expected to contribute to the party at each meeting. We had to go door to door to get petitions signed and we had to place roadside signs at election time and take them down after. We also had to go to $50 a plate fund-raising events. Why would anybody other than a person seeking public office to this job? Typically, I was the only non-town employee at a monthly meeting. When I was thrown off for sickness (chemo) the entire town committee were town employees. We met at Town Hall at 6:00 pm so they could just stay late from town work one day a month. Town employees participating on the committee was an effective way of brown-nosing the boss, the town Supervisor, who needed a staff to keep getting elected.

There would probably be no political parties if it were not for "petitions." A petition looks like a legal document with unreadable fonts and lots of legal jargon if one uses a magnifying glass to read it. The concept of a petition arose from the need to restrict frivolous candidates for office. For

232

example, in my city I ran into two people running for President of the United States as write-ins. It is legal to have a person elected to office without any party affiliation but having a petition requirement of 5% of the voters in every election district limits elections to serious candidates. A friend of mine in Poland told me that they have 200 political parties, and this makes a democracy very different. The United States' two-party system, though greatly flawed, eliminates the obvious problem of running a consensus government to appease 200 political persuasions.

In any case, in the United States, each state is like a complete country, and they will have their own election laws. However, they still operate with two predominating political parties. In the United States Senate, in 2020, there is only one senator not affiliated with one of the two major parties. In the House of Representatives, the number is usually less than 3 or 4.

A typical party A petition looks like the following:

Party A Designating Petition   *Sec. 6-132*
Election

The undersigned do hereby state that I am a duly entitled voter in Party A and entitled to vote at the next primary (or other) election of such party, to be held on November 4, XXXX; that my place of residence is truly stated opposite my signature hereto, and I do truly designate the following named person (or persons) as a candidate (or candidates for the nominations of such party for public office or for election to a party position of such party.

1a. Name of Candidates   *Public Office or Party Position*   *Place of Residence*
     Candidate #1   *State Senator*
       XXXX

Candidate #2   County Legislator
         XXXX
1b. I do hereby appoint XXX Address, XXX address, XXX
address as a committee to fill vacancies in accordance with
the provisions of the election law. In witness whereof, I have
hereunto set my hand the day and the year placed opposite
my signature.

1c.   Date   Name of Signer (Signature Required)
       Residence   City/Town
1.   XXXX   XXXXXX
       XXX   XXXX
2.   XXXX   XXXXXX
       XXX   XXXX
3.   XXXX   XXXXXX
       XXX   XXXX

1d. I (name of witness) Person Carrying the Petition state I
am a duly qualified voter in the state of XXXX and I am an
enrolled voter in Party A. I now reside at Address of the
Person Carrying the Petition.

1e. Each of the individuals whose names are affixed to this
petition sheet (fill in number) XX signatures, **** to **** in my
presence on the dates above indicated and identified himself
to the individual who signed this sheet. I understand that this
statement will be accepted for all purposes as the equivalent
of an affidavit and, if it contained a false statement, shall
subject me to the same penalties as if I had been duly
sworn.

                    _____ date
_____signature of
                    witness

234

_____

_____   (2) *Notary Public*
or Commissioner of Deeds
*On the dates above indicated before me personally came
each of the voters whose signature appear on the petition
sheet containing _____ signatures who signed same in my
presence and who, being by me duly sworn, each for
himself, said that the foregoing statement made and
underscored by him was true.*

_____

_____

____
   Date   *Signature of Official/Title*
of Official Administering Oath

The format of the petitions that I carried for 50 years was the same. The legal jargon that started the petition was never read by signees. Section 1a which listed the candidate names was always read by signees. Section 1b was in unreadable font and it contained things like sending people to the state convention and all sorts of things that election law required or that the party officials were trying to hide. In my opinion, it made the entire process dishonest and partially made the petition-bearer complicit to a crime. The signature part of the petition was readable, and we had to ask people to sign the way they sign when they vote. Section 1d and 1e are more legal jargon. The final section: 2 shows that a notary public has to sign this.

I often questioned who checks to see if 5% of voters signed their petitions. I never got an answer from party leaders. I suspect that the election commissioner checked the signature count for the whole town. If that was at least 5% then the ballot could go ahead. I think nobody checked to see if a specific election district had their 5% satisfied.

We usually had 4 to7 different petitions that we asked people to sign. For some unknown reason, some sheets would contain 3 to 4 candidates; some sheets only contained 1 candidate. However, it was really difficult to get people to sign so many sheets. I used to say: "Hello, my name is XXX; I live on XXX drive, and I have the petitions to put the Party A candidates on the ballot for the fall elections. You do not have to vote for the people, but 5% of registered voters have to sign these petitions for there to be candidates for election." If they agreed to sign, I waited for them to sign the first sheet and then told them there are five more sheets for different candidates. Each sheet held 15 signatures and each petition signing took about one hour to obtain. I usually had to go to 5 houses to find someone willing to sign. We serfs of the political party were assigned certain streets in an election district by the party chair. If you were in good favor with the party chair you were assigned houses near your house. Most of the time, I was assigned to neighborhoods far from my house. We only knocked on the doors of enrolled members of Party A and we carried a booklet showing the political party registration (and age) of the people living in every house in an election district. The list showed party, house number, and name. The major parties were Democrat, Republican, Conservative, Independent, UB, Right to Life Party, and BNK. They are election law rules for allowing party names on election ballots. For example, if a party obtained 50,000 votes for a candidate on a state election, that party would be listed on the next ballot.

The overall message on political parties is that they exist to produce candidates for elected office and getting citizens to sign designating petitions once or twice a year is their principal task. What is absurd about this is that only able-bodied men can do this and thus able-bodied men are the only people in the United States who can participate in the selection of candidates for elected office at every level. Of course, women can circulate petitions, but in my 50 years on a committee in a town of about 100,000 residents I never saw a woman go door-to-door with petitions. We always had a few women present at committee meetings, but I suspect that they got their petitions signed at women's club or church group meetings rather than going door-to-door. Going door-to-door is simply tough work. I remember being smacked in the face by a huge door while the woman at the door signs five petitions. I also remember having a rifle shoved in my face when a door opened. And of course there were countless dog incidents.

About 60% of houses in my town do not have a working doorbell and 32% do not have a working entry door to knock on. People in my neighborhood enter their houses from their garage. They stop their cars in the driveway, click the garage door opener, drive in the garage and close it. They never use their front door and never answer the door. In my neighborhood 68% of all houses harbor one or more visitor-eating dogs. Of course, going door-to-door is also an absurdity in gang-dominated neighborhoods and high-rise apartment buildings. The United States' petition requirement system is obsolete; it is the primary cause for our pitiful choices for elected office. Nobody of stature will go door-to-door with petitions. Rich people hire people to do their petitions. Thus, only desperate career politicians and rich people can run for office in the United States of America because of the party and petition requirements in election law. And that is a huge problem – my opinion.

Conclusions

1. The Constitution of the United States of America is still a valuable basis for the United States' democracy.

> Basis: It has worked for 225+ years and it has not been changed in its original concept of strong states and careful power checks on the federal branches of government.

2. The weak link in our democracy and the constitution is to allow non-elected judges for life to make decisions that belong to the people and the legislature.

Basis: Allowing abortion is against the constitution and against the will of the people. Supreme Court judges created a law that so far has allowed 30 million Americans to be murdered. This is not interpretation of laws.

3. The constitution states that all men are created equal, yet countless laws are based upon birth circumstance

Basis: Affirmative action laws make institutions discriminate against people with certain skin hues and genders.

4. The political parties control the candidates for elected office in the United States, but they are "closed" organizations that are not open to public scrutiny or participation.

Basis: You cannot be a member of a political party committee unless you can physically go door-to-door with designating petitions (if not wealthy). And you have to be asked to join. You cannot apply.

5. Political parties often nominate people for elected office that no voter wants to support.

Basis: The 2020 presidential election offered a person with personality faults that irritated some voters and a lifetime politician who was beyond too old for the job.

6. There are no non-partisan election watchdogs to keep the process honest.

Basis: Election Commissioners are appointed by two political parties not the public.

7. Civics is not taught in United States Schools; Americans do not know how their democracy works

Basis: I went to U.S. schools and was never offered a course on how the democracy runs.

8. The federal government contains countless functions that are not needed or wanted by U.S. Citizens

Basis: Citizens never get to vote in referendums to delete specific government functions like HUD and certain commerce department functions.

9. Government regulations from every level of government make it almost impossible to start new businesses or developments or even build a house.

Basis: I bought a building to expand a business; the government prevented me from using it for two years and made me put in a sprinkler system that cost more than 2 times the building itself. It took me two years and $10,000 in permits to build a $50,000 building for another project.

10. Judges at every level are designated by political parties without basic vetting for qualifications and character.

Basis: I voted to elect candidates for judgeships after hearing him or her talk for two minutes as a party A Committee Person.

11. A full, independent, unbiased press is needed in a democracy and the United States of America no longer has one.

Basis: The 2020 presidential election had all media decide on the truthfulness of every statement made by politicians. Their job should be to state what was said not refute what was said.

12. America lacks the technology to allow citizen voting for elected officials as well as issues.

Basis: The 2020 presidential election showed there is complete chaos in voting functions in most states and no agreed-to way of recording votes.

13. America's two political parties are ill-defined

Basis: Neither political party will state orally or in writing what their party's philosophy or platform is. I dare them to tell the people what they stand for.

14. America's public schools at all levels are in failure mode

Basis: International comparison of SAT scores and the like test results who that the United States is behind 40 or so other countries in academic achievement.

15. Healthcare is unavailable to most working young people in the United States of America

> Basis: 53 million Americans work in low-wage jobs (less than $15 an hour) out of a total workforce of 156 million. It is estimated that 20 million people work for the government where they have complete and extensive individual benefits. This means that 40% of working Americans have to buy budget insurance for $500 a month with a $6,000 deductible. They cannot even go to a doctor. Yet 75 million non-working Americans get free health insurance under the Medicaid program.

Governments are often the enemies of the people. They were formed to unify, protect, and guide the people, but often lose sight of their mandate and become a slave owner. They become "authoritarian". China quickly controlled the 2020 pandemic in their country because they could order and enforce appropriate controls. The United States of America had the world's highest infection rate because they have little control over what people do.

The other important aspect of government is trust. The Chinese people currently trust their leader. In 2018 or so they altered their constitution to allow Chairman Xi to be their supreme leader for life. Russia did the same with Vladimir Putin. People want a strong leader since life on earth is a competition. Our forbearers, the primates, were a species where a dominant male may protect a harem of eight with up to 40 offspring. The tribe of 50 had a hierarchy and worked as a unit under the dominant male. The dominant male fights intruders and rivals. If the dominant male falls in battle, the rival will take over the harem and kill the defeated rival's offspring. This is how nature works. It is the same with countries. Citizens want a government they can trust to protect them and allow a peaceful and plentiful life.

A true democracy, where citizens decide on all state matters cannot survive on a large scale. It is difficult to get 10 people to agree on anything; it is impossible with 100,000,000 or more. Planet Earth in 2020 consists of about 200 "countries" Maybe 10 of these have real monarchy where the monarch makes all important decisions. Some countries are absolute dictatorships like Cuba. I only know of two countries in 2020 that still affect Communism in its strictest manifestation: Cuba and Belarus. Some countries in 2020 have no functional central government like Afghanistan. They are simply an area inhabited by competing tribes. They are still back in primate mode. Most of the 200 countries have some semblance of citizen participation.

If the United States is to survive as a sovereign nation, its system of government must change in character; trust must be reestablished. I was a curious youth during "The War." Everybody pitched in to help the country and the government at every level. I helped the war effort by weeding and tending our "Victory Garden." Everybody had one; everybody did what they could to help with our war effort. My aunts and uncles, my parents, everybody united to save America. There were reporters at the front to keep us informed every minute on how we were doing. The daily newspapers kept us informed, without opinion. We trusted them; we trusted our government; we trusted our neighbors; we were a united people.

This unity needs to be reestablished. My world as a youth was Reece Street. It was a short street between two major city-center streets, only about 20 houses. We were as diverse as could be. The Evans were rich. The Colbys had a beautiful lawn that they trimmed with scissors (it was tiny). The neighbor next door "worked for the city." Two families were supported by firemen and one by a policeman. Six of the twenty houses had kids my age. They were my playmates. We played in the street and in each other's yard and life was centered around our neighborhood. All of our stores for everything were in walking distance. My mother's job was in the factory that abutted our backyard and my father's factory was one block to the right and then to the left. The Catholic Church and School was four blocks away and our public grammar school was on the next street parallel to mine. We were a community centered on these two schools and multiple churches. Maybe that is the missing ingredient in America's current government.

Conscience certainly is missing. Morality is missing. Spirituality is missing. Government must be based on the common good and decisions on all matters based upon the mean of the people. Education must be designated for mean intellect; highways need to be designed to mean driving skills, laws to mean behaviors. Government must govern to the mean of the Gaussian distribution. The Constitution of the United States was designed to prevent influence from factions. America is currently run by factions and that must end. Unity can never be achieved catering to factions. We had no pampered factions during the War. We must go back to that state to survive.

I have often admired the titular monarchy of the United Kingdom. The citizens maintain a "monarch" as a figurehead and the Royal Family serves as the branch of government that takes care of social interface with their citizens and the world. However, this concept only works if the royals continually produce royal-quality offspring. In my lifetime the Queen of England has been the most stable and unifying force in that country. She is the country's continuity. She is a symbol to the world of how they want to be perceived. She maintains commensurate decorum and appearance. She epitomizes what all English people would like to be, the life that all English people would like. Besides the symbolism, this monarchy for decades has been one of the greatest financial assets. For all of my life, England has been a top tourist attraction in the world. People have to visit and see all of the vestiges of their monarch.

I have always felt that the United States of America could use a Queen of England-like entity to take the social load off of the President. The President cannot do a good job of running the United States of America when he or she has social events and schmoozing sessions scheduled each day. Maybe the constitution can be amended to give that job to the President Emeritus. In 2020, the President Emeritus would be Barack Obama. He and Michelle would do great in the job of visiting orphanages, entertaining visiting heads of state, visiting hospitals – doing all of the non-business functions of the President of the United States. Also, the president spends about half his or her term running for reelection in the final term. Again, this is a catastrophic distraction. A single term of 6 years, like senators, would solve the problem. Of course, this would require a constitutional amendment.

This morning on my commute to work the sign in front of the Town Hall (my local government) read – "Open for essential services – Wear a Mask." I could not help but think about that statement. The only "services" in the building are the building department which makes people pay the town to improve their property and then raises the owner's property taxes as well, some service. There is also the town clerk in the building which collects taxes and sells hunting and fishing licenses. Town hall also contains the Town Assessor who decides how much your property taxes will increase this year. There are no "services" other than taking your money to support more and more public employees to take more and more of your money. There are no services in City Hall—only costs to taxpayers. Government does not have to be bad. It is a tradition in the United States and many other countries. All bad government comes from bad leaders coupled with citizens who are inattentive. What can be done to provide good government? The process for developing good government starts with educating citizens. Americans do not understand the mechanics of political parties and how candidates for office are chosen. Every four years there are presidential elections that may involve primaries in some states, but primaries are very, very rare in most elections. Candidates for office are selected by committees from Party A and Party B. The party election process is far from democratic. Americans at every stage in life need to be educated in civics --how America is supposed to work – how any country is supposed to work. Students need a civics class in grades 8-12. America's schools need to be rebooted. They have morphed into baby sitting in early grades and into places to pick up bad habits and practices in later grades. There is no emphasis on learning trades and fundamentals needed for a work life. The emphasis on sports and non-essentials has made them ineffective in conveying useful knowledge. America must return to teaching reading, writing and arithmetic (and civics).

Secondly, political parties need to be opened to the public. Americans think that candidates for elected office and ballot issues appear from "the cloud" or some source in the cosmos. They do not realize that political parties select candidates for office in a closed room of party leaders at every level. Citizens or even committee members are unaware of the backroom bartering that is going on to grant an endorsement. In my 50 years in Party A, I only witnessed one elected position candidate that was selected properly. The position was advertised to the committee. Interested committee people or others could make a presentation to the full committee and a secret vote was conducted to give the party endorsement to the winner.

What happened all other times was that the party chair named the position, stated that the screening committee (the people in the back room) endorsed so and so. All in favor of giving the party endorsement to so and so say "aye" opposed say "nay". The "Ayes" have it. There was no voting. In the early days we had a parliamentarian, but when he died so did Robert's Rules of Order and democratic candidate selection. I suspect candidate selection is the same in the thousands of towns, city, county, and state party organizations.

The United States needs laws that make political parties open to the public with stated functions, operating procedures, offices, and public accountability through an annual report available to all citizens. This must be done at every level. Currently America's two political parties are not much different than the drug cartels that currently control some countries (and millions of people). The behavior of both USA's parties in the 2020 elections is verification of this statement. These were angry people and angry people are not rational.

The 2020 presidential elections in the United States of America brought out another critical flaw in the United States of America's government, lack of the ability to maintain law and order. When U.S. cities were ravaged by looting and rioting that was permitted by local governments for the purpose of getting the votes from the rioting and looting mobs. It worked, the political party supporting looting and rioting won the presidency, but America lost most of its city centers.

In my city we had a riot in 1964 over nothing but the police trying to bring order to an over-sized street party on a hot summer night. The rioters burned and looted most of the city center. The city started to rebuild, and in 2008 or so people and businesses started to return. It was rebuilding right up to 2020. After the 2020 riots and looting the city center is back to below what it was in 1964 riots; it is an unbelievable situation.

Why do political leaders allow these things to happen? Votes is the answer. Career politicians will sell their spouses into prostitution for votes. Their hunger and thirst for power, fame, and wealth transcend all moral ethics. This is a career politician. This kind of behavior is a product of America's closed political parties. People who are not government employees or career politicians are not allowed in. American needs a citizen watchdog on the operation of political parties. They need a limit on contributions to candidates and political parties. The 2020 presidential election cost 2 billion dollars, Senate races typically cost 100 million and in 2020 a corrupt local politician had 1 million in his campaign fund. Who gave this congressional candidate a million dollars? The answer is well concealed. This may be America's biggest flaw in its democracy. Candidates for office are bought because of the enormous costs that are needed for advertising. Many democracies have collective campaign limits for candidates and that is what the United States needs: $100 max from any individual or entity with printed newspaper notification of all donors for every elected office.

Another ever-increasing impediment to the survival of the United States of America is monopolies. We now have them for just about every human need. Amazon has closed or will close every retail establishment in the United States. You will only be able to buy things, even food and medicine, from Amazon in the future. All companies who make things or grow things will have to sell through Amazon or go out of business. Clearly the government of the United States needs to breakup up Amazon, Facebook, Home Depot, Lowes, Google, Microsoft, Apple and other incontrovertible monopolies.

A key part of having a democracy is free press. We are all told this. Now (2020) the United States does not have a single unbiased source of news, not a newspaper, not a TV channel, not an online news source, not a magazine. So-called news reporters preface every statement with their own

or their company's opinion. When my city was being burned and looted in 2020. The local newspaper reported: "Peaceful protests have been happening daily in the city center."
The solution is an unbiased source of news. When I was in high school my English teacher told the class that the only unbiased newspaper in the United States of America was the *Christian Science Monitor*. It is long gone, and America must get a replacement or dissolve.

In summary, the USA's democracy is in finitude and if US citizens want to see it survive until our extinction, they need to participate to a fuller extent than present. The problems that I observed in my lifetime are fixable, but not without special effort on the part of every citizen.

Chapter 7
Communication

"Light yourself on fire with passion and people will
come from miles to watch you burn"
John Wesley

Communication is a very inclusive word. It means transfer of information and there are many ways that information can be transferred. They range from a frown to a 10,000-page USA tax code. All that we are depends on communication. Our knowledge was communicated to us by teachers and experiences. Our success in life is a product of our self-marketing. Our legacy depends on how our accomplishments are communicated to those who follow.

I am at end of life and I believe that the net worth of my life has been my communicating of the learning of my materials research to others. I usually presented at least two papers each year at technical conferences in my field (tribology). This year (2020), the Covid-19 pandemic caused all conferences worldwide to be canceled, but last week I presented a paper at a virtual conference to in some way make up for my loss of in-person communication. Communication is important.

It is the purpose of this chapter to elucidate on how a person's communication skills determine his or her success and happiness in life. The chapter objective is to increase our reader's evaluation of communication skills and to make suggestions on how readers can improve their communication skills.

The chapter subjects include:

- The origin of communication
- Types of communication
- Writing
- Reading
- School
- Public speaking
- News
- Television
- Electronic devices
- Effective communication
- Misinformation

The Chapter concludes with conclusions and thoughts on the way that communications should work.

Historical Evaluation of Communication

Whenever I see an animal documentary on TV, I learn about the incredible things that animals do to communicate with each other. A lot has to do with mating, but it is none-the-less incredible. For example, one documentary showed amazing sand sculptures on the bottom of the ocean. They resembled rosette windows on famous cathedrals. Researchers found that some species of fish makes these sand sculptures by wiggling fins and the like and their purpose is to attract a female for mating. The grander the sculpture, the better the fish's chance of success. A fish may spend days making his masterpiece. He is communicating that he is ready and available to the female.

Primates communicate hierarchy within tribes. Many animals, even dogs, communicate their territory to all others. That is the purpose of a dog's bark. You entered the dog's territory and the dog is communicating to you that you are about to be eaten by the dog. Many wimpy little dogs have the loudest communication skills. A growl may be an even higher level of communication than a bark. Most animals have developed ways of communicating to each other and this communication is usually key to their survival as a species.

Words- Anthropologists have opinions on when humans started to talk. Apparently, Neanderthals did not have the jaw movement and the throat features to talk. A different skull shape with a more flexible jaw had to evolve before humans could talk like us. No doubt women were the first to talk: dinner's ready. Every grouping of humans developed their own words/sounds for their situation. A documentary on Australia's aborigines suggested that their language may go back 30,000 years. They communicated orally down the generations. They had to live off the hostile and often barren land, and how to do this have been passed down verbally from generation to generation. Tribal groups all over the world did the same. Native Americans and First Nation people in Canada often passed on traditions and survival knowledge verbally.

Verbal communication is fraught with problems. Someplace along the line, I participated in an exercise in a group of about 30 people. A teacher read a paragraph to one of the 30 in private and told that person to pass it along verbally to member 29; member 29 passed the paragraph on to 28 and so on. Then the group leader asks member 1 to write down the message that was conveyed verbally to the 30 people. Needless to say, the message received by member 1 was significantly different from the original message that member 30 received.

The most valuable communication from early man is probably cave drawings. Some go back tens of thousands of years, and they communicate hunting and living in pictures. Some early humans developed a written form of communication as in hieroglyphic scenes and figures carved in stone to communicate to succeeding generations. The Egyptians were masters of this form of communication. The point is that communication to others was a part of humans living in groups.

Early language - Facial expressions probably preceded verbal communications. Someplace in our evolution, smiles and frowns occurred. From the moment that a baby is born, parents cuddle and do things to make babies smile or coo. Babies communicate right from birth with smiles, frowns, and crying. So even before any attempts at learning words, humans have communication skills that they use to improve their physical comfort. A smiling baby is full and comfortable. A frowning baby does not like something (peas) or somebody (Uncle Ralph); a crying baby is communicating the need for some immediate response.

Facial expressions and body language remain to this day one of the most important forms of communication. I use one that I call "render invisible." This means avoid eye contact with an individual. I seldom use it, but it is my most severe form of communicating displeasure with a person's actions. I used it once on a person who worked in the laboratory where I worked in a large corporation. He was running an outside business on company time. All of us workers knew about it, but the boss was oblivious. My rendering him invisible let him know each time that we passed each other in aisles or were in the same meetings that his behavior is not to my liking. I avoided all eye contact and all optional talking with him. I have no idea if my actions had an effect on him, but I felt vindicated in that I communicated my displeasure with his dishonesty. I could not report him to management because it was well known that reporting on another, ends one's career at that company.

A smile is the most widely used form of communication. People are territorial in group events. They take the same seats in conference rooms, churches, and other places where they repeatedly meet. Everybody does this in the USA. So, at church, the same people always sit around my spot and I smile at them to acknowledge their presence. They smile back. Our current pandemic required face masks to be worn at church so now the people that smiled at me give me a subtle hand wave. How nice. Some people smile with their eyes. If your mouth is shaped into a smile your eyes reflect this.

A frown is the usual way of communicating displeasure or lack of understanding. Some people frown so much that their frown becomes permanent in their facial wrinkles. Habitual grouches may have a permanent facial frown. A wink used to be a way a man or woman signaled interest in each other. In the USA in 2020, if a person winks at a stranger he or she may be arrested for assault and sued for mental anguish by the wink recipient. A covetous look will likely result in arrest and imprisonment in an America that is addicted to political correctness and making something of nothing.

Finally, there is sticking one's tongue out. This is another time-honored way of communicating displeasure. In a similar vein, I was once mooned; I was in a city that I never visited before, innocently walking down a residential street and I never could figure out why I was mooned by a passing car. I did not know anybody in that city. Maybe the mooner recognized me as a visitor and she worked for the visitor communication center. It was an effective communication, but the message was unclear.

Petroglyphs - Petroglyphs are line drawings or sculptures and such. They are typically found in caves that probably served as shelter for long-gone peoples. Archaeologists read and interpret petroglyphs to deduce who made them and what kind of society existed when they were made. The Egyptians produced incredible petroglyphs to give us details of their civilization, but they also had a system of writing. They were more technically advanced than earlier societies that did not have writing.

An example where petroglyphs are the only communication from a lost civilization are the Mayan ruins in Mexico and other places in Latin America. These people were very technically advanced, and their civilizations flourished in what is now Mexico and Latin America from about 900 A.D. to about 1300 A.D. There were large cities along hundreds of miles along jungle paths or roads. I visited the Mayan City of Chichen Itza once when I was vacationing in Cancun Mexico. The public buildings at Chichen Itza were all embellished with scenes of their rituals, sports, and other activities carved in the local stone. All of the buildings were made from these stones. They were probably a type of sandstone.

One day I found myself exploring a deserted section of the beach that led to an outcropping of stone like the Mayans used for their building. To my surprise I could carve this stone with my hotel room key. I was in a bathing suit and this was my only tool. But this explains how these people could do so much stone carving. It was easy to carve with a tool with only the hardness of brass.

The temple or pyramid at Chichen Itza was made from huge stones and resembled the Egyptian pyramids. The petroglyphs suggested that the pyramid was a place to offer sacrifice to their gods. It was integrated with their sports stadium. The petroglyphs described what the game looked like and also showed that the winner of the sporting event lost his life. That was the reward for winning. The petroglyphs also indicate that these people waged war with other cities and that they were well versed in astronomy. The petroglyphs communicated many things about these people except the details of what happened to their advanced civilization. Nobody knows for sure. There are many theories, but because there were no written records nobody knows what happened. The Mayans did not become extinct. Mayans still live in the jungle in huts like they have for a thousand years, but their cities, their institutions, their religion, and their civilization have disappeared.

Prayer- Many cultures pray to gods. Prayer is communication to others through thought. It is something that we do in our brain, and the people who pray believe that this is a way to communicate with the dead and with one or more deities. Where do prayers go? Secular societies often forbid prayer in government functions, but now allow moments of silence for a minute or two at least in the USA. What is being communicated in a secular moment of silence? Can thoughts leave the thinker's brain? Those of us who were married for very long times know that a spouse can transfer a thought to the other spouse. I knew what my wife was thinking about; we both knew everything having to do with each other and household matters and she knew my thoughts on all matters. We would go to lunch or dinner together, and we seldom talked. She knew all of my stories, my dislikes, my likes, my thoughts. We did not have to talk. Married telepathy does exist. However, the proof that prayer communicates to a higher state probably rests with the individual. I received many miracles relating to prayer requests. Thus, I believe that prayers go to the intended. People who never got a prayer answered may not believe in praying as a form of communication.

Writing

Some people, (my philosophy tutor) believe that Sanskrit is the oldest continually-used written language. It allegedly started to be spoken and written as long ago as the 3rd millennium BC. The interesting part of a written language is that allows transfer of information that can be permanent, when spoken language can disappear. I recently took a philosophy course and the instructor tried valiantly to give us a perspective of the philosophies of Native Americans. She could not find any books written by Native American authors before 1945. Traditions by first people in many countries had to be handed down by word of mouth. And in the USA, some of the Native American tribes lost their language because the people who could speak it fluently died off.

Writing may have started something like Japanese writing, where each character is really a sketch of something. For example, the character for "elephant" looks like an elephant; "house" looks like a house; "rain" is the house character with dots above it. Sanskrit writing is beautiful, but it does not look like a sketch of "things". There is an alphabet, punctuation, usage rules. It is quite sophisticated and middle-eastern writing looks to me to have come from Sanskrit.

There is no American language or written form. The USA uses English, and it appears that the world is adopting English as a global language. On my first visit to China, I was surprised to hear Chinese officials taking to Japanese visitors in English. I thought that their languages were similar because they both use characters rather than words made from an alphabet. Apparently, they are not that close as language or as a writing system and the Chinese, being the purveyors to the world, have to deal with about 160 countries. The Chinese people can do anything because of their numbers, but as a nation they decided it is best to use only one language for their global activities; they chose English, and they teach English in grammar schools.

Another curious aspect of language and writing is that worldwide schools teach other languages as part of general education. I took three years of French and four years of Latin in High School. Why study a dead language like Latin? It is the official language of the Catholic Church which has members in every country. Sanskrit is the official language of Hindu scriptures and chants.

Writing allows presentation to others of things locked in one's brain. One can have incredible knowledge, but it will be for naught without a way to communicate that knowledge to others. Spoken word is flawed. Written word can be forever. The hieroglyphics on the Egyptian tombs will be read and interpreted as long as there are intelligent beings on planet Earth. Homers *Iliad* will be read for as long as there are people. The religious scriptures will be read for as long as there are followers. The written word probably has more power than anything else on the planet. It must be cherished and used with maximum care and caution.

Today's electronic devices can send typed words to millions of people at the click of a button or a swipe. These words are forever, just like Egyptian hieroglyphs. They are carried into digital databases and your words can come back to haunt or ruin a career. Anything written on an electronic device should be suitable for publication on the front page of a newspaper. This applies to every email or text.

Reading

Writing provides a window into one's soul; reading fills one's soul with who you are. Reading produces a transfer of information from an author to a reader. For most of us, it is something that is taken for granted, but until civilizations started to school their young, reading (and writing) were the purview of the wealthy or those in important positions. Today, we start children reading and writing as part of learning to talk. As I understand from talking with schoolteachers, reading as something to be learned, is supposed to be "all done" by maybe the third grade, and from then we are exposed to books and writings of other subjects like geography, religion, philosophy, etc. We rely on comprehension of written word to see if we were gleaning the critical points from documents that we were assigned to read. Our ability to read, somewhat follows our knowledge of words.

I never knew that there were tests to measure how many words a person knows until I took such a test. It was administered by the personnel department at the company where I worked at the time. I was told that I knew 25,000 words and the average person knows about 20,000 English words. My boss also took the test and he knew 29,000 words. He reads a lot. The more words a person "knows" the easier it is for that person to comprehend complicated writing.

I used to brag that I have never read a book that I did not have to read. In other words, I have never read a book for the enjoyment of reading. I buy books only to learn specific things. For example, I could not figure out how China's economic system worked. I saw a book on this subject advertised in *The Wall Street Journal*. I bought it and read it. Unfortunately, I never found out how China's economy works. The author meticulously recorded who was finance minister of China since 1930 or so and all their five-year plans and such, but it failed to answer my question: How can China have a "free market" that produces millions of products when no person in a communist society really owns anything. The government owns everything. But this is how I read books. Each is read with a learning goal, and I do not read any books for relaxation or enjoyment. I never read a fiction book except when it was assigned reading in school.

Some people read books for enjoyment. My sister was a "book worm". She read every novel she could get her hands on and then put it in her extensive library and likely read it again. She derived great pleasure in reading, getting into the minds of others. Reading can be relaxing. You are sitting in a comfortable chair, in a quiet corner; you are transferred into the world of the writer. It can be like meditation.

My wife used to subscribe too many "women's magazines". I never told her that I also read her magazines. When she died, I continued her subscriptions (and her magazine philosophy). To this day I probably get 20 magazines a month. I read all of them and pass them on to a friend and she passes them on to others. They get very read. My wife's magazine philosophy, however, is a well-guarded secret. Ignore all magazine subscription notices until they are $10.00 or less. But this secret must never be shared. Magazine subscriptions start at $29.99, then $19.99, etc. I have had some go as low as free. Their advertising revenue is a function of their readership. They want to keep subscribers.

I read two newspapers and one or more magazines a day. I read newspapers for business information. I read magazines mostly for pure enjoyment. I like women's magazines because they usually provide stress-free reading, comfort reading. Newspapers produce stressful reading because of the issues that they deal with.

For many people, reading is the go-to method of communication and for many it is also a major form of enjoyment. Reading is good. Today, as I mingled with holiday travelers at a major airport, I encountered a young man (fellow traveler) wearing a tee shirt emblazoned with "Read or Die". I agree.

Public Speaking

Some people like clerics, politicians, teachers, entertainers, and public relations personnel, make their living by speaking to various groups and audiences in public. Some people would rather have a root-canal than speak in a public forum or to any kind of group. Public speaking is an acquired skill. All people should have at least rudimentary training in this skill. It should be a mandatory class in high school, but when I was in high school, "Public Speaking" as a subject was only available by joining the debating club as an after-school activity. Debating at any school was a competitive "sport" where debaters were given a topic to be "pro" on, the competition would argue the "con" on the same topic. This is really not public speaking, but competitive speaking. Participants had to often argue for something that they did not believe in, like abortion. True public speaking involves expressing your beliefs, you're learning, your platform, and your passion to others.

My only formal training in public speaking was a mandatory public speaking course in undergraduate engineering school. It was a tough course for me since I never spoke in front of groups of any kind. We had to give 3-minute extemporaneous talks on assigned topics and 15-minute talks for exams. The school had about a dozen "speaking rooms" for practicing. They were like over-sized phone booths. They were soundproof and each contained a microphone, recording equipment, and a full-length mirror to talk to. To this day I believe that all schools, high schools, and colleges should offer public speaking courses. The rationale for making public speaking mandatory was that all engineers in their careers would be called on to make presentations to managers to get project funding.

My professional career has been characterized by presenting papers at technical conferences. About 15 years ago I decided to write a book on public speaking for one of my technical societies. It sold OK for the first two years, then I encountered one of the strangest things in my writing career: negative royalties. Apparently, the publisher gave me too much in one royalty payment, so they started deducting royalties from the other book of mine that they published. I think that they have stopped the negative royalties since both my books with them are near death. Chapter heads in my public speaking book were:
- Audience accommodation
- Researching your subject
- Preparing an oral presentation
- Intellectual property considerations
- Selecting and preparing visual aides
- Delivering your message
- Message strategy

Whenever you speak in public you need to establish in your own mind what you want to achieve by speaking out. If you are teaching, you need to decide what information or learning you want to convey. Then you need to decide how to do this. What facts to you need to review? What examples do you want to show? Sometimes the public speaking situation may be as simple as a public forum at the local town hall. If you wish to convince town leaders to consider your suggestion, you need to decide on the best thing that you can say to convince them. You may only have minutes to do this, but it is important to think about what you will say and what do you want to achieve. What do you want the audience to take away from your talk?

Audience accommodation
Your talk/presentation/presentation should be tailored to the situation. If you are making a presentation at a meeting with a dozen participants, chances are you want your remarks to be brief to allow the others at the meeting to speak. If you are giving a formal paper at a conference you need to talk for only the allotted time and you need to speak to the audience and not to a slide on a projection screen. If you are speaking at a public forum you need to follow the format rules. Most of all, you must consider the nature of the audience. If you are presenting a paper to research peers, there is no need to define all terms. If you are teaching students, you need to speak to their level of understanding. If you are speaking at a public forum you need to consider the makeup of the attendees. What do you want them to know? Speak to their level. Always keep a talk of any type as brief as possible. Nobody listens to a tome. Research your subject – nobody wants to listen to a talk without substance. Professional politicians often read their talk. This

tells the audience that they are presenting what a speechwriter came up with. TV news conferences by members of Congress are almost always their insincere attempt to garner votes. To be effective in presenting a message, one needs to research the subject, select appropriate facts, and use your knowledge of the subject and collected facts to make your point. If you are speaking at a public forum on a proposed apartment development in your neighborhood, gather facts about the project and make your point using these facts.

Always write what you want to say (if the situation allows it). Then throw your written talk away and give it as you remember it. A public speaking goal can best be met by conveying knowledge of the subject to your audience.

Preparing your presentation -Extemporaneous talks are fine and appropriate for many situations. Meetings at work are often called with inadequate information on why the meeting was called. Once you learn the purpose of the meeting, you may want to quickly formulate your path forward on the subject, and present it to the group. This is an extemporaneous situation, but you still need to consider what you want to say and what you want to achieve with your presentation. If it is appropriate to use a slide presentation, PowerPoint and the similar software on most personal computers produces an excellent basis for preparing to talk. Make a statement with your title, present background material, purpose, objective, and talk format, and you will quickly end up with a complete slide talk.

I do this for formal papers at conferences and then I go over the slide presentation daily for about 10 days before the presentation. If you do this, you will need no notes and you will know what slide is next and you will have the confidence you need to make an effective presentation.

Intellectual property considerations - It is becoming easier to copy and use the work of others. However, it is illegal to use any published information without the written permission of the publisher and for some countries, the publisher, and the author. It is very common at technical conferences for a speaker to compare his or her findings with previously published work. They show a graph of the published data; then they superimpose their data to compare. This is illegal without permission. Even citing the reference is insufficient. Copyright laws demand permission and most publishers require payment for permission. It may only be $10.00 but it must be paid.

You can mention work of others in words, but not reproduce any published words, graphs, data, photos, or equations. It is also becoming common in technical presentations for researchers to list the manufacturers of test equipment used in the research. This is dead wrong and extremely unprofessional. It seems to be a post-2000 standard in many technical fields, and it needs to end. It is unnecessary information unless only a certain piece of equipment can do what you are talking about. When you weigh a test specimen, you do not need to state the name of the manufacturer of the scale. There are probably 100 manufacturers of a scale that will do that job.

Use of visual aids - I published a manual on preparation of visual aids for speakers at an international conference that I have been a part of for about three decades. It is most irritating to me in an audience participant when a speaker shows a slide full of words, or so full of graphs that nobody in the audience can discern them. People prepare visual aids on computer screens. It is very easy to copy and drag graphs and photos onto a slide format and you can see everything sitting 16" away from your computer screen, but video projectors make everything grainy, and sitting 20 or 60 feet from a projection screen makes many slides useless to an audience.

Years ago, when we had a manufacturing economy, I worked for large companies that had art departments that would professionally prepare slides for me for formal presentations. They had guidelines on everything from font to maximum number of words on a slide, to permitted use of colors. As an example, 10% of the world is color blind and it is now common to project graphs with data plotted as line graphs in different colors. Ten percent of your audience cannot differentiate the green graph from the yellow graph. Art department professionals had guidelines on graphs, data presentation, - everything.

The following are the most egregious mistakes made in visual aids for talks:

1. Too many words on a slide – 6 lines max, 20 words max per line.

2. Too many images on one slide – two images (photos, graphs) per slide.

3. Never make a slide of the output of an analytical instrument - talks are summaries of data, not displays of computer-generated data to be interpreted by talk attendees.

4. Graphs plotting multiple parameters – two parameters maximum – no colors - use solid and dashed lines to discriminate.

5. Slides cluttered with company logos – do not take 20 or 30% of your slides' real estate with your company or institute's advertisement.

6. Tables of numbers – nobody can make sense of a table of numbers in a 30-second slide exposure.

7. Starting a talk with acknowledgments – acknowledgments should be a few lines at the end, not at the beginning of a talk. Acknowledgements are distractions; limit their use.

8. Equations without the symbols defined- complex equations are incorporated in every talk, but if they are presented without the definitions of each element in the equation, they convey the message that you are trying to "snow" your audience. It destroys your credibility.

9. No end to your talk - it has become common for speakers to end a technical talk with "future work" and no conclusions. If you had no conclusions for a talk then it should not be given. Restatement of what was done is not a conclusion. Conclusions are global statements deduced from a body of work.

10. Inadequate procedures - technical presentations must include a background, purpose, objectives, and format, body (procedure, results, and documentation), and an end: your conclusions. The procedure, what you did, should be presented in sufficient detail that it can be duplicated by others.

In general, visual aids should not be used unless they help to convey a message and they will not convey your message if they are too busy and unreadable.

Delivering your message - If you did all of the preparatory things that we discussed, now it is time to deliver your presentation. How do you proceed? Look at the audience; talk to them; make your point; answer questions and sit down. Sounds simple, but many people fear speaking in front of a group. Practice eliminates the fear component of public speaking. If you prepare and know what you are going to say, fear diminishes. Your confidence can overcome your fear. All speakers will have anxiety before a talk, but that is normal. At conferences I always feel "at ease" after I present my paper.

If it is at all possible, give your talk to another person, a colleague, coworker, or spouse to get their impression. Did they get your point? Was your talk interesting? Boring? Too long? Too short?

The most important talk that I gave in my lifetime was in 2000. I was selected as Engineer of the Year by the local engineering society and the award is given at a black-tie affair of the "who's who" in our city and industry. There would be about 1,000 in attendance including my bosses and my family. I wrote my talk and had my secretary type it. She did not like it. I tried to make it a humorous account of how engineering degraded over the past decade or so. Fortunately, I accepted her criticism and scrapped the talk and wrote another; this one had a positive spin on how engineering had improved over the past decade. It was a big success. If I did not get a critical review from my secretary, I would likely have had one of the worst nights of my life. There is nothing better than getting an opinion on a presentation by a trusted non-involved person.

Nervous ticks and other avoidable glitches commonly ruin speeches and presentations to groups:

- Saying "ahh" often, or "you know", or "like" every few words
- Talking to a projector screen (instead of the audience)
- Talking too fast, too slow, too weak
- Poor visual aids
- Talking with your hands
- Not adhering to time limits
- Reading your talk from a script or from slides
- Distracting appearance

Giving a speech to another person is the best way of identifying any nervous ticks or blunders. Confidence in your message will almost always carry you through a public speaking challenge and you can have confidence if you address the issues that were discussed.

Photography

A picture is worth a thousand words. This statement is old and worn-out but true. My most prized possessions at this point in my life (end of life) are the photos that I hung on my various walls. I live in a one-room barn so I have limited display space, however my collection of antique black and white photos are on the bathroom walls. My dead wife's photos are all over; on my desk, on the refrigerator, by my bed, about any place that I had. My dead granddaughter's photos are in my workshop as are my family and my wife's family.

When I traveled the world, I would take the single best photo from a trip, enlarge it, frame it, and put it in my gallery. When my wife was alive, and we had a big house I used a large bedroom as my gallery for photos, art, and antique technical instruments. My travel photos hung there. When my wife died and I sold the big house, I put my travel photos on the many walls of the lab building where I work for my youngest son. We have 15,000 square feet and lots of walls and my lifetime of travel covers many walls. Every time that I use the men's room, I see the Shogun Palace in Kyoto and the rugged coast of Oregon. On my way to the rest room, I pass a photo of fishermen repairing their nets on Coca Cabana Beach in Brazil. My lighthouse collection is by our hardness testing equipment. Sacred memories are captured on photos. The really old ones are black and white; they are from my 38 years at Kodak, most are matte Kodachrome prints and later ones are Fuji thermal prints.

I look at photos on the wall daily and they remind me of what a wonderful life I have had. And this produces brain action to lower stress. These memory photos produce psychological health benefits. Spousal death can produce debilitating grief in the remaining spouse. Photos of my wife all over the house make me feel that she is still with me. Of course, I communicate with her all the time and still blame her for bad things that happen, just like when she was alive. Photos can be calming and therapeutic.

My tribology research is such that I use photography to record test results and important material changes to explain test results. My six engineering books are rife with photos illustrating different modes of wear, fracture, corrosion, and the many different applications that are present in engineering materials. The photos are called photomicrographs and they are taken on special metallurgical microscope. I use these microscopes daily at the tribology lab where I work. Photomicrographs are recorded on memory sticks and hard disks, but I still take the thumb drive to the pharmacy and obtain prints. Long-term storage of my photomicrographs is accomplished in my technical books. One is an atlas of 20 years of friction, wear, and erosion examples.

The point of this discussion is the supreme importance of photography in life and how it seems to be on its way to irrelevance. People take photos on their cell phones so much that photography has become trite. My granddaughter took a photo of every meal she ordered in a restaurant. I have no idea what she did with them or who would want to see a photo of a Monte Christo sandwich, but that is what she did and what her peers do. They misuse photography. Making videos of whatever a police officer does, (through the use of video cameras that they wear), in 2020 has resulted in the destruction of many city centers in the USA, including mine. It was finally being rebuilt from its 1964 race riots, and now it is back to the state of public avoidance of that area.

The Chinese video app TikTok in 2020 reportedly had 80 million users in the USA. A user posts a frivolous video and hopes that it gets lots of views. App users may spend hours a day screening posts to find the most stupid, or funniest, or who knows what type of video. These misuses of photography are sucking the lives from people.

Photography used to be the way to chronicle one's life. Prints were put in albums or made into framed photos for display. I have many of my parents and grandparents that I look at daily. My dead wife's photos are everywhere in the house. These photos quell my mind. They make me recall happy times, people that I respect, people that I loved. They honor the dead.

In most instances, storing photos on cell phones and computers results in the loss of those photos. I had countless photos stored on an old computer. Rather than transfer them to new computer equipment, I stored my old computer in the attic. When I looked into getting images off my old computer and I learned that I had forgotten how to turn the machine on. My 1983 Apple 2C did not even have upper and lower case. I have lots of floppy discs with no place to play them. Electronic devices are obsolete in a matter of years often with the images that you would like to save.

Black and white silver halide prints are permanent. I have some over 120 years old and they are as perfect as on day one. I have black and white movies of my parents' wedding in 1925. Color silver halide prints fade in sunlight, and they are best kept in albums. Currently most photographic prints from pharmacies are thermal print. Colors are "melted" together from base colors a paper support. I have many that are 30 years old, and the color seems to be holding.

What happens to your lifetime of photos when you die? When a dear aunt reached her 95th birthday she took her lifetime of photos and distributed them to her children and people she knew would want them. She gave me precious photos of my parents. Photos I had never seen. As I mentioned, my lifetime of photos are special parts of family history. In addition, when I send notes to people, I use 4x5" prints from my travels as notepaper (the backside). I identify the image and people seem to be delighted to receive hand-written notes with bonus photos.

In summary, photography can supply the prints on our walls that chronicle life. This form of communication is sacred and each and every human should try and chronicle their moment on earth for their descendants. A stored computer in the attic will not suffice.

Telephone

This will be a brief section because I believe that the telephone is the lowest form of communication. A phone call always interrupts the recipient. And that is why my cell phone is always off and why I do not answer the phone at work, and I have no phone in my house. Email is my preferred means of written communication. The recipient is not interrupted. And he or she can respond when it is convenient.

I use my cell phone only for emergencies or for travel. However, I guess that I am in the minority. Every place that I go I encounter people walking in malls and on sidewalks talking to the air. They are wired to be on the phone as they do something else. About one third of the people in the supermarket are talking on the phone while shopping. In airplanes 97% of the people pull out their phone and call someone when they land. They also report when we take off. One time I was sitting next to a man who could not find anyone to tell that we were taking off. I counted at least five numbers that he tried to find someone to tell that he was taking off in an airplane.

I have taken complete semesters in my philosophy school on "attention". The school teaches that attention to the task at hand is key to success, success in the task, success in life, success in obtaining inner peace. The phone addicts should step back and consider what they are doing. How ridiculous they are; how annoying they are to others (with their blather) and how lack of attention to a task almost always results in failure.

In addition, most mobile devices access the internet where one's time on earth can be wasted in nonsense: posts on politics, photos of meals, in tweeting opinions that nobody asked for. Beside all of these nonsensical phone activities these phones offer an evil in the form of pornography (child and other), gambling, selling stolen merchandise, (Ebay, etc.), even threatening politicians. A person in my town was given a 10-year sentence in federal prison for posting that he intended to do harm to a person running for elected office. He was convicted and jailed even though he had no way of carrying out his threat.

The evils of mobile devices however, go much further than the gambling and pornography. We already mentioned how cell phone videos by incident bystanders have destroyed the city centers in most American cities in 2020. Rioting and looting continues nightly in my city (in 2020) over phone videos of police responses to incidents.

Then there is the vehicle accidents caused by distracted drivers, people texting and looking at cellphones while driving. Just this week a 35-year-old mother of two was killed across from the building where I work. She was walking to the store on a sidewalk some 30 feet from the roadway when a distracted driver ran her over and plowed into a house. The point of impact with the house was more than 100 feet from the roadway. Then the driver fled on foot. News reports are rife with horrible incidents that are caused by distracted driving due to phones and other electronic devices.

Loss of a life by phone is easy to fix. One only has to stop operating the device when you are doing something else. Even the stupidest person on the planet knows that talking on the phone in a public place is inconsiderate to others and should not be done. Only an idiot would text or phone when driving. The dumbest persons on the planet use their phones for pornography, sex, gambling, and dishonest activities.

I am at a loss for the superlatives to use to discuss the lunacy of the 2020 mobile-device situation. Maybe it is sufficient to say that nothing good can happen when these devices take your attention from the task at hand. Similarly, the inconsideration to others produced by public use of these devices assures an eternity in hell for the people who do this.

A friend of mine works at a factory making military equipment. All cell phones must be checked at the entrance. Public schools in my city have a similar policy. I am a principal in a small company. Of course, cell phones are not allowed on the premises. The damage to the human race caused by mobile devices makes these devices more destructive than all of the bombs and explosives used throughout history— even the atomic bombs. And every user has the power to reign-in their misuse. Life can be quite wonderful in controlled mode. My flip phone is off in my briefcase wherever I go. I know that I can turn it on and use it for emergencies. It is quite useful and gives me peace. It does not do internet; it does not do idle conversation; it never distracts since it is off unless it is the object of my attention. Please ponder phone misuse and lack of consideration of others.

Computers

As I write this (in 2020) the United States is in crisis mode because somebody hacked into the software used by the military and 10,000 of their suppliers and now this unnamed entity controls the military supplier costs relating to the United States military budget which is about one trillion dollars a year. Everybody who uses a computer knows that every digit is stored someplace and is available to everyone in the world who has a computer connected to any system. I was well along in my professional career when personal computers evolved. My first PC was an Apple that cost me $4,300 in 1983 and it did not even have upper and lower case. Capitals has a shaded background. It did very little, but we all know how powerful computers can be in 2020.

The world now runs on computers, but is this a good thing? I love the communication possibilities of computers connected to the internet. I absolutely refuse to perform any financial transactions online and I have never and will never buy anything online. I have never streamed anything or taken a computer course.

To explain my weird philosophy on computers: tenet number one is anything that you save to a computer or enter in any way is there for the world to see and use for purposes not intended by you. When I write anything on any computer I do so assuming what I wrote will appear on the front page of tomorrow's *Wall Street Journal.* This is the philosophy that I ingrained in my three sons. Many famous people and high elected officials have lost their jobs because of something they wrote on a computer. President Trump lost his reelection bid because he irritated so many people with his daily tweets.

Most online purveyors of anything want you to fill a shopping cart and pay for it with a credit card. My niece and her husband lost all of the money in their bank accounts buying things on the internet. Their banks eventually reimbursed them, but it involved months of personal finance agony. Such stories are everywhere. Everyone knows somebody who was scammed by computer theft of their personal and financial information. When I register at technical conferences, I use bank transfers instead of a credit card input into a computer.

Online shopping is in my "verboten" category. The reasons for this are many, but in my opinion buying from the online shopping monopoly is buying stolen merchandise. World leaders are committing national suicide by allowing the online monopoly into their country. It has destroyed almost all small and big businesses in the USA. People who make anything are forced to sell it on terms dictated by the monopoly and the only things available to inhabitants of any country are those offered by the monopoly.

If a manufacturer or purveyor of something starts to be successful it will be bought by the online monopoly and that will be the end of the development or new products from that company. The stealing part of online shopping started decades ago. A friend of mine used to shop all of the furniture and clothing and appliance stores in the city to select what he wanted to buy; then he would order the items that he selected at the local stores directly from the manufacturer. Of course, it was always cheaper than the store price however the stores had to add their costs. He was stealing from the stores. He used their design and display costs without paying for them. This is what the online monopoly does. It takes the manufacturers products and offers them to customers without any of the costs or risks associated with being the manufacturer. It is much more insidious when it comes to the shopping fraud involved, but suffice it to say, online shopping using computers has effectively destroyed all manufacturing of just about anything in the USA. The monopoly is now moving into food and drugs so it is well on its way to eliminating food stores of every size and the United States pharmacy system. Elected officials worldwide really need to ponder the effect of the online monopoly on their economies. The effect on humanity may be even worse. People as a species have something in their DNA that prompts shopping and mingling with others. In all of the countries where I have visited where people tend to live in cities, relaxation means going to the city center, browsing stores and markets, eating at restaurants and in general mingling and enjoying the sights and sounds of community living.

Buying online has decimated city centers, malls, and all other places where retail and restaurants existed. When I was in graduate school, we lived in a town of 5,000 people that was located about 300 miles from the nearest city. We had to buy clothing and anything else that we needed through catalogs; the once famous Sears catalog was our sole source of supply. There was no need to go to the city center on weekends; there were no stores, no restaurants, no attractions. The remote location was in snow country, about 300 inches per year. I am a skier, so I skied at the school's ski slope when I had some free time, but my wife the shopper, hated our stay in the frozen north United States.

Online shopping steals an essential need of homo sapiens: gathering, browsing, and bartering. Online anything promotes separation which is devastating to the human species. Isolation is counter to our biological needs and essence. Humans are hard wired to be out and about.

In my opinion, computers have also seriously degraded health care in the United States. I have many serious diseases (heart, cancer, etc.) so I go to about six doctors on a regular basis. These are my doctors I have been with for more than 20 years; they are all part of health-care monopolies. Over the past 20 years, my contact with "my doctors" has degraded into a situation where they treat the computer, not me. I get a bevy of lab tests a week before visits and a "doctor" visitation consists of the doctors looking at the test results on a monitor and typing of his or her interpretations of the results. There is usually no eye contact whatsoever with me, and the visit concludes with something like "Well, your cancer is still active, we better see you again in three months. Goodbye.

Years ago these doctors would ask "How are you? Do you have any concerns?" I submit written questions to my primary care doctor, and she quickly goes down the list and says a few things and goes back to typing and looking at my medical record screen.

When my wife was dying in the hospital, I would often find her laying soaking wet in bed and all of the nurses on the floor were on stand-up computers on wheels in the hallways. They seldom left the computers. One time the person in the room across from my wife was yelling, "Help me! Help me!" I went to the nurse at her computer in the hallway near the man's room and told her that a man is calling for help. Her reply was "He always does that" and she continued her typing on her computer. Hospitals are not the place to go if you are sick, only computers get attention. Of course, they are doing this for protection for lawsuits. In the United States, health care and other patient records matter more than outcomes. Computers, not people get attention.

Music/Art/Beauty

Music is something that probably evolved from animals. If you go near any swamp or forest at night, you will hear a cacophony of sounds that are the products of creatures serenading to lure females into mating or some other such reason. Most animals are equipped with sound sensors. They are part of an animal's preservation system for the species. Sounds alert the animal of possible danger (as in being eaten) and they take action. In any case, homosapiens came equipped with sensory ears that produce brain responses from harmonic vibrations in the air over a certain range of frequencies; we have hearing. Someplace in our emergence from chimpanzees, music became part of homo sapiens way of life.

The wonderful artifacts that exist from the "BC" era suggest that musical instruments were well known and in wide used at that time, at least in the form of wind instruments and drums. Today we have lots more ways of making pleasing (and not so pleasing) music. Music alters mood and thus it is a very important part of communication.

As in the case with most skills, there is a difference in one's genes that produces the ability to be a musician or singer or actor. But everyone with a brain can be affected by the harmonic machinations that constitute music. Many people weep when singing their national anthem. Hard Rock can evoke anger in the soul (or in me), opera can be an exciting (I love it) and classical music annoys some and soothes others (me). Country and Jazz are acquired tastes (not to my taste). The important part is that music is an available tool to favorably alter one's mental state and as such it should be encouraged and promoted. Music is good.

Art can alter mood like music. The range of responses to art are similar to people's responses to different types of music. I like modern and traditional art. Some people do not like modern art. I used to make abstract welded sculptures and jewelry. Mostly I did this because I like to weld, braze, and solder and making these sculptures gave me the opportunity. I gave the better ones to people. However, a significant piece of art can have a profound influence on many people. For example, one time I stumbled onto an incredible collection of artifacts from Egyptian tombs in a museum in Torino, Italy. There was a 10-foot-high black stone sculpture of an Egyptian queen that I will never forget. It was such a beautiful work of art.

Beauty in buildings, beauty in statues, beauty in the sky, can be mind-altering. I ski because it provides a rare opportunity to witness hills and forests blanketed with white decoration. The sights from ski trails can be wonderful. Winter snow and ice can be incredibly beautiful. When I lived on the shores of Lake Ontario, the ice sculptures created by winter storms were amazing to see.

Music, art and beautiful things can communicate many different mental responses and they can be key to achieving a happy life. Life without these true essentials is meaningless to me. Every individual needs to establish an appreciation of art, music and beauty and use that ultimately to make one's trip through life more wonderful.

Television

I was amazed by TV when it came to my city in about 1950. My aunt and uncle who lived several blocks over were the first in the family to get TV - a 10" diameter Zenith. My sister and brother and I used to get permission to go to Aunt Helen's to watch wrestling and the Ed Sullivan show. Of course, it was black and white. Several years later we got an 8" rectangular screen Air King TV. Now we could watch Howdy Doody and Ed Sullivan at home. When my sons were young, we had color TV and many shows available, but they seldom watched it. I almost never watched it and my wife watched it after the day's work was done and she relaxed before bedtime.

The role of TV in communications depends on each household. My wife and I discouraged our children's TV watching. The available shows were of no educational or any other value. In 2020, I live alone, and I only watch the 6pm local news and the 6:30 national news. It is my quick scan of what is happening. The advertising for medical cure-alls and lawyer ads is so annoying and that TV in general is unbearable to watch. And that is a shame since it could be used to inform and educate. The first time that I visited China, the TV was 100% educational with no commercials; it was wonderful. Of course, the news was and still is not news, but the government's edited "information". I particularly loved shows on how to make things and manufacturing operations. The last time that I visited China in 2017 or so, I did not have time to see how their TV had evolved there, but I know for certain the America's TV has evolved into "uselessness". What a shame.

About a year ago I discovered a use for TV that I believe should be the way for education to go in the future: courses on DVD played on TV's. They could play on any device that accepts input from a DVD. However, the TV has the biggest screen, so I use it as the display for the courses that I am taking. Hundreds of courses are available from the company that I use and their cost ranges from about $50 for DVD format to several hundred dollars per course. Their courses are usually taught by college professors and the subjects covered could be from different college majors. The courses that I have completed have been on philosophy or biology since they are part of my current interest. Each lecture is 30 minutes in length, and the number of lectures in a course varies from 12 to 24 or more. There are no exams, but it is very apparent that exams could easily be part of these courses. I explore health and philosophy issues mostly for my writing work.

As I write this we are in a pandemic and many United States schools are closed. Some say they are doing remote learning, but I have yet to see evidence that such a thing exists. What I envision is grade school and high school subjects offered to the world by the very best instructors on DVD. Grammar schools and high schools could commence (once the virus is contained) much like they exist now except teaching would be done by DVD courses by the very best instructors and schools would have tutors to answer questions, offer air to those who need it, and be a resource on the subject of the DVD. Most instruction would come from the" best lecturers" shown on TV or device screens.

The English college system (based upon my experiences over the years at Cambridge University) works something like this. Students go to master lectures at the university center and reside in small colleges. The colleges have tutors to meet the needs of individual students. Cambridge University consists of more than 35 such colleges. In any case, TV could be an incredible learning tool, but in the USA, I believe that what is offered is a monumental waste of a person's life. The United States has a channel that is labeled a "public channel" but like commercial TV, but it is controlled not by the public but by a political faction. And all programs promote the interests of the faction. For example, all news is controlled by the liberal political faction and only their views are presented. "Newscasters" present opinions; they do not report on happenings.

The situation in the United States is that most households have a TV on for most of the day and it is sort of used as background noise. I have not heard a person claim to have a favorite TV show in at least a decade and I personally find it mostly impossible to watch. Even sports are rendered unwatchable by inane commercials and blather from sports has-beens off to the side of the game. I no longer subscribe to cable TV since there is nothing to watch. When I travel, the hotels where I stay often have 70 channels to watch. It is usually impossible to find anything remotely entertaining, informing, or educational in all 70 channels. After 75 years of existence, it is time to move on. My worldwide travels suggest this is the case in many countries. What is offered up is not even worthy of critical review.

Electronic Devices

In 2020, the word "devices" is used to mean the myriad of gadgets that people carry on their person and these devices convert electromagnetic waves in the air about us into words, images, or videos. Devices range from eyeglasses that display images and sounds in a partition of your glasses to handheld screen that can play full-length movies. The average American spends upwards of four hours a day on his or her electronic devices. Millions of people devote their entire lives to games that are available on electronic gadgets. Our local technical college even offers a degree in gaming: development of electronic games.

When PC's became available to the general public in the United States of America, most came with a game called "PacMan"or something like that, where balls with a mouth would eat each other. Current games are the same, but the eating can take more forms: death rays, guns, bombs, lasers, AK47's, etc. Needless to say, every second spent participating in one of these adventure games is part of one's lifetime lost.

In 2020, the incredible aspect of gadget use is that many games and "apps" require a subscription. People addicted to their devices may have to pay for dozens of "apps" per month. Electronically many are amazing, but for what purpose, to what end? I'll never forget riding on a ski gondola up a mountain where the other 3 people (family members) were all watching their devices as we ascended the mountain. They were watching our increasing height above sea level. I asked how high this slope is. What is its height above the base of the gondola? None knew what the height of the parking lot above sea level was so they could not ascertain the vertical drop of the slope that we were going to ski down.

They were also bragging about their speed in the last run. One woman claimed that she traveled 60 miles per hour. At that speed, one error of form can cost you your life. Many skiers at this resort had cameras on their ski helmets. They recorded every run down the mountain. I cannot believe that these people spend hours reliving skiing down a slope, but what else would they do with the videos shot from their ski helmets. It seems to me that electronic devices in the hands of skiers suck the joy out of skiing, the beauty of the slope, the crisp air, the sights and sounds, the stillness of a pause on a wooded trail.

Overall, the 2020 preoccupation of Americans and many other countries with electronic gadgets is diminishing the entire human race. Their gadgets are amazing in what they can do from the communications standpoint, but their diversion of one's attention from tasks at hand and surroundings cannot be good. Relying on these devices for everything from daily schedule to social contacts can atrophy one's brain. Why study any subject or anything at all when you only have to ask Google or Alexa for anything that you may ever need to know? When the latest iPhone comes equipped with an artificial intelligence app there will be no need for universities or schools of any sort. Your phone will be omniscient.

Conclusions (excuse the following format. Use of different computers made this numbered list impossible; this is an example of how computers seldom work as intended. Sorry)

1. Communication with others in your species is innate

   Basis: all animals do it as part of DNA-based survival instincts

2. Writing/drawing is the oldest form of communication

   Basis: Much of what we know about our world, about each other, about our planet exists because of written words and drawn images.

3. The ability to read and write is necessary to live and work in our current civilization.

> Basis: Governments publish rules and regulations that must be read and observed, or terrible harm will befall you. You cannot drive if you cannot read traffic signs (as my son found out when he drove into Montreal for the first time' he did not know what "Arete" meant.).

4. Public speaking is an acquired communication skill that is necessary for many careers

> .
> Basis: Public speaking gets politicians elected; teachers use public speaking to teach; clergy use public speaking to inspire, etc.

5. Visual aids are part of public speaking, but too many visual aids miss the mark; they do not help if they are not prepared properly

> Basis: I attend up to 4 week-long conferences per year and I have been doing this for more than 50 years. Many slides are unreadable, too long, or contain too many words.

6. Photography is often the most effective way to communicate.

> Basis: In 2020, most city centers in the United States were damaged and looted because of media-released videos of police incidents.

7. Photographic prints are a way to prevent loss of treasured memories
.

   Basis: Wedding and event albums have been used since the start of photography to preserve important photos. It works. Electronic storage of digital photos often fails because of equipment evolution (Remember floppy disks, and photos on CD's, etc.?).

8. Telephones used to be essential to conducting business. In 2020, they are mostly for recreation and idle chatting. Their use steals attention from the task at hand.

   Basis: Because mobile phone users talk on the phone wherever they are, I hear their communications- they are not business, it is idle chatter; waiting for a flight at any airport is to participate in the personal discussion of almost every passenger waiting to board your flight. Everybody is on the phone saying "I'm at the airport we will board shortly, blah, blah, blah.

9. In 2020, cellphones with texting and internet capability have made addicts of many, maybe most, users.

   Basis: Surveys show that the average user spends more than four hours each day on their devices. People walk in public areas holding their devices as if the device is determining their direction. Groups in restaurants look at their devices rather than whom they are sitting with.

10. Computers control daily life in the United States of America, usually at the expense of human interaction and tasks at hand.

Basis: Call anyplace to get a service or product you will get a computer answer that sends you to another computer. Usually, you will not get the objective of your call. You apply online for jobs; buy online; pay online get medical care online. In the company that I work for, the owner (my son) answers the phone, and we believe that is why we have been in business over 20 years; we do not use an answering machine or service. You get to talk with a live person when our phone is answered.

11. Arts in the United States are continually diminishing, and most forms are economically challenged.

Basis: I have been actively supporting classical music, opera, art galleries all my life and I witness one after another gallery or concert flounder; in 2020, it is nearly impossible to make a living as a musician or an artist.

12. Television in 2020 has to be replaced as the source for news and entertainment. The offerings are so poorly designed and delivered (reality TV, cooking shows, news, etc.) that watching TV is too irritating for most to endure.

Basis: The advertisements for prescription drugs are so disgusting and repulsive as to drive any sane person crazy. Streaming has largely replaced TV

Effective Communication

This chapter has painted a relatively grim picture of the 2020 state of communication in many areas. The number one problem is cellphones with internet connections. They are destroying personal intercourse, education, civility, etiquette, honesty, morality, and family life to name a few of their negative consequences.

As a widower, I dated a woman for several years and decided that marriage was out of the question because of her cellphone addiction. Our dates usually constituted of going to a bunch of nice restaurants. She would put her cellphone next to her plate and often end up talking with others several times during our dinner dates. Her profession was real estate agent, so she had some business calls, but since I listened to all of her calls, most were friends, her daughter, or her grandchildren. She could not shut her device off for two hours.

Some acquaintances fact-check everything that I say. If I say "Sea turtles can live as long as 200 years", she will counter that the Humpback Turtle actually lives 229 years. Or I say that it is hot out; she will supply the complete that-moment weather from her device. Why do these people ever talk with other humans, they have their devices? There is no need for anything else in the world. Their device is omniscient.

Virtual meetings and classes have replaced the real thing because of the 2020 pandemic, but if it ever ends there are many schools that will opt for virtual classes forever and many organizations will forever meet virtually.

Entertainment, movies, sports, and the like will likely stay virtual post pandemic. It certainly is easier to stream a concert rather than have 3000 people and 150 musicians showing up at an auditorium. Football looks better on TV than in person as do most sports. There will be no need for stadiums and tailgating.

My philosophy on the future of communication is to strive to return to the basics: reading, writing, meetings, school, speeches, and electronic gadgets for work only, educational TV, personal interaction, and elimination of electronic gadgets that distract. Life does not have to be as horrible as it is in 2020. Restoration of civility, however, starts with addressing device addiction.

Hopefully what I see in the United States may be a passing fad. When TV came to the masses, everybody watched a lot. Then came transistor radios, everybody carried one around listening to it. Then came MP3 players with earphones. Maybe the United States' addiction to cellphones will diminish. I witnessed proper use of cellphone technology on my last trip to China. Every shop keeper that I encountered who did not speak English whipped out his or her cellphone to use for translation. I spoke what I wanted into the phone that they placed it next to my face for a reply. The phone translated their reply to me in English. I have never seen any display of voice recognition in the computers or mobile devices used in the United States of America. This is an example of the beneficial uses that could be possible if Americans stopped using them for idle chatter and inane videos.

The 2020, most mobile devices and computers in the USA are freely used for all types of business transactions. A basic tenet of the use of computers for any purpose is that whatever you put on the internet can be viewed and read by all internet users worldwide. Somebody, someplace, will devise code to allow them access to whatever you are using the device for.

Computers not linked to the internet work fine. My home computer has never been linked to the Internet and I have no internet at home and that solves all issues with hacking and the like. The internet has become the server system of the world. We all use it, but like any server's system it comes with the potential of carrying infectious diseases. In fact, the word "Hacking" was invented by computer people to describe electronic intrusion of others into one's electronic communications. It is electronic burglary. Much of the human race depends on computer networking for their very existence. All of the essentials in life in the United States of America are dependent on supply chains operated by computers, our vehicles are controlled by computers, but nobody knows what a computer is actually doing, but the individuals who wrote the software. I would venture that young people in the United States are fully addicted to devices before they have any comprehension of how they work. We all have come to accept the internet. I remember its start. US universities were among the earliest adapters. Of course, they educated the people who were part of the development of computers and the internet. I remember the start of both. The PC was invented in my hometown by a researcher at a prominent manufacturing company that was the business enemy of the manufacturing company that I worked for at the time. The inventing company never commercialized it. Somebody else did.

The internet started in the United States in Universities. At the time I was doing research that was still being done at many universities and at our meetings the professors told me how they delighted in using the internet to see salary information on colleagues at their universities. They also peeked at communications between deans and university leadership. Thus, from the very start, the internet was being used for nefarious reasons. That is still the situation. If I pay for a restaurant meal with a particular credit card, the next day I will receive an email from the credit card company asking me how I enjoyed the meal at the restaurant and offering me a coupon for some other restaurant.

All actions on the internet are sold by others for reasons not to your benefit. Anything that you want to do on a computer that you do not want to share with others should be done on a computer not linked to the internet, and that is the absurdity of the United States' electrical grid, government use of internet, even voting. All Americans know that something went amiss with the 2020 presidential election. Twenty percent more people voted than in the past 100 years. The difference between the 2020 results and the others over the last hundred years was voting by mail and computer tallying of votes. Only computer programmers know what is being done with input data. There is no way to check. Sensitive communications should never be put on the internet.

The use of Twitter cost the President of the United States his presidency. He spoke his mind for all the world to see on

Twitter and this negatively affected most of the country. The use of social media is a fad that needs to end. It has caused the near completed breakdown of our civilizations. How can civilizations survive when nobody is paying attention to tasks at hand?

In summary, communications in the United States of America and much of the world have reached a low point in the history of human beings just about everything that humans have developed has been compromised. The "free press" no longer exists. In the United States every source of "news" is owned by some billionaire and his "news", not the real news is their product.

What is being communicated to students in schools is not fact or truth, but what current bureaucrats want to infuse into the mind of naive voters.

Television has been bought by pharmaceutical companies who advertise expensive drugs to the point where people will believe they have whatever the drug is for and then tell their doctors to prescribe it to them. Why else would drug companies advertise drugs to an audience that cannot legally buy their drugs? Just about everything on TV is dishonest or intellectually diminishing.

Books in general have become trite. Publishers only publish works of previously published authors and celebrities. It is extremely difficult to find a non-fiction book with a fresh concept or something that helps humanity in a significant way. This book is the first since my last one.

So what is a citizen to do about our not-so-good state of communication? To start with: Read only *The Wall Street Journal* for news, never buy anything advocated on TV, and sue every drug company for any illness that befalls you. It was brought on by advertising indoctrination. As an aside, a local member of the United States Congress tried to pass legislation banning prescription-drug advertising, just like the United States bans liquor advertising. He disappeared from the face of the earth, no doubt at the hands of the prescription drug lobby.

Overall, people need to ponder communication as it exists in 2020 and make rational judgements on how to make their future communication more effective and how to fend off the improper communication that is all around us. The need is urgent. Finitude has arrived in many of our existing modes of communication. The loss of believable news is particularly damaging to world democracies. Preoccupation of the masses with electronic gadgets has reduced cognition levels in homo sapiens to levels not seen since we were in the chimpanzee stage of evolution. The human race is really in big trouble in the area of communication and the problem could be mostly solved in an instant. Life can be wonderful (and prolonged) when your hands (and minds) are free.

Chapter 8
Health

A celebration of life
A euphemism for "funeral"

This chapter recounts my life experiences in dealing with various issues involving health and suggests a philosophy to properly deal with them: don't put contagious sick people in a building full of feeble old people who rely on caregivers for everything.

The format of this chapter is like it has been in previous chapters: we will discuss issues, deduce conclusions related to these issues, and suggest a philosophy that effectively deals with prevailing issues.

Children's health

The earliest health issue that I recall was having my tonsils removed in a basement operating room at a doctor's house. I was about six years old. At that time, parents were told that their children's tonsils should be surgically removed early to prevent some later disease. I still do not know what that disease was. My mother brought me in my pajamas the big house where the doctor had an operating room in his basement. They laid me on an operating table and put a rag soaked in ether over my nose and mouth. It produced a bizarre dream that I remember to this day. I was in the boiler room of a large steamship and a person was shoveling coal into the open fire of the boiler. The boiler fire was glowing red. The boiler room was full of piping, valves, and gauges. It was very noisy. A truly remarkable part of this experience was that I had never been on a boat of any kind in my life. I never saw a boiler room or valves or gauges of any sort. How did I dream these things that were totally unknown to me? Two years ago, in one of my philosophy classes, a student stated that dreams can be based upon previous lives. Maybe we are recycled.

In any case, the other part of this first medical experience was spitting up blood for a day or two. It was after the war and the nurse gave me a khaki army towel to spit blood into. Also, I think that I was vaccinated for something in the 7th grade. I got sick and that was the last time that I was too sick to go to school of work. I never missed a day in high school, college, or 44 years of factory jobs.

However, when I got married at age 23, we started to have babies and I had to figure out where they were coming from. We had to deal with the health issues of my three sons. We also had to deal with some handicap issues, since after college we lived with my in-laws with two babies while our new house was being built. My father-in-law was a quadriplegic, so I had to learn how to help care for a person who could only move his head.

We lived in married student housing at a university a thousand miles from home when we had our first two boys. My wife was a thousand miles from her mother and my mother, and she had to learn how to deal with perceived health issues with the babies. During our first year as parents, my wife sought help from Dr. Spock's famous book on babies to find out if any baby peculiarities were causes for medical concern. How babies react to situations; what should their weight gain look like? When should they stand? What if they frequently wake up at night? Dr. Spock answered most of these questions. However, eventually we learned that one of our neighbors in student housing was a medical doctor from Canada. She could not practice in the USA, but my wife directed all her baby held questions to her and she would say: I cannot give you a professional guidance in your state, but some people view this rash is such and such. She would steer my wife in the right correction on what to do. Our doctor neighbor was there to help her husband get his degree in mining engineering. She practiced in a mining town in Canada where they both lived.

When I finished grad school we will back to our hometown and the only health issues that we had with the boys in grammar, high school, and college was chronic ear infections in the part of one son at about age 8 years old. We dealt with these by going to an ears, nose, and throat specialist. There was also a broken arm from skateboarding and an out of socket arm from skiing, but in general, my wife became an in-house medical expert with a handful of trusted doctors. Thus, an effective way of dealing with traditional baby health issues is to have a mom with common sense, a Dr. Spock book, parent guidance, and some trusted doctors.

Of course, this favorable medical situation was made possible by a wife being a stay-at-home mom and good health insurance produced by a good manufacturing job. The company covered all medical costs. Such benefits are almost nonexistent in USA's private sector in 2020. The healthcare of one's children from infancy to young adult is the parents' responsibility, and with the loss of manufacturing jobs, family healthcare can be a family's number two expense after shelter. There is no way to deal with the absurd cost of medical treatments if a dependent gets a chronic disease like multiple sclerosis or diabetes etc. The proactive approach to dependent health is to use your role as parents in charge to prevent your children of any age from lifestyles that compromise their health like obesity and drugs. Along these lines, my wife forbid our three sons to have motorcycles and dirt bikes. I kept finding them in a shed out back when they were teenagers and when I asked them about them, the story was always: we are just fixing it for Michael G. I suspect that they were their bikes and they were sneaking them out to ride in the woods near our house. Fortunately, they did not have any injuries that we knew about.

Monitoring your children's health in college can be challenging. Prayer is about the only recourse if they are out of town. You need to pray that they do not do anything stupid, like fraternity drinking parties. My oldest son found his wife in undergrad school. This was great; she kept him out of trouble; they have been married for 35 years now. Prayer and worry however are not necessary if you did a good job of instilling good judgment and your children in their formative years

Healthy Eating

I attended two 50-year school reunions: eighth grade, and high school. In both instances, I only recognized about three percent of my classmates. My 8th grade girlfriend looked just the way she did 50 years earlier, but her two best friends from 8th grade, who were both pretty girls at the time, looked nothing like their eighth-grade appearance. They had become matronly overweight older woman. The same thing happened, only worse, with my high school reunion. My 8th grade reunion only had 60 classmates; my high school was several hundred. I recognized the class president and a few individuals that I had continual contact with, but most others were unrecognizable. This was mostly because of obesity or general overweight. Weight is a huge health issue and one that everyone can control.

Genes play a role, but eating and exercise plays a predominating rule. After my recent course in molecular biology, I learned that most of our proclivities and characteristics are predetermined by the molecular makeup of our DNA. We all know that a parent with curly black hair will produce offspring with curly black hair. I have my father's nose and he and his brothers all had my grandfather's nose. My sons have the same nose. On my one trip to Poland which is where my grandfather came from, I toured a historic castle and saw a painting on the wall of a man with my family nose. Without a doubt he was one of my ancestors. Thus, genes determine physical attributes, but so does the feeding of the humans with those attributes. Too much feeding can produce negative results.

Weight control is simple mathematics. A person needs to eat 2000 or so calories a day to live. Any more goes into fat; any less goes into weight loss. Eating produces positive brain reactions, that is if you like food, and it quells stomach contractions from hunger. Hunger is a product that the brain, and people have the power to control their brain. My daughter-in-law has breast cancer and a doctor advised her to fast before and after radiation treatment. This fasting allegedly increases the effectiveness of the radiation and chemotherapy. I do not know if this is true, but for the past two years she has fasted one or two days each week and today she still believes that it has been helpful in keeping her cancer in check. She finds fasting easy, and it helps her feel good. We Catholics used to fast regularly. They diminished this requirement in my lifetime to one meal on Ash Wednesday and on Good Friday, but fasting is an ageless tool for weight control. When I have a big lunch at a restaurant, I usually do not eat dinner. I fast (dinner is a martini and peanuts). My weight has ranged between 165 to 180 pounds for the past 50 years or so. However, I have concurrently done what I call bull work. Bull work is heavy lifting, shoveling, carrying rocks around, shoveling dirt, etc. It is work that makes you sweat. This is not formal exercise. I am always building or repairing something. I currently maintain two houses, a building lot and a 15,000 square-foot commercial building. My eating habits do not include calorie counting, and I believe that my weight is controlled because my lifestyle incudes bull work along with daily exercise.

I once watched a show on television about working off excess calories. Medical technicians instrumented an athlete was a gadget to record the number of calories that he burned doing various exercises. It was incredible what this guy needed to do to burn off 500 calories. For example, he only used up 500 calories in two hours of running on a mile-long school track. You can eat 500 unnecessary calories in one donut. In other words, the exercise required to burn excess calories caused by eating one donut makes them never worth eating. That is why I only eat one per week. I ate one per day before I saw the video.

What you eat makes a difference. I know very little about nutrition, but in 1998 I had an angiogram and I learned that I had a hundred percent blockage in one of the three main arteries to my heart and 45% blockage in the remaining two. This learning may be stop eating food high in cholesterol. I did not voluntarily change my eating habits; my wife changed her feeding-me habits. No more bacon, no more pizza, and no more cheese covered things, no more cakes/ pies and almost everything that tastes good. My wife used to say. If it doesn't contain fat, it doesn't taste good. How true. However, reduced intake of fat-containing foods is good for reducing the propensity for plaque buildup in body's circulatory system. It is prudent to monitor your fat intake in eating. I do not measure anything, but I always take note of the fat content of what I eat. A breakfast habit that I developed about 30 years ago is now a favorable breakfast from a nutrition standpoint. My wife never worked outside the house, and she used to get up at 6 AM cook my breakfast. One day, she decided that she would rather sleep until she naturally woke up at about 8 o'clock, and that I need to start fixing my own breakfast. I was not given another option. What resulted was instant oatmeal with apple or blueberries and light milk. And this is my take on eating. Everyone needs to ponder what goes into your mouth. Net doing so, can make you unrecognizable at your 50th school reunion.

Work

Some forms of work can have health risks. Fortunately, there are regulatory bodies in the USA that allegedly can be petitioned if it is thought that there is a job that poses risks to oneself. My second factory job after high school was a poster child for work related health risks. I was an inspector of steel desk pedestals, the sides that support a desktop, after they were painted. A person would deliver a skid load of freshly painted pedestals, about 10, and I inspected them for spots, scratches, and other types of paint defects. If any needed rework, I took them off skid and piled them into a rework area. My inspector job did not have any health risks other than those associated with lifting 50-pound steel desk pedestals. The health risk came when the workers that brought me the pedestals to inspect would quit. They typically only lasted a few days in the oven retrieval job. That job was putting the desk pedestals into the paint-baking oven. The oven was the size of a single car garage with two steel doors that opened out. It was maintained at 400°F. Once an hour, a fresh skid load of pedestals had to be put into the oven and the one in the oven had to be pulled out. The skid of pedestals was pulled with a 6-foot-long steel hook. The skid had small steel wheels and the floor of the oven was steel. The wall and ceiling of the oven were brick, and all of these surfaces were at paint curing temperature: 400 F. The skid of pedestals was about 8 feet long. You had to walk into the oven, try to hook the skid and pull it out without touching anything because all surfaces were 400F. Also, you had to hold your breath and close your eyes or else your eyes and lungs would get burned. There was no protective equipment.

This is why oven tenders did not last more than a week, and I had to fill in between new hires. The painters on the paint line had a similar situation, but their physical harm was not as immediate. They sprayed paint containing volatile hydrocarbon solvents. Continued breathing of them would make a person faint, so they were allowed to go to the bathroom for 15 minutes out of every hour to gasp for air out of an open window. Of course, all the solvents that they used were later found to be carcinogens.

Thus, there are jobs that can pose health risks. Now in the USA, you can demand to see a safety data sheet and any chemical that you must handle on the job, but these data sheets are written in legalese and may require a special lawyer to interpret. Every person needs to assess their work situation and try to remediate health risks. If you are subjected to chemicals for a significant amount of time, identify them and find out if they are harmful, in the long term. Do you have a job that requires you to push, pull, or lift loads larger than your frame can withstand? Government regulations control these you have to research limits. If it is an outdoor job, you may be exposed to weather extremes, you must acquire and wear appropriate protective gear like a sun hat and sunscreen or heavy canvas leggings for the winter etc.. Overall, think about work risks in choosing a career or applying for a job.

Exercise

Like scotch, exercise is an acquired taste. My wife of 50 years would never touch exercise that was not camouflage as something else. The medical basis for the need for personal exercise is: move it or lose it. This year I had my first broken bone it was the thumb on my right hand. It got caught between two large rocks that I was moving. I had my hand in a cast for seven weeks. My thumb healed OK, but I lost the use of my right hand. I had no grip strength and there were sore spots in my palm. I'm in the middle of a building project and I quickly learned that I did not have enough strength in my hand to hammer nails or carry cement blocks. I could easily carry a concrete block in my left hand but not in my right. Needless to say, I started looking into exercises to bring back my hand. I purposely nailed things that should have been screwed in order to exercise my right hand. I carried as big of a rock as I could in my right hand just this week. I restored my hand by carrying a 20-pound barbell in my hand for 24 laps around my house each morning.

I still do the sports today and that I have been doing since college: golf, sailing, biking, and skiing, and I believed that they provided me with sufficient muscle activity so that I do not need planned exercise. However, in 1983, I spent three weeks in China as a guest of the Chinese government as part of as part of a scientific mission. We stayed in Chinese facilities, and we were immersed in their culture for the whole visit. One observation that impressed me forever is that at sun-up, everybody went outside and starting to do stretching exercises. Everybody did something different, but everybody was alone, and every motion was slow and smooth like Tai Chi. I was so impressed with this wonderful daily ritual that when I got home, I bought a book on Tai Chi and developed my own sunrise exercise routine. I do it daily before anything else accept coffee. I make a cup of coffee sip it a bit and start my routine. It contains Tai Chi moves, Qui Gong moves, exercises that I got from my doctor's wall, exercises from my optometrist's wall, as well as new exercises as needed, like carrying barbells to strengthen my grip. I do these exercises wherever I am (except the ones requiring the barbells) in the world. I usually find a discrete park, but sometimes I do them behind a column in an airport. I have published my exercise routine in my books and will do so in this book if I remember. I tried going to the local gym and using exercise machines, but I was driven away by the sanitization procedures required after using each machine.

I have a permanently damage back from a lifting incident in one of my factory jobs. It goes out if I do not keep doing my bull work. My avocation is stone mason. The lifting and digging in mason work keeps my back from going out. One time, I started getting sharp pains in my upper back doing nothing at work. X-rays showed tiny fractures in my spine. I was diagnosed with osteopenia the precursor to osteoporosis. I asked the doctor how I can rebuild my fractured bones. He said bones tend to strengthen under compression. There is no other way. So, I added walking around my house with a 40-pound bag of sand on my head. This became part of my daily routine for several years. It worked; after about two years, my bone scans improved and have not had any fractures for 10 years or so. Thus, directed exercise can possibly cure things.

My purpose in recounting these incidents is to try to convince readers of this book that developing a daily exercise regimen can do wonders in preventing loss of mobility with old age. I am never sore the next day after doing heavy work. The Tai Chi routine that I stole from the Chinese is a vital part of my life. It is in the same category as a daily shower and brushing my teeth. This is not a chore; it is not really work; it is getting your mind and body ready for the new day. Please consider a sunrise routine for better health.

Mental health

This aspect of health is equal in importance to exercise. Your brain controls your body, your actions, your thoughts, and your life. It is your operating system. I recently completed two DVD courses in the working and neuroscience of the brain, and I learned that medical researchers studying the brain keep learning about what part of the brain does what. However, the parts of the brain that respond, for example to pain, are different for people of different age groups. They use nMRI to measure blood flow in the brain to study trends, but overall, it is my opinion that neuroscientists have not figured out how the human brain responds to stimuli or how it stores data. They know many things about the brain, but not how it makes you who you are. Good health requires good mental health which in turn requires internal peace, a peaceful mind, a brain at peace.

In 2020, the Covid-19 pandemic produced mental problems, like fear and anxiety in a significant portion of the world's population. After 18 months of fighting the virus on many fronts, US citizens are not in agreement with acceptance of the available vaccines. Almost a third of America's population is reluctant to receive the vaccine as I write this. This response is mostly due to fear of negative effects. Fear is a product of one's brain, as is addiction, neuroses, suicidal behavior, aggression, anger, and the like. These are negative brain "responses". Things that quell mental issues include, attitude, family, pets, socialization etc. This section will discuss a variety of issues relating to mental health. However, the final chapter on "Self", will discuss some of these factors further and propose the use of self-inquiry to chart a course of life, the physical and mental aspects of life.

Consciousness- Quotation:
The only thing that we are sure about consciousness is that
is soluble in chloroform,
Lisa Turve, biophysicist

Consciousness has been a study pursuit of mine. I took a DVD course in it by a distinguished professor from Oxford University and after 12 half-hour lectures, I concluded that nobody really understands it. Yet, as living creatures we invoke it daily for our very existence in the form of sleep. How does the brain switch from cognition (consciousness) to non- consciousness? This phenomenon can happen in a femtosecond or may take hours. I can personally vouch for the existence of the femtosecond route. On the way home from my junior prom in high school, I was driving sleep deprived. I had not slept in about 30 hours. I remember going through an intersection near my house and the light was green. The next conscious event was a screeching sound. It was the tires on my vehicle trying to drive my beloved 1952 Mercury convertible farther up the telephone pole that was 100 feet from the intersection that I consciously observed. Falling asleep at the wheel can be one of the fastest things on the planet.

What is happening in the brain when non-consciousness occurs, and I repeat non-consciousness; this is one of the few things that I learned in my consciousness course. Unconsciousness occurs when you receive a brain-damaging blow or too much alcohol. Non- consciousness is the natural phenomenon that produces sleep. Medical professionals know well what chemicals or gases can produce loss of consciousness, but they do not know the mechanism. Chemically inducing non-consciousness has been known for very long time. Anesthesiologists know what works and what doesn't work and repercussions. They know how to make the patient's brain switch from consciousness and cognition to non-consciousness. Biophysicists are now exploring the possibility of quantum effects controlling the mechanism. Maybe the chemicals in anesthesia produce changes in the spin of electrons that are associated with atoms that make up the molecules that make up the proteins of which we are all made.

The evidence in support of consciousness being related to quantum effects is the unexplained antics of wildlife. How do birds navigate? They can fly 2000 miles without GPS and find a particular island in the Pacific Ocean. The Earth's magnetic fields could be the source of their scientifically unexplainable behavior. Magnetic fields could be causing quantum effects in the atoms of the molecules of the proteins in their brains. Sea turtles are more amazing. They may swim 3000 miles to get back to the beach where they were born, all this without GPS help.

The mental health aspect of consciousness is sleep. To fall asleep can be a health challenge for many and without a biophysical explanation or understanding of how it works, average people often must employ tricks, rituals, or intermediaries to achieve sleep. And of course, sleep is needed for our very existence. Every night I go through a ritual to bring sleep. I get comfortable on my back, then I turn on my right side, and then think about my current non-work project. I suspect that my building projects alter the quantum states in my brain, or as Albert Einstein once said:" quantum entanglement of atomic particles is "spooky" action at a distance".

Mental illness seems to me to be the non-conscious part of the brain, overpowering cognition, and the conscious part of the brain. Mind-altering chemicals like alcohol, marijuana, and opiates also allow the non-conscious part of the brain to take over. A person does things that are incongruent with normal behaviors. Clinically diagnosed mental illness, like depression, suicidal tendency, and dementia, similarly produce abnormal behaviors. Sane behavior requires cognition and use of the conscious part of the brain.

Addiction- Addictions may be the biggest mental health issue in the USA. It seems to be all over the country. People get addicted to alcohol, nicotine from cigarettes, psychotic drugs, obtuse sex, even coffee. There are many additions. Addicted people lose their free will, their non-conscious brain takes over. Neuroscientists know the science behind major causes of addiction to substances. The brain requires an electrochemical reaction to complete connections between neurons and addictive chemicals like nicotine, alcohol, marijuana, cocaine, OxyContin etc., mess up the electrochemistry needed to make neuron connections. Addictions of all types are caused by neurotransmitter problems and the only way to stop an addiction is to change the body chemistry and return the neurotransmitter situation back to normalcy. It takes 21 days to produce an addiction and it takes 21 days to get rid of an addiction. At least that is my belief. I was severely addicted to smoking for 30 years. It was only three weeks to get cured, but it was a very difficult three weeks.

Dementia - Dementia is a mental illness that will affect many of us. It usually happens when you get old and sometimes when you're not so old. My first exposure to dementia occurred at one of my nieces birthday parties. My sister's husband has a large family and we attended celebrations with my family and her family and her husband's family. We were a big group. In one of these celebrations, my niece's uncle Ralph was behaving a bit strange. He was going about smiling and singing to everybody. I did not pay much attention to this because he was a big friendly guy. However, several months later I learned that uncle Ralph had to get a medical leave from his job because he had dementia. He could no longer work and he was only 55 years old.

Then I started to see dementia in friends and neighbors. A good friend who lived maybe 10 houses away from me started to do strange things. She stopped driving and retired from work and I would see her walking down the highway pushing a wheelbarrow. She was pushing the wheel barrow to the neighborhood convenience store to buy food. She was never married and lived alone, so there was nobody to notice that she was not behaving normally. One day, as she was pushing her wheelbarrow past my house I went out to talk with her. She did not recognize me. She said that I looked familiar, but she could not remember my name. Well, she was very familiar with me because we were in politics together and she was a source of secret information about people running for office. She knew everybody and she knew all the dirt. And she told me all of it. We were close in civics. Eventually she moved out of her house and I don't know where she went, but a do know that she lost her cognition for about a year before she moved away.

In my technical activities I use to visit and have dealings with a famous professor at MIT. He was sort of a mentor to me. We worked together on my company's problems. One time, at a technical conference he was scheduled to give a talk at a dinner and to my surprise his wife gave his technical talk. He was sitting next to her with kind of blank look on his face. I did not know what this was all about. Later learned that he had severe dementia and could no longer teach at MIT and do his tribology research. He was still healthy looking, maybe 60 years old. So dementia can affect very learned and bright people, people with great intellectual activity.

My personal brush with dementia occurred after I had just finished publishing another technical book. I wondered if I might have dementia of some sort and that what I published may have been gibberish. This was the ninth edition of my college textbook and the publisher no longer sought outside reviews of the content. I wondered how I know that what I'm telling readers is factual. What if I have dementia and my writings are wrong. At my next physical by my primary care doctor, I asked him if I have dementia. He said I can answer that question. He pulled out a sheet of paper from his desk drawer and it was a test of 30 questions. He said that this quiz will do a rough screen for dementia. If you get more than 24 questions correct you don't have dementia; if you get 19 to 23 correct, you have mild dementia; if you get 10 to 18 correct you have moderate dementia. Most of the questions were simple like what's today's date, what season is this, what is 2+6 equal to? As I recall I only got two questions wrong, However, I said: do you have anything more definitive.

As I mentioned previously, my primary care doctor loves to refer you to experts for anything that he is not expert in. He said I will refer you to this doctor and he will give you more complete testing to determine if you have any dementia.

Several weeks later I went to this doctor that he referred me to and he just asked me a lot of questions. However, my answers did not lead to a diagnosis. He said we needed to do some more tests. Well one of the tests that he did was the worst experience of my life. He said we were going to do an MRI of your brain. I told him I was claustrophobic and didn't like being put in the MRI tube. He said no problem, we use an open MRI machine. So I went for my MRI only to learn that they used an open machine, but my head had to go into an iron mask that was out of the famous novel: The Man in the Iron Mask. It was sheer terror for the 45 minutes it took for this MRI. Apparently what he was looking for was your brain shrinking away from the skull. Alzheimer's can do that. The next visit with him I had to bring my wife. In my final session, he asked me questions and they had to be verified by my wife. While driving to this session my wife told me: you better be nice to me, I can put you away. The doctor that was doing my dementia study was a psychiatrist and the tests were administered in the county home for the insane. I passed all of these tests and was declared sane for the time being; my wife covered for me.

Thus, there is a simple test to determine if you have dementia as well as a not so simple test and studies. However, dementia is still subtle compared to many other health issues. There is nothing definitive like a blood test that can show reduction in cognition. It can be a problem and everyone should be aware that the brain, like many body organs, can lose some of its vitality and operational characteristics. Having a mate or close care giver can make detection and coping easier.

Sexual proclivity - I read an article in a woman's magazine written by a 20-something nice looking woman in the big city and she made the statement that men have two states of mind: hungry, and horny. I respectfully disagree with this young woman's opinion. I am not hungry for two or three hours each day. As a lifelong male, I cannot make any statements and woman's editorial toward sex, but I believe it instinctively they must feign all sexual advances of men, but subconsciously or consciously invite them. When women walk about in public with these leggings or whatever they call them, that are spray-painted on, they are advertising to men that they want to be coveted. Well, to the women legging wearers in the world, it works well. As a widower, my closest association was sex is shopping at the supermarket were the" good ones" shop. It is better than the "men's lounges" that used to populate most inner cities.

The need to copulate is in the human and animal genome. There are protein sequences in our DNA for self-preservation of a species. In one of my brain courses, the lecturer explained why the praying mantis eats her mate after copulation: it provides nourishment for pregnancy and successful birth of an offspring. All animals have instincts from their DNA that are designed to preserve the species.

Unfortunately, the human species is not doing well in this area. My professor in molecular biology (in the DVD course I recently took), concluded his 24 lectures with a doomsday prediction for the human race. In 2020, the human species is on a path to extinction. There is still as much sex as years passed, but sex is not producing offspring because of increasing homosexual activities, contraception, abortion, and gender dysphoria. Some estimates of the problem

317

predicts that China, the world's most populous country, may be smaller in population than the USA by 2050. I had never thought about the effect of the so-called "family-planning" on the preservation of a species, but apparently besides being a sin, contraception, abortion, obtuse sexual proclivities, and the like are significant causes of our impending extinction.

A growing percentage of people in the United States are migrating to sexual orientations that do not produce offspring. Homosexuality has been recorded to be around for centuries, possibly since biblical times, but it affected may be only 1 or 2% of the population. It did not inhibit population growth. However, 2020 in the USA, people afflicted with obtuse sexual proclivities are promoting their way life in every way possible.

The US government is teaching in public schools that gender is optional. You can be male, female, neither of either, non-binary, or butterfly. They are telling young impressionable minds that it is okay to ignore your genetic instinct for self-preservation and live a life that does not produce offspring. In 2020, some countries are already experiencing negative population growth. More people are dying than are born. As mentioned previously, abortion and other birth control measures are mostly responsible for the reduced birthrate, but obtuse sexual proclivity is certainly contributing to our impending extinction.
Gender dysphoria in 2020, by some estimates, is affecting as many as 20% of some high school classes. Up to 20% of the girls in high schools want to change their gender from female to something else. This of course cannot help our extinction problem. My only granddaughter was lost to gender dysphoria. She took her life at age 19. She was my

only grandchild. My three sons have incredible engineering talents; those talents will not be passed on. They are forever lost. She was my only grandchild.

Sexual proclivity should be "governed" to the mean of the Gaussian distribution of sexual proclivity. That is, most people (median) want sex to be between male and female and that its objective is to produce offspring. Anything else is a nail in the coffin of the human species. People who engage in obtuse sexual proclivities know that they are doing is "species unnatural", but they promote their behaviors as a way of rationalizing. Sex outside of marriage between a female and male is immoral and against the civilized living of our species.

Attitude- Many behaviors and actions can have a positive effect on mental health. Attitude is a significant one. This quotation regarding you and your brain points out that an individual can control both the conscious and non-conscious brain:

If you are distressed by anything external, the pain is not due to the thing itself, but your estimate of it; and this you have the power to revoke at any minute.

Markus Aurelius

Marcus Aurelius said this quite some time ago. Pain and suffering are products of brain activity. In my years of studying philosophy rooted in ancient India, there is great emphasis on controlling one's brain. That is a primary goal of meditation. If done properly, you purge your brain of spurious thoughts. Focus on your mantra eventually makes spurious thoughts disappear. One philosophy text stated that an ordinary person may experience 30,000 thoughts per day. Some of my philosophy classmates called this "monkey brain". Things pop into your mind. Your mind is really your brain. You can somewhat control your brain by your attitude.

About two years ago, I reached the age where all the men in my mother's and my father's families died. So, I decided to go into self-hospice. I am likely to die at any time so I declared that I was putting myself into "self-hospice" and I made a list of features of "self-hospice"; a notable one was: "It does not matter". As it turned out, 2020 was the worst year of most people's lives because of the Covid-19 pandemic. I have accepted masks, social distancing, and aloneness, but my "it does not matter" concept has kept my mental attitude calm. If I die from the pandemic, then so be it. I am in self-hospice anyways and I have done everything on my bucket list. I'm satisfied with my situation. I cannot change the past or dictate the future. I live in the present and I am thankful for every moment of life. Life is a hoot. Being satisfied with one situation is key to robust mental health.

Socialization-Your brain is a product of your genes, and some individuals tend to be introverts; some tend to be extroverts. I am an extrovert, I guess. I have always had one or more best friends and I belonged to groups and organizations my whole life. Having friends and acquaintances gives me mental quiet. I have had many "girlfriends" since my wife died nine years ago. I have averaged about two dumpings (don't call me again) a year from these so-called girlfriends. I rationalize my dumpings by saying to myself: They dumped me because I do not want to get married again. I do not know that is why they dumped me, but this explanation satisfies me. All of them have been a pleasure and a significant part of my life as a widower; they gave me necessary socialization. Most aging-brain experts agree that socialization improves mental health. Introverts and extroverts need to take steps to assure continued socialization.

Family- My parents came from big families; I father was oldest of nine; my mother was the youngest of eight. I had lots of family growing up since most of my parent's siblings lived in my city. I have a brother and sister, and I have always revered both. My brother is a year older, and my sister is three years older. My sister was very smart; she read every book that she encountered. Our grammar school required everyone to read and write book-reports on 50 books in order to graduate. I achieved great popularity with my male classmates by sharing my sister's 50 book reports with others. Yes, plagiarism was alive and well at that time. I used them as well as most of my friends. I suspect that Sister Martenella discovered the plagiarism, but let it go since I was the ringleader of the bad boys, and she was happy to see us go (graduate).

I also copied everything that my older brother did. We played on the same baseball team, went to the same high school and college; we sailed together during high school summer vacations. He moved to another state after college and sometimes I would not see him for several years, but he was always the older brother that I to tried to imitate. When I got married, my wife and her family merge with my family. She was one of six siblings, so we had plenty of family. Many are now gone. The family is super important in mental health in preventing aloneness. And aloneness can hurt. It is why I started dating two weeks after my wife's funeral. We were so together for 50 years, and now she was gone. I sought solace in one of her single woman friends. She did not really dump me; she just moved away for better weather. At least that is my explanation for what appeared to my family to be a dumping. Good mental health requires good family relations and most of us must work to ensure that they always remain good.

Pets- In the USA in 2020, there is a very strong tendency for American to use pets for mental health reasons. Airplanes resemble Noah's Ark because of the overabundance of people who need a comfort animal to survive a plane flight. I will never forget watching a husky young man on an airplane trying to get himself and his120-pound German shepherd dog into the plane restroom. It took him minutes to close the door and no telling what he did with that animal once the door was closed. Every Sunday I encounter a young man at the church I attend, who brings an ugly 120-pound dog that barks during Mass. At least he has a "service dog" sign on him. These people are using the animal's brain for conscious behavior rather than their own.

Some animals will offer unconditional affection as long as you feed them. As mentioned previously in this book, my wife had the belief that owning a pet was slavery revisited. I suspect that pets do not really want to be incarcerated 24/7. Pet ownership is really animal cruelty.

So why do people need about a pet? People have pets to achieve affection on demand. However, it is my belief that the affection and care given to pets may better be given to family. Use of pets for mental health reasons is not a righteous path. They do not want to be your slave. Mediation can calm the brain better than a dog or cat. The environment also will thank you for not having a pet. The media reports that there are about 100 million dogs in the USA. This means at least 100 million pounds of untreated animal feces in our drinking water each day. Many pet owners pick up after their animals, but they dispose of animal waste in the trash which goes to landfills untreated. This is how the animal waste ends up in the world's potable water.

Another mental health aspect of pets is the distress that animals suffer when locked up all day while their masters work. I live in a small enclave of about 80 houses. I suspect that all houses have at least one dog. The dogs cry, whine, and bark for the entire time that their masters leave them alone. They are really distressed as are the neighbors who do not need a dog for mental health reasons; that would be me. Daily incarceration of pets is animal cruelty. Pets all evolved from wild animals, and they are born with genetic instincts to hunt and do animal things. Putting a Halloween costume on a dog and putting it in a baby carriage to be ridiculed by all who see it, is incontrovertibly animal cruelty. Pets may improve a master's or mistress's mental health, but the animal cruelty and environmental damage involved should be pondered. Really, meditation works better and you do not need to walk it.

Appearance

Every day I try to watch a particular evening news, but I have to switch channels when the "ugly women" appear. Their reporting is fine, but their appearance is so distracting that I simply cannot watch. Appearance matters, and people can control their appearance even if they are ugly. One the most famous announcers on TV is a shriveled old man with wrinkles on his wrinkles, but his appearance is not distracting because he looks like the old man that he is. He does not make himself distracting by weird clothing, obesity or a toupee that does not fit.

Maintaining a favorable appearance in public and at home is part of good mental health. People who look like a balloon character from Macy's Thanksgiving-Day parade are telling the world that I do not care enough about myself to keep myself presentable to others. When I was in grammar school, we had a family of about 7 kids who were unwashed, wore disheveled clothes, and smelled. All of them were dirty and smelly. Their house was directly across the street from the school. The house looked like them. Of course, most of my classmates and me did not become friends with members of this family. Incredibly, when my three sons were in grammar school, they had a similar family of smelly kids near their school. Poverty had nothing to do with the family across from my grammar school. We were all poor in my neighborhood. It does not take wealth to wear clean clothes and take baths.

Poor appearance is a mental health issue. It usually means that a person does not have sufficient self-worth or self-esteem. A successful life requires self-esteem. You must believe that you have worth and make your appearance testify to your self-esteem.

Happiness

In 2020, I received an anonymous homemade Christmas card that stated" The basics of happiness are: something to do, something to love, something to hope for". I agree with this wholeheartedly. Idleness can produce the worst punishment for person. A person locked down alone is the ultimate punishment. There is nothing to do, but stare at the walls. Some life situations create nothing to do for some people. In the USA, some nursing homes are such that meals are the only thing that a person can look forward to during their waking hours. They have no work. They have no place to go. They are often alone. Meals together are often the only "something to do" for the elderly people.

Handicap people are often in a similar situation. There is nothing for them to do. As mentioned, a number of times, my father-in-law was a quadriplegic; he sat in his lounge chair alone in the living room all day. My mother-in-law would get him out of bed at 6 AM; she would pick him up with a hydraulic life (he weighed about 200 pounds), wash and feed him, put him in his chair and be off to work at 9AM. He would only have TV to watch until the mailman came to take his bathroom break. He would talk with my father-in-law every day. What a wonderful, wonderful gesture of kindness on his part.

My mother-in-law would come home from work for lunch and feed Dad and his afternoon break was a visit from his physical therapist. The government caused his paralysis, so they paid for a person to come in and exercise him five days a week so that his muscles did not atrophy.

However, I believe that my father-in-law was happy; it was as happy as a person be in his situation. He also had something to do. He had a telephone that he could access with a chin switch; he took care of the house maintenance and family matters over the phone. He also had the second item on the requirements for happiness list: Somebody to love. His wife was a saint. She accepted what she had to do to keep my father-in-law home and there was great love between them as well as with their six children. The kids helped until they married and moved away. Also, he had something to hope for, surely you hope to regain some mobility in his arms and legs. Every two years or so, the government would pay for him to go to New York City to a famous rehabilitation institute. They worked with his muscles and nerve connections every day. When he came home from the hospital he would have some use of his arms, but it disappeared within a month or two. The rehab Institute would take him places like Broadway shows the like, so he liked going even though the exercise regimen was brutal.

My father-in-law's example illustrates how the three basics of happiness can go a long way in making everyone happy. They work in my life. I have too much to do. However, I relish it. I officially retired from industry 19 years ago, but immediately started working full-time at my son's testing company, Monday through Saturday.   I retired on a Friday and started work at my son's on Monday. I have something to do.

I have somebody to love; I had my wife and partner in all matters for 50 years in person, and now in-memory, and my three sons. I have two daughter-in-law's and for 19 years I had a wonderful granddaughter. I am currently older than dirt as they say, but I have high hopes for the future. I have a technical book that was published in 2021 that I am promoting, and I hope to live long enough to at least self-publish this book. What I would add to the three basics on my Christmas card list would be: be satisfied with your situation.

Of course, you can and should try to improve what you can; whatever your job is, give it your best and do not let something obsess you. Also note that we did not include wealth and possessions in our discussion of happiness. Possessions are meaningless if you are not happy. Last week in the newspaper, they reported that a billionaire committed suicide at 55 years old. He had many possessions, but was not happy. Happiness is as a product of your brain and as Marcus Aurelius stated: you have control of it.

Medical intervention

Things will happen to one's health in life that cannot be resolved by meditation and self-cure processes. A medical professional will be required. How should a person deal with health issues that require medical intervention? Until the Internet came available, people would try to obtain a trusted primary care physician and have that person direct him or her in all medical issues. Outcomes usually depended on the choice of the primary care physician. With the Internet and TV ads at every disease known to mankind, people tend to self-diagnose. You can input a medical issue and Google, Alexa or some other on-line function will recommend a solution. The source of the Internet solutions is not to be questioned. The Internet is omniscient.

My professional field, tribology, has expanded into medicine in the form of "biotribology". I had to include a chapter on biotribolgy in my tribomaterials book, so I did some research in this area. The biotribology subject that peaked my interest was materials for joint replacement. A patient seeking a hip replacement can choose various rubbing couples: a stainless steel ball versus a Teflon socket, a cobalt chromium metal ball versus ultra-high molecular weight polyethylene socket, a titanium ball versus ultra-high molecular polyethylene or a ceramic ball against ultra-high molecular polyethylene. I asked a surgeon whose specializes in hip prosthesis how he selects one of these material couples for a particular patient. He told me that most of the patients do an Internet search and decide on the best mating couple by themselves. Often their choice, not my choice, determines what I put in their body.

I tried to use Internet material selection myself for my hernia operation. The Internet showed that I could use a cotton, Dacron, or Kevlar, screen to keep my bulging insides from popping out. I selected Kevlar because I like it is a sail material on my sailboats. When I told my selected surgeon of my screen selection, he said if you want this screen material use another surgeon. I've had all sorts of problems with Kevlar and none with Dacron. If you want me to do the operation you will get Dacron. I said OK since he does 500 of these operations a year. Sometimes Internet answers are not the best way to decide a medical intervention.
About 30 years ago I started to get annual physicals. I became a patient of a primary care physician and fortunately he has kept me alive to date. He believes in specialists; so, whenever an ailment arises that he is not expert on, he sends me to an appropriate specialist. So, in addition to my primary care doctor, I have an endocrinologist for my osteoporosis, a cardiologist for my coronary artery disease, a dermatologist for my skin cancer, an optometrist for my

cataracts, a hernia specialist and a urologist for my prostate and bladder cancers. As a team they kept me alive for more than 20 years since my first cancer death sentence. Thus, I highly recommend this approach to medical event intervention: use of specialists as needed. And all should be board-certified in their field.

Unfortunately, in the USA. The luxury of a bevy of doctors for every need , can only be accomplished with great wealth or great health insurance. I have the latter. When I worked in corporate manufacturing in America all insurance was free. In retirement I kept my doctors using the US government's Medicare system and a supplemental policy, both of which are free. My youngest son is self-employed, and he has essentially no health insurance. He cannot go to a doctor for his debilitating eczema and other ailments because of insurance's $6000 deductible amount. So-called affordable care is the worst penalty anybody could conceive of on working people. The 40+ million Americans who opt not to work for a living get no-deductible health insurance free. Government employees get complete coverage in all sorts of benefits free, but medical intervention is unavailable for many private sector Americans.

Overall, the medical profession in the USA is incredibly talented and dedicated. They charge a lot of money for services, mostly because their liability insurance costs. This problem could be solved by our government, but it will not because many US politicians are members of the trial lawyer's association which is a major source of campaign funds for politicians running for elected office.

Medical research is mostly done by pharmaceutical companies and the only work on things with a high profit potential. New medical research initiated by doctors and hospitals is mostly unfunded. Two years ago, I was invited to a cocktail party and technical sessions at a university medical school. I went out of curiosity. It turned out to be a group of doctors at the university trying to get funding for a good idea that they had regarding cancer surgery. There were working out of a broom closet at the hospital and using their own free time and money to carry out this research project. There was no funding from the University to do the job right. Those doctors did not know that I had no money and I think that I was invited to this session because they mistakenly thought I might've been a source of funding for their research. How sad it is that this situation exists.

Conclusions

1. Good health and adequate healthcare for children depends mostly on parental responsibility.

> Basis: a lifetime of observation showed a correlation of children health with the seriousness in which parents accept the challenge of caring for their offspring.

2. Children in USA are developing mental illness from the introduction of sex and sexual relations at the kindergarten level in public schools.

> Basis: a grammar school mother told me how her children were taught to masturbate in the third grade.

3. Social media is destroying young minds and creating permanent mental health issues. For example, pornography, promiscuity, hate, war, how to commit crime, revolution, bomb–making, how to behead, and disregard for others is offered to every child with a cell phone.

Basis. My granddaughter told me about what was available when she got one at the age of 7. Of course, her having a phone was against my wishes.

4. Most Americans, I think at least 80%, are overweight or obese by the time they reach age 50 or so.

Basis: observation of Americans in any public venue will confirm a too-high level of overweight or obesity.

5. Fast food and regular restaurants in USA tend to make offerings that are too large for a single meal.

Basis: the number two meal at a popular fast-food restaurant produces your calorie limit for the entire day. A significant number of people leave restaurants with the box in hand. Their meal was too large.

6. It is nearly impossible to work off calories.
Basis. Workout data shows how many calories are used up and biking, running, basketball, etc. It takes an awful lot of biking to work off a single donut.

7. Most jobs, even sedentary jobs, have health risks that need to be identified and dealt with.

Basis: my 45 years on the factory floor have shown me many job-related health issues. My loss of hearing in my left ear can be attributed to working inside a sandblasting booth refinishing large chill rolls for making paper. My permanently bad back is due to a crushed vertebrate produced by carrying a broken pump at work that weighed too much to be carried by humans.

8. US government agencies that are supposed to address workplace health issues will not address the single person's concern.

Basis: I tried to do something about dangerous workplace situations only to learn that the government agency only records the number of complaints for a particular type of injury and takes action only when the number of complaints exceeds who knows what level. Maybe a minimum of 12 people has to die before action is taken.

9. Personal exercise in the USA seems to require a gym or a cellphone app.

Basis: health clubs are on the rise. There is one on almost every corner and every city.

10. Regular exercise is needed to maintain any muscle-related body function.

Basis: I broke a thumb and it cost me loss of my right hand for a year. My hand was in a cast for 6 weeks and it took 10 months to get my grip back.

11. Addictions are a significant mental health problem in USA and the availability of addictive substances is the root cause of this problem.

Basis: alcohol is readily available. It is in every USA grocery store and marijuana will soon follow suit. USA government promotes addictive substances like cigarettes, alcohol, marijuana etc. for the tax revenue.

12. Addictions can only be cured by the brain of the addicted. The addicted party needs to want a cure.

Basis: two of my sons and one daughter-in-law are alcoholics and some do not will to end their addiction. The addicted brain is in control of their lives.

13. Cell phone addiction is rampant in USA and has caused the USA's loss of world leadership and technology. Americans cannot direct their whole attention to any task.

Basis: USA can no longer manufacture any complete product. Almost every item that we consume comes from another country. USA does not have the technology to make most of the necessities of life. Average addicted Americans spend up to seven hours per day on their electronic devices doing nonsense.

14. Family is a support structure for mental health issues, and it is diminishing in the USA.

Basis: divorce in the USA is over 50% and families can lose importance in divorce. Also, a large percentage of children come from a single-parent family. Children need a father and a mother.

15. Pets are increasingly being used for mental health purposes.

Basis: In 2020, over 100 million Americans harbored pets. Pets seem to be needed to guide their masters on plane trips, car trips, trips to the grocery store, trips to the lumber company, trips to the mall etc. Many Americans have ceded their human cognition to animals.

16. Personal appearance in the USA in 2020 is reached about as low as is possible.

Basis: People shop in pajamas; people go to church in work clothes; CEO's of large companies address their employees in tee shirts and sneakers.

17. Happiness for the "Selfie" generations has become possessions and the number of friends on social media.

Basis: the Selfie generations cannot seem to focus on anything, but the device in their hand.

18. Fear of death is at an all-time high.

Basis: The Covid-19 pandemic has frightened most everyone in the USA to the point of panic. They do not want to die from it; they fear finitude because many believe that there is nothing after life. There is nothing, but the cell phone and possessions.

A path to better health

Something has significantly changed in the rearing of children in my lifetime. I never heard of attention deficit disorder or special needs children when I was growing up or when my children were growing up. In 2020, one in five children in USA has some kind of learning disability. Why after thousands of years of children learning how to become productive self-reliant adults do so many young people need special intervention to learn things? Is it lead in the drinking water? Is it fluorine compounds in the drinking water? Is there a brain disease out there?

My observation is: inadequate parenting. I travel a lot, and thus I am subjected to a diversity of babies and toddlers and airports, and I find it unbelievable how parents take orders from 2 to 5-year-old children. The children say I want something, and the parents jump to fulfill the child's every wish. Parents ask their children what they want to eat, what they want to wear, if they want to hold your hand or not, everything is done only with the child's permission. They give toddlers mobile phones at age 2. They lessen the natural cycle of life. Children need to be told what to do in all matters as long as they live in their parent's house and eat their food. This is the nature of life. In the animal world, the offspring listen to and obey their elders, or they become the evening meal of their respective predator. To let children and adolescents call the shots in matters of upbringing is to deny parental duty. We are all products of our life experiences; and young people do not have anything to base a wise decision on. Parents are supposed to have the wisdom necessary for that job.

Public schools in USA are failure at every level because they teach students the political policies of the day. They no longer teach what students need to learn to bé productive adults. Public schools under elected politicians will teach only what the party in power wants the students to learn to support their political policies and their continued control of power. Labor unions also control how everything is taught in public schools. In addition, all US schools aggrandize sports over academics.

I was schooled by nuns and priests who taught things that young minds needed to become responsible adults. I went to Catholic grammar school and to a boy's Catholic high school. The nuns in grammar school were completely dedicated to the success of every student. We had no special needs students or attention deficit students. All students succeeded. The priests in my high school were similarly completely dedicated to creating well-educated and successful adults.

All schools should operate like the parochial schools that I knew as a youth. The teaching nuns and priests have all but disappeared, because of the decline of religion in favor of secularism. However, charter schools are trying to emulate parochial schools and concepts. Education of young people will continue to fail, and mental health issues will increase until the USA government goes to a voucher system that will allow Americans to send their children to the schools of choice. Learning disabilities will recede as parents return to the acceptance of responsibility for rearing children.

Healthy eating and exercise are essential to personal health, and education is the way to make proper practices part of life. If schools taught counting calories and personal exercise from kindergarten on, there will be no obesity problems. If young people become aware that one donut will equal a whole lunch, they might not eat so many. Because I started working (newspaper delivery boy) at age seven and played sports from age 10, I never had to exercise. After college I continued sports and they gave me required exercise: golf, sailing, skiing, and biking. I continued to do these in my old age, I also do my Chinese-style daily exercise. This exercise can be easy and eating can be controlled if people are educated in the basics of nutrition and exercise. Weight control doesn't have to hurt.

Work is essential to a happy life. People need something to do. Work is holy. Work is what you make it. I am still working in the field that I started working in 60 years ago. I do applied research in a near virgin technology, tribology, so there is no end to projects. When I finished one project, I published the results and move on to a new project. Not everybody can work in what they want to do as I do. However, if you accept what you do and give it your all, you will gain happiness. I really believe this. I have worked with many people over the years, and it has been my observation that a person can derive happiness from most any job with the right attitude. I stop for coffee each morning on my way to work. I go to the same fast-food drive-through every day. The two women who are tending the window always offer a smile and a cheery greeting; they make my day. They have a job that is not one to bring fame and fortune, but they have the attitude of doing that job well, and they appear to be happy to me. They are always smiling and helping each other as they scurry about to fill orders. This is meaningful work. They're fulfilling a significant need: morning coffee, and they radiate their happiness to customers. How wonderful work can be for one's mental health.

Love of something or somebody is also one of the basic essentials of happiness. Love means that you want good things and happiness for a person. Love of something is similar, but if the thing is an inanimate object like a tree, of course there is no way to know if the tree is currently happy. We have stated previously that possessions do not bring happiness, but possessions can be part of one's happiness. Every person will have certain things that they love. When I downsized from my 14-room house to my 800 square-foot nanobarn, I retained only the furnishings, clothing, and tools that I loved. Marie Kondo, the decluttering expert on TV, teaches to get rid of clutter by assessing every item in your possession. She says: pick it up and ask: do I love this? If the answer is not a firm "yes", then toss it. I tried this; it did not work on consumables like toilet paper and soap, but it did work on: clothing, furnishings, household clutter and many other things. Every piece of furniture in my nanobarn is irreplaceable and comes with a story. My houses now contain only things that I love.

The people that I love are many. I have best friends; I have lunch partners; I have research colleagues, I have technical society colleagues, I have family. I have teachers that I love. I only want good for them. There is a Buddhist saying that suggests people love each other:

May all be help happy, healthy, and free of pain and suffering?

I subscribe to this as well. I dislike all people who are inconsiderate of others, but I do not hate them. Hate is the opposite of love and I reserve that for terrorists and their ilk who practice mindless acts of violence towards others.

Is it is good for one's mental health to love all others with emphasis on a select inner circle, like family and best friends? Love comes from the brain, thoughts formulated by one's brain. Hate and ill-will disturbs one's brain, like stress and anger. One cannot have rational thoughts when angered. Love brings peace to an individual.
Death is part of health. It is part of every person's life; one's attitude about finitude can have a lifelong effect in oneself. If a person believes that there is nothing left of a person after death, he or she may have a lifelong fear of dying. The 2020 pandemic has millions of such people paranoid over catching the covid-19 virus. It may kill them, and they believe that that is the end of everything.

 Some Hindu, Muslim, and Christian religions promote the belief in an afterlife of varying descriptions. Followers of these religions usually have a lesser fear of death if they believe that they are in the right path in their religion. Yesterday I had a surgical procedure that required that I be anesticzed. There is risk of death every time that extraordinary measures, like anesthesia are used. I was very aware that I could die from my surgery, but I simply took efforts to notify my health care proxy, my location, and where important papers were located. I was at peace with my possible finitude. I have strong religious beliefs, and such beliefs and prayer make life's challenges easier.

We will discuss religion, beliefs, spirituality, and other life prerogatives in the last chapter. We conclude this chapter on health with repeating the words of Marcus Aurelius:

If you are distressed by anything external, the pain is not due to the thing itself, but to your estimate of it, and you have the power to revoke at any minute.

All of the mental health issues that potentially affect people are products of one's brain. Meditation, religion, and one's beliefs determine your brain's response to health issues. It is a medical fact that some people who take part in drug evaluations get cured even though they took the placebo. The brain produced the cure. Your brain has the power to alter your body's homeostasis and cure very real health issues. A brain at peace is one of the very best adjuvants to health issues.

Chapter 9
Economics

If it does not make money, don't do it

Harley Ruft

Introduction

Happiness in life is predicated on having enough. Enough
may mean food and shelter. Enough may mean great
wealth. For all of human history, people have been
managing the output of their situation. Economics deals with
the cost and distribution of goods and services. The word
"economics" comes from a Greek word that means
management of a household. When we were hunters and
gatherers, the economy meant trading an animal hide for a
stone tool. When people started to live in cities, their
economy was often based upon the output of the city or
region where they live. The cities traded with one another,
and in 2020 we have a global economy where goods and
services can come from 100 or more different countries.
The supermarket where I shop always has oranges, apples,
strawberries, blueberries etc. when some of these items are
locally unavailable. Strawberries in deep winter in the north
USA means grown in South America. Planes and container
ships distribute products from a country or region worldwide.
Is a global economy worth the cost? We will discuss this
question in this chapter.

The purpose of this chapter is to review the economic happenings in my adult lifetime essentially from 1952 to 2021. The objective of this chapter on economics is to suggest a path forward for leaders on how to have enough. We start with a review of historical economies, then society options, economic theories, economic measures, government regulations, then current economics, fiscal responsibility, and end with" in the best of times", what happened in my economic lifetime.

Civilizations and early economies

The first city state occurred about 8600 BC. Archaeologists believe that it was a city with hundreds to more than 5000 residents in what is now Turkey. Before the likes of cities and states, people lived possibly as families, bands of families, maybe even tribes. However, there was no civilization. Civilization requires some type of structure to control the humans. It is hard for we "advanced humanoids" to comprehend that there may not have been a language for your name to communicate with each other. Mom may have been two grunts; your brother may have been 4 grunts. Hard-core evolutionists claim that we originated as tadpoles from the swamp. It may have taken us a million years to develop to frog status and maybe 100 million years to evolve to chimpanzee status. For all that time, we communicated with each other with grunts. Some chimpanzees excelled at grunting and words evolved, but each group of chimpanzees had their own grunt words. Some indigenous peoples in North America, still can speak ancient languages, but one by one they are disappearing because many had no written language. Sanskrit is reportedly the oldest written language still in use and it dates back to maybe 5000 BC.

I suspect that humanoids could not live-in groups until they had some sort of language. Everything was easier for the creationists. Adam and Eve could speak as-created, and they could even talk to snakes. In any case, humanoids evolved and maybe 10,000 years ago people started to live together; and this 10,000 years is only 1% of the time that humanoids have been existing in humanoid form.

Someplace in history, people started to stay in one place rather than follow game or other food sources. They taught themselves farming and herding. They domesticated some animals like sheep and goats for food and clothing. People started living in bands. Bands were probably less than 30 people; when food production got plentiful, bands became larger" tribes". Both may or may not have had a leader. Bands and tribes made it possible to go after game that may have been too large for a single hunter like a moose. First nation people still band in the Arctic to catch whales and walruses. Living in bands and tribes also provided increased protection from predators and even humanoids who may want to eat the food acquired by others. Commerce in the form of barter originated with living together. If a hunter had a good day hunting, he may trade some game for fruit that a gatherer obtained.

I recently viewed a documentary on some "Bush" people that exist in a jungle in an unidentified location, and they are still 100% hunters and gatherers. Hunting is done in a group of about 10. Since they mostly get their protein from small game, they deplete the immediate area around their encampment and forage ever farther each day. Mostly they rely on plants in the jungle for most of their food and their protein comes from small game hunts. As advanced as we believe that we are, there are human beings today that live a happy life doing hunting and gathering as it existed maybe hundreds of thousands of if not millions of years ago. I just hope that the people made that documentary did not tell the hunters and gatherers about Facebook and Amazon.

According to my American archaeology professor, chiefdoms followed tribes and tribes evolved into states; states were the start of civilization. Civilization requires some kind of structure to make the people who came from the bands, tribes, and chiefdoms want to consolidate further into states. Many times, the state was ruled by a king or priest. Religions were formed to hold the state together. The pharaohs of Egypt are good examples of an early state and some of the pharaohs made themselves gods. Sometimes the rulers of states made themselves like gods by predicting what the weather or stars would do. They taught themselves astronomy and this knowledge was used to impress their citizens. Economies like we have today in principle, started when multiple civilizations sprung up where food and resources allowed their existence. For example, Egyptian cities formed along the Nile River because the river annually flooded allowing crops to grow in the flooded zone. In addition, the river supplied water, fish, and transportation. Each city state used the nearby resources as the basis of their parochial economy, but it was not long before travelers told residents of a city about the iron tools made in city "B" from meteoric iron. Their tools were better than their copper tools. This started intercity and interstate trade. City A traded avocados for iron tools from city B. No doubt, the pharaohs of Egypt did a lot of shopping to get supplies for their chariots, horses, and pyramids.

Humans have always traded and bartered as individuals, but the emergence of civilizations made economics far-reaching. For example, lots of early civilizations had copper available for tools. However, copper does not make a good tool. It is too soft and malleable. However, alchemists and metalsmiths learned that adding the metal tin to molten copper made bronze. This alloying greatly increased copper alloy's strength, hardness, and performance as a tool. Somehow city states in the Middle East acquired tin and from England to make bronze and eventually the whole civilized world had advanced bronze tools available. A global economy started. A similar thing happened with iron. People maybe 10,000 years ago made iron implements that came from meteors. That was the only source of iron. However, humans learned how to smelt iron from plentiful iron ore. Some 4% of the Earth's crust is iron. Use of iron furthered the global economy. By the first century A.D. most existing civilizations had access to metalsmiths that could make iron or bronze tools. Eventually metalsmiths learned how to harden the iron to produce swords and knives and the like that were very durable. Then the trouble started.

Concurrent with the formation of the states was the invention of war. War probably started in the bands over a disagreement on sharing a woolly mammoth and it grew to various degrees around the populated world. Wars were mostly parochial when bows and arrows and spears were the only weapons. However, some states made up of nomadic people learned to use horses for war and they made it their business to conquer pastoral states, the farmers. Pastoral states settled an area and farmed it for food. The marauding nomadic armies conquered pastoral states. They took their food, their possessions, their females and made slaves of the conquered men. Their economy was based upon bartering the conquered booty with other states or they simply continued to conquer pastoral civilizations. The Egyptians fended off marauding armies for centuries. Their cities were located along the Nile River. Desert protected the cities on the sides, but the Nile River provided access to enemies at both ends. Cities at both ends of the kingdom were susceptible to raids. Again, slaves from wars were part of the economy. The pharaohs used captured people as slaves to build the pyramids.

War economies changed with the development of available weaponry. Horses were known to very early humans, but they were like deer to them, and they hunted them for food. However, some crafty humans learned that horses could be bred and trained to carry people and pull sledges. Soon marauding horse people waged wars on pastoral civilizations. Some pastoral cities acquired horses and armies and wars could be spread over larger areas. It is reported that 10 bowsmen on horses could dispatch 500 people fighting from the ground with bows and arrows, but no horses. And they could do this in ½ hour. Wars became more widespread because horses allowed movement of men and supplies over greater distances.

War economies advanced again when the husband of the woman who invented the potter's wheel decided to put two of her used potter's wheels on an axle to make a cart. Pretty soon wars included charioteers. Now they could fire arrows from the platform of a chariot, and this made more hits possible than from horseback. Some civilizations paid marauding armies gold to go away. Some marauders liked the slaves and booty better. Some made the slaves join the marauding army.

Around the first millennia BC, iron weaponry and armor further enhanced the war economy. Many forts were built; then wars were taken to water when people learned how to build ships. Some civilizations hired mercenaries to fight off marauding armies. Some civilizations hired mercenaries to fight their wars. However, civilizations soon learned that if you could not meet the payroll, the mercenaries would just destroy your civilization. They would dispose of the leaders and intelligentsia. It is thought that this may have happened to the once-great Mayan civilization in South America.

The next great advancement in the war economy was the use of gunpowder to propel projectiles. Apparently, the Chinese invented gunpowder, but only used it for fireworks at celebrations. Somebody learned how to use it for cannons. This phase of the war economy involved building of forts and all sorts of protections. Castles and the like sprung up all over, especially in what is now Europe. Then they put cannons on boats and we evolved into naval wars. The Americas did not participate in the armor/sword and gunpowder types of wars until the invaders from Europe with ships, guns, and cannons arrived. Native-American wars were mostly parochial wars with bows and arrows and spears until they acquired their own guns in the 19th century.

Between wars, economies were based upon trade of goods; each civilization came up with their own goods, but most civilizations were supported largely by their agriculture. Ordinary people were farmers and herders for at least 2000 years or so. By 1900, most civilizations lived off of farming and the manufacturing of things needed for farming, making supplies, and transporting people and goods.

We started this discussion by saying that civilizations have existed for only 1% of human existence, yet wars seemed to predominate that 1%. Wars that killed thousands or hundreds of thousands started around 3000 years ago and thy have not stopped. Incredibly, slavery is still part of the economy in parts of the world. In 2020, we still have marauding armies beheading people and destroying civilizations. A significant part of the budget for every civilized society goes for defense in the form of an army or another way to keep from getting conquered. Humans seem to always have war or the potential for war as an economic driver.

Economic theories

The Christian Bible tells us to there was coinage and taxation in the time of Christ. Jesus asked: whose image is on this coin? He also selected a tax collector to be a disciple. It is believed by some that the ancient king Croesus invented money in the form of coins. This was in the first millennium. Taxation in the form of tribute as a share of one's farming product, went to support the leaders of the civilization allegedly for public works.

Money and taxation are key ingredients to having an economy and a civilization. Money is good because barter is messy. A chicken for a shoe repair is unwieldy. Thus, it is a good economic theory to have money as a foundation for an economy. Money has taken some not-so-positive turns in the last few decades, but this will be discussed later.

Taxes go back to the formation of cities and states. Cities needed roads, drainage, and other public works; states needed a military and bureaucracy to run the state. Farmers and workers generally accepted the fact of taxes as long as it was not that burdensome. My burden limit is 10% total (good luck with that). States continually at war, like Israel, may require a high tax rate, like 50%. In any case, taxes are part of every current country's economy.

Communism - Private versus state ownership of everything has always been and is today a key issue of any civilization's economy. Communism is an economic theory that proposes that the state owns everything and gives out money as needed: from each to the level of his or her abilities, unto each as needed. Communal owning of property is not a new concept. The Catholic Church started out that way in the time when Christ's disciples were forming the Catholic Church. Converts sold what they had and gave it to the church treasury. The church gave to the people as needed. This model did not last that long with the general membership, but many monastic orders still live a communal existence. The only monastery near my house bakes bread for sale and this supports the monks. They do not receive a salary, but all of their daily needs are met. Religious participate in a communal living because their goal is spiritual satisfaction and not worldly possessions. However archaeological evidence shows communal living in the early civilizations. Archaeologists discovered many large buildings in a city/state that existed about 5000 BC. They concluded that they were used for communal storage of grain. For centuries, farmers and settlements congregated around walled villages often surrounded with a moat for protection. The wall and moat had to be a community or communal activity. No doubt this was for protection; it also illustrates vividly the role of war in the economy. The earliest settlements were in Mesopotamia, and they contained evidence of trade in the form of fancy pottery found in most villages. This pottery was too fancy for ordinary people; thus, they were evidence of wealth and trading over a fairly large region, about a 500 km radius. These early civilizations dabbled in some form of communism and also capitalism in the form of inter-village/state trade of products by entrepreneurs (fancy pottery).

At the time of this writing, communism existed in China, Cuba, North Korea, North Vietnam, Laos, Belarus, and some smaller countries. In 1993 when I visited Belarus as a guest of their government, they were communist. It is now a communist dictatorship. I was part of an academic mission, and we were guests of the Belarus government. They showed us their best. Their technical capabilities and academics appeared to be above par, but it was quite obvious that most people had nothing. The capital of Minsk is all concrete and ugly. The only good-looking buildings were government and offices. People were moving goods about on city streets with pushcarts and donkey carts. Buildings stood half- completed. The exchange rate was 26,000 rubles per US dollar. Dinner for six at a restaurant cost over 3 million rubles and their largest bill was $10,000. I took a photo of the pile of money that we left for dinner.

Things were much worse in 1983 in a similar academic mission that took me to China. At that time, all people wore Chairman-Mao uniforms and rode bicycles. The only stores that had anything worth buying were closed to Chinese and open only to visitors. In some cities, people lived in small huts heated by a coal fire on the dirt floor. Children could not go to school in the winter because the school building was not heated. Everybody worked in a government factory or doing some government function. You could opt to work for yourself, but the penalty was the loss of all government benefits, like health care.

When I went back to China in 2017, Beijing was more modern than any US city and people could own an automobile and an apartment. However, their capitalism appeared to me to be a facade. People bought and mortgaged apartments in high-rise buildings, but it was apparent that the government really owned everything. All private possessions can be taken at the will of the government. Communism really cannot work outside of religious communities and the like. It is foreign to human nature. Why work hard and excel, when you can get the same wages and benefits is a laggard who does very little.

Free-trade- As previously mentioned, archaeological finds showed free trade between cities in Mesopotamia occurred as early as 5000 BC. The herders who lived nomadic lives got tired of eating their goats and the farmers surrounding the cities got tired of chicken and wanted some goat. They started to trade food. The problem with unfettered trade in all matters is that it can make one civilization dependent on another. It can also deplete a country of its natural resources. Ireland today has few trees. It was heavily forested when first inhabited. The English navy bought/acquired all of the good trees in Ireland to build ships when it was the world's naval powerhouse. As I write this, the Amazon jungle is being destroyed to allow farmers to grow cash crops and the Amazon Forest was the largest supplier of oxygen for breathing. Unfettered free trade is also completely depleted certain species of fish; limits had to be set by countries to prevent extinction by overfishing of certain species. Unfettered free trade sounds nice, but economically it is unwise. History has shown that many resources can be totally depleted with unfettered free trade. Some regulation is required by governments.

Capitalism -The word capitalism means that businesses, and major productions of goods, are owned by private individuals or corporations. Individuals supply the "capital" for the business. The opposite of capitalism is state-operated businesses and factories. Capitalism started before cities and states as evidenced by the archaeological findings that we mentioned (how special pottery was found over a huge area near some ancient cities). Then when writing was in use in various civilizations in around 3000 BC, tablets discovered over wide areas confirm that goods were being sold over a large area as a global economy. States all developed a bureaucracy, but capitalism always existed in ancient times because it is part of genetic makeup of humans. All animals have genetic codes for self-preservation and capitalism is part of the genetic code. All animals, including humans, learn to barter food for protection etc. People learned how to develop businesses. When a person made a product that others wanted, he or she became an entrepreneur. He or she sold or bartered the product. People made and sold things so that their family had enough.

In 2020, capitalism means businesses owned by individuals and corporations, but in the USA, corporations can be one person. Many USA states permit limited liability corporations, LLCs, which means persons can become a limited liability corporation (LLC) to shield his or her personal assets from lawsuits and judgments. I have two LLCs. One is for my book writing business, and one is for my real estate rental business. There are other types of corporations in the USA, with the big leap in ownership of businesses is making a business a publicly-traded corporation. A businessperson will sell shares of his or her business to gain capital for building the business. At least, that is the theory of becoming a publicly traded corporation. An individual cedes part or all of his or her ownership to the people who bought the offered stock. This supreme risk of becoming publicly traded is that a competitor can buy all of your stock and close your company down.

I'll never forget going to a busy steel strip mill which got bought by its competition. The buying company immediately put the entire facility up for sale. I toured the plant to inspect items that they listed for sale. We examined pieces of equipment while employees were still operating them. The mill had a backlog of orders; the equipment and employees were working around the clock to fill these orders as the new mill owner was selling everything. I felt so bad to buy the microscope that a longtime employee was using to measure steel grain size. We even bought the chair that the lab technician was sitting on. His job was over as soon as all of the equipment and site was liquidated. This is the state that the distasteful aspect of capitalism. If you are a publicly-traded company, you are for sale at all times. Public ownership of businesses sounds like a great thing, but since the advent of the stock market and related gambling techniques, viable companies are often bought for dishonest reasons, like destroying your valid competition.

Monopolies - In 2020, the Western world is dominated by monopolies. USA is mostly monopolies in all economic drivers. A monopoly traditionally meant only one source of a product or service. In the USA, each state, city, town, and village established monopolies and essential services such as water, road maintenance and construction, fire protection, streetlights, public parks, etc. Citizens generally accept this kind of monopoly, but they are wrong for the same reason that all monopolies are wrong: innovation and cost control disappear. In my 60 years of association with leadership in my town, I witnessed incompetence in most government functions. For example, the town will pave a road producing results that would never be acceptable to professional road paving companies. The town employees do not have the required skills to pave roads since they only pave roads as fill–in work. Similarly, the town continues to fill the same roadway potholes each year and not fix them properly. They do not have to meet any quality standards because they are a monopoly. Citizens have no way to monitor or control a government function because of their monopoly status.

Business monopolies are supposed to be prevented by governments. In 2020, in the United States and much of the world, monopolies control a significant part of all human activity. Companies like Facebook, Google, Microsoft, Apple, and Amazon now control the lives and work life of most USA citizens. The social media companies control the news for most people; what is fed to users is censored to reflect company policy. Why do governments permit incontrovertible monopolies to take over aspects of life? The simple answer is that in so-called democracies, money plays a huge role in determining who is elected to office and large companies are major sources of political campaign contributions.

One economic theory that emerged about 30 years ago was the rule of three. Buy up all competition, but allow three companies to still supply a particular service or product. The theory of this is that three companies making a product will prevent government monopoly intervention. In the USA, we have seen this theory espoused in many areas. However, two of the most glaring examples are in building supplies and pharmaceuticals. Most cities in the USA have just two suppliers of both commodities. The USA stopped addressing monopolies in 1990 or thereabouts and now we have what I call "duopolies" in every city – just two suppliers of a critical commodity.

The USA federal government of the 21st century treats monopolies kindly because monopolies are part of the way that the country runs at every level. The Constitution of the United States created a monopoly for the federal government to maintain a military function and deal with foreign governments. This one is okay to most US citizens. They also gave themselves the monopoly of waging war with other countries and with issuing currency. Again, most citizens can accept this. There are countless other monopolies in USA federal government, and I have been a victim of most.

A local monopoly that is particularly damaging to America is state and local highway departments. Only governments can design, build, and maintain highways and city streets. They often do not have technical expertise to do these jobs. Heads of highway departments are patronage jobs as are the jobs that many of the people involved in building highways. There are precious few materials engineering people in the whole system with the engineering training to do these functions. Fortunately, many major highway and bridge projects are subcontracted by the government monopolies to private engineering firms that do have technical expertise and personnel to do these jobs. However, in my 60 years association with the town and city and county government where I live, I certainly witnessed many public work projects that were debacles.

Sometimes government monopolies and public works are so egregious that people die because things relating to public safety and health are controlled by patronage department heads. Probably every city in USA gets its water from a municipal corporation or some such name, but again these are government monopolies headed by people who got their job by supporting the elected officials. In 2015 or thereabouts, in the USA, water-monopoly bureaucrats decided to switch the water supply of the city of Flint Michigan from one of the Great Lakes (Lake Huron) to the Flint River which goes through the city of Flint. I lived in Flint for about five years when I was in undergraduate engineering school. My fraternity brothers and I would play golf on a course that followed the river for half a mile or so. It was common knowledge to consider any balls even touched that River to be considered lost. Never try to retrieve the ball from the shallows because it would be so full of toxins it would burn a hole in your golf bag. That river had been an industrial sewer for at least 50 years before I started playing golf there in the 1950's. It was brown to black in appearance, and it mostly resembled used motor oil. And the government water monopoly in that area gave this water to residents to drink to save money. Of course, what should happen in the case of necessary government monopolies, is that governments should subcontract all aspects of projects pertaining to public safety to qualified private engineering companies with necessary technical competence.

I lived through a time when USA's federal government declared some industries monopolies and broke them up. I worked for 38 years for a photographic film manufacturing company. We had at least four significant worldwide competitors, but in 1980 are thereabouts the United States Justice Department went after my company with a vengeance. We had to sell our crown jewel plants by government order and we had to give $1 billion to one of our competitors. This was when a billion dollars was a significant amount of money. The entire photographic film industry was only worth about 4 billion dollars annually at that time. This breakup ended with both 100-year-old companies (mine, and the one that got our billion dollars) eventually going bankrupt out of business. In 2020 in the USA, we have gone the other way to such an extreme and almost no company can grow beyond initial success. The company designs a new product that everybody needs, like an infallible Covid-19 virus test kit that people can do themselves and costs two dollars. As soon as the company goes public to get needed funds for scaling up production, it will be bought by one of the prevailing monopolies; it will be dissolved or only allowed to make product for the monopoly.

In the USA, monopolies and duopolies are "Golden". Monopolies are treasured as long as they generously contribute to the political parties in power. Overall, monopolies stifle innovation, cost jobs, promote inferior practices, fix prices, and in general, negatively affect citizens in the countries where they reign supreme.

Family- The oldest economic theory is: family is the fundamental economic unit in society. Many species of animals have a family unit as their basis. This is a genetic thing having to do with self-preservation. Mama bear protects her clubs; mama feeds and protects her babies; there are family units. Some species have the male stay and help with the raising of the young, but most animals have a family unit comprised of a female and her offspring. Economically she provides sustenance of the offspring. Male birds of prey often participated in raising offspring. Humans have followed suit. As hunters and gatherers, the family unit was usually self-sustaining. Food, shelter, and caring for offspring was a family affair. When humans started to band together, there was trade and barter interface with other families.

When I was growing up, everybody had a family, often an extended family. All economic decisions and practices happened at the family level. The family decided where to live, how to support themselves, what schools the children went to, what social sphere they would live in. I never knew a divorced person until I finished college and started to work in a big factory. There were some divorced people at work; later I learned about what is called a single-parent family. My wife's brother became a single parent, of three girls and a boy, after his divorce. He maintained a family as a fundamental economic unit, but of course it was much more difficult alone. He had to be the breadwinner, confident, cook, the chauffeur and all those other things normally shared by parents.

A family is a microcosm of a civilization. It is a group of people with the structure, laws, traditions, income, liabilities, buildings, and property and with negotiations with other such microcosms of civilization. A proper family will function similar to a successful state. Anything that interferes with the family as the fundamental basis of the economy is harmful to civilization and to the continuance of the human race. Having a family unit matters. Families are an essential part of any country's economy.

Government regulation of the economy

The United States has countless branches of government to control all aspects of the economy. At the federal level, there are regulations that control the money supply, interest rates, lending, financing of the government, etc. These organizations are often run by people who were academicians in former lives. They often taught economics and related subjects. They usually believe that models predict economic results. US citizens have no input into how our Federal Reserve and those kinds of functions operate. However, all citizens are affected by government regulations that interact with the economy. What I have witnessed in my lifetime is the loss of manufacturing in the United States. This has had a profound effect on our status as a nation. Also, as a small business principal, I have been the subject of business suppression by unnecessary and wrongful regulations.

During my lifetime most factories that had a smokestack were shut down by government environmental controls. When I started my career in engineering and manufacturing, there were cast-iron and nonferrous foundries in almost every American city. There were maybe 500 in the country. Many had more than 50 employees. Some had thousands of employees. In 2020, the number of foundries remaining in United States that can make metal castings can probably be counted on one hand. This work and the technology associated with it went to countries that will permit the burning of fuel to power furnaces. Mining of minerals like iron ore to make steel involves the digging of open pits or underground tunnels, chemical processes to separate ore from rock, and smelting ore into metal. The US federal government as well as state and local governments ended this activity because nobody wanted a mine or steel mill near their house. We can buy steel and other metals from other people. America had many companies that developed and made plastics. Most plastics are made from petroleum-based chemicals and US government regulators have been merciless in attacking these industries. Almost all of the plastic companies that United States had were sold and moved to countries that consider the United States to be an enemy. When I was a child, plastics were mostly used for cheap toys and they broke easy. But we had plastic manufacturing in USA with many options for using plastics and engineering applications. They advanced to being called engineering plastics and many had amazing properties. We were the leaders of the world in plastic technology by 1980 or so. In 2020, United States is back to having plastics that break at first use. It is no longer a reliable material for construction. The technology is lost. The USA imports plastics from countries with lesser technology than we had when our plastic companies that were shuttered.

At the small business level, I can speak to the economic effect on my small business. Like many startup companies in the USA, we started operating out of the garage associated with a house. After about 10 years, a commercial building became available that we could afford, so we bought it. Then government regulations stepped in to near bankrupt us. We paid cash for the building, but the town would not let us use the building until it was upgraded to code. This means that if you have a 50-year-old building you have to rebuild it with things that came into existence over the past 50 years etc., even though every aspect of the building was in good shape and usable. The worst part is town's assault on our business was a mandate to install a sprinkler system. There was a monopoly on such systems where our building was located. We had to use this particular company owned by a large corporation in Europe. They were incompetent so it took two years to get the system approved. During the installation and approval, we could not use the building for our business. In addition, once you have a sprinkler system you have to pay another government agency quarterly for having the system. You also must hire a sprinkler inspection company for an annual inspection. In our town, the sprinkler inspection companies are staffed by retired or moonlighting firemen. And we also have to submit to unannounced inspections from town fire marshals at any time.

We had a fire marshal inspection today. We were terribly busy, and we had to stop client work and go around the building with the town employee is he finds things wrong with fire extinguishers and inspection paperwork. This particular government related regulation in my opinion is costing millions of jobs each year and is totally unnecessary and meaningless. There is no data presented by government agencies showing that sprinkler systems save buildings our lives from fire. At the time of our installation, I asked for the data on the benefits of the sprinkler. I was told that the average cost of a fire with the sprinkler in place was $17,000. The cost of fire without a sprinkler system is $18,000. So we had to pay hundreds of thousands of dollars for the sprinkler system that would save maybe $1000 in case of a fire. In reality, if the sprinklers in our building went off, the water damage to our electrical equipment would be worse than any fire. The story gets worse. I did some investigation into sprinkler mandates in the USA, and I learned that the national head of the agency that makes everybody buy sprinklers was a retired member of the House of Representatives. Of course, he knew how to develop laws to mandate their product to be used everywhere. At the local level, fireman retire after 20 years of service. So, they can retire in their 40s and form or work for sprinkler inspection services and also get a government pension. They retire at 70% full play and work full or part time inspecting government mandated sprinkler systems. In addition, I learned that the fire stations in my area did not have to have sprinklers; they were exempt, and one firehouse near where I live burned to the ground while I was interacting with the sprinkler mandate for our building. However, what infuriates me even more than the unbelievable dishonesty of fire protection agencies is that every piece of pipe, every valve, every fitting, in the system was made in China and one of the installation mechanics told me that the system will corrode out and fail in 10 years. Then we get to put in the new have to put in a replacement. I do not know how the fire protection people involved in America's perfect scam (sprinkler systems) can live with themselves. This is government regulation at its worst. This is humankind at its lowest.

Overall, unnecessary and technically wrong codes and regulations in the USA make success of any small business just about impossible. The Arab spring in the near East in the 2000s started over a government bureaucrat taking a vegetable scale from a street vendor. Worldwide, absurd government regulations are an economic problem that may outweigh all other problems that exist in economics. In USA, these codes and regulations exist only to create inspector jobs for friends and family of elected officials. I suspect that the bureaucrat who confiscated the scale in Tunisia that started the Arab spring was a brother-in-law of the reigning chief. Reduction in government regulation should be in the platform of every political candidate wherever there are elections. Every regulation on everything needs to be reviewed and reapproved every five years. Every political candidate for office should have a platform of reduced government.

Computerization of everything

No transaction can be done in a business without use of a computer. And anybody who spends every day of their lives on a computer knows of these devices daily do something other than what you want them to do. For example, I use a flatbed scanner frequently and it pre-scans the document, decides what the document is, and then does the document scan. Sometimes it decides to make the copy 50 percent of the original size. Sometimes it rotates the image 90 degrees; sometimes it only prints half of a document. It has a mind of its own. This is typical of all computer gadgets. These devices operate on a program established by a person who likely has no concept of what you do in your business. The economic losses from computerization of everything have to be equivalent to all the money every government minted for all of time. As I write this, we are in a pandemic and all businesses are shuttered and lots of businesses are trying to have employees work from home. Some things can be done at home on a computer, but ultimately what one does on a computer has to generate sales someplace, somehow. Somebody needs to pay money for touching keys on a keyboard. Companies that perform government studies as a business, for example, have paperwork as a product, but the economy of all countries generally depends on physical goods and services.

 Years ago, when I working as an engineer in the large manufacturing complex, I was working on production problems that involved a team of about 10 other engineers. As a materials engineer, I worked in the lab full of equipment, instruments, chemicals, microscopes, machine tools, and related technicians. I had a computer, but spent most of my time doing lab work. One time on a project, the team that I was on was meeting in a production building and the building's computer system crashed. The other engineers panicked. "We cannot do anything without our computers". The problem that we were working on was product contamination from an unknown source. It was not coming from the computers in the building or the computers on the desks of the engineers. However, these engineers were so accustomed to spending their entire day typing messages and moving data around on the computer they didn't know what to do when the computers stopped working. It is very easy to spend an entire workday on the computer and may contribute absolutely nothing to making the product that supports us in the company and pays our salary.

Another time, at the same manufacturing company, we were in the middle of an economic downturn (recession) and the company established a policy of reduction in force that basically said: If you do not physically touch product in your daily work, your job is on the line. Needless to say, I immediately put more emphasis on solving production problems rather than my fundamental research projects. I survived.

Another example of total reliance on computers that, to me, was quite unbelievable, happened in my neighborhood supermarket. This store was part of a prestigious chain of hundreds of supermarkets. One day, I was there shopping for my cereal and the store's computer system crashed. The manager came on the PA system and told us shoppers to leave our carts where they were and leave the store empty-handed. They had to close the store until they brought in a computer geek to try and restore the computer system. My store had about 200 workers on the site at the time. After the customers were cleared, the employees were sent home with no pay. As I recall the store was closed for two days. The supermarket chain was wealthy, but what about a supermarket computer crash at a mom-and-pop operation?

Of course, the same type of horrific failure of complete economic systems happens on a regular basis when it comes to electricity and some other utilities. I recall a significant amount of time that New York City went without power for computer failure. Just two weeks ago, around 20 million people in Texas were out of electricity for up to a week because the jet-stream dipped lower than usual and brought below freezing temperatures to the state for a few days. Reportedly, the freeze froze the blades on wind turbines that provide 10% of their electricity. They also had problems with the computers switching power from one part of the grid to another. Some people died. They froze to death because of computer glitches.

In a related story, one time I was at a funeral, and I sat next to an attendee from out-of-state. I asked what he did for a living, and he told me that he was a computer security expert for the power grid. This is the grid that covers the United States. He told me that there are three computer network hubs to control the whole grid for United States and that if an enemy or snarky high school student hacked into one of these sites and messed up the computers that replacing one of the hubs would take six months. The entire United States will be without electricity for six months because of a computer hacking. How about that for a scary situation?

A reporter interviewed the person who controls the computers that controlled electrical grids that lost power to millions of Texas during the 2021 cold week and he said that there were within four minutes of a total failure of United States electricity.

Another incredible reliance on computers in recent times is the loss of hundreds of lives by computer-generated crashing of Boeing 737 MAX airplanes. The plane was designed to have an on-board computer fly the plane in preference to the pilots. The pilots lost their lives trying to take over from a faulty computer. This to me is an absurd application of computers.

I could go on forever citing examples of how total reliance on computers for economic transactions or any critical operation can lead to disasters that are beyond comprehension. I use computers daily, but I do so with enough backups to accommodate system failures. Software failure or malfeasance is another factor. The 2020 presidential elections in USA produced election participation results that are incongruent with the participation for the past hundred years. For 100 years, the citizen participation was never above 60%. In 2020 it was at 72%. What caused this huge surge in voter participation? Was the Democratic candidate, Joe Biden, much more popular than fellow Democrat John Kennedy? The votes are all counted and cataloged by computer software. The only person who knows how the computers count the results is the author of the software and there is no way to check what she did. Most people that I know believe that there is no longer reason to vote in any election since there is no way to know if your vote was counted. I suspect that the introduction of computers into current "democratic" elections has ended the concept. There are no checks on computer tallies.

My three sons were in high school when calculators became affordable. I would not allow them to own or use one until they were in college. I completed seven years of engineering school with arithmetic and a slide rule. If humans cede their decision-making to computers, humans become unnecessary. Why live? Computers should be viewed as a tool and used as a tool, like a socket wrench. A socket wrench is absolutely necessary for some jobs, but humans are always in control of it. No batteries or electricity is needed, and they work fine by human action.

The global economy

The term" global economy" is a euphemism for "made in China". Supply-chain is a euphemism for" transportation from China". United States and many, if not most, of the countries in the world have become victims of made in China. I hate to admit it, but I may be may have contributed to this problem. I mentioned in previous chapters that I participated in a scientific mission to China in 1983. The objective of the mission was to upgrade China's expertise in my field of tribology. There were six of us in the mission and I was selected because I authored a seminal textbook on selection of engineering materials in 1979 and it was deemed an internationally important work. We visited maybe 10 universities in each of us gave lectures to students and researchers at these universities.

What I witnessed at the time was a country that was far behind the USA in every aspect. They were hardly any roads, no freeways, no interstates, no cars, only institution vehicles, and no private cars. To get a driver's license you had to work for three years is a traffic control police officer. Everybody rode a bicycle and there would be thousands of identical bikes parked by completely huge gray factory buildings that were state-run businesses. Everything was Spartan; everything was drab. People all wore the same Mao uniform. In one city, Shenyang, people lived in tiny huts heated by coal fires in a dirt pit. This was a city of 6 million people. When they would get a meter of snow, the citywide loudspeaker system ordered all 6 million people out to shovel snow with whatever tools they had, maybe just a bucket.

The equipment in their research Institute was modern and on par with Western countries. And a large percentage of researchers were Western-educated. Our host told us that the budget for his institute was 10 percent for salaries and 90 percent for capital. His Institute had 3000 researchers in the field of metals and related materials. One day, on a field trip, we passed a giant construction site in our bus. It was off-limits to foreigners and the site was surrounded by signage from a Japanese company. I asked our host why they were having Japan build this refinery. I thought that China was not too friendly with Japan. His reply was: they will only build one of these.

That statement summarizes how China has come from an inefficient backward country to the world leader in manufacturing of everything. They copied the best technology in the world. Every nut and bolt in the Japanese-built refinery will be copied and China will build 100 refineries like it of course without paying royalties. After my 1983 trip I sent copies of my materials text to some of our Chinese hosts. About five-year years ago I was attending a conference in Atlanta and as is my practice, I was staying in a low-budget hotel well away from the conference hotel. I needed to use a taxi to get to the conference hotel. I asked the person at the desk to call a taxi and I went outside to wait. A taxi showed up in minutes and I thought it was mine. I want to get in and a group of three Chinese conference delegates came out and said that it was their cab. Then, one in the Chinese group noticed my name on my conference badge. He said we know you. You write books. Come ride with us. I did. However, this incident confirmed one of my fears that the Chinese illegally copied my engineering materials text. I wrote nine additions of that book and likely they copied all of them and never paid the publisher (or me) anything. I believe that they stole my work and used it to teach their engineers. I just suspect this; of course, there is no way to investigate. Who would investigate the matter? Who would I ask in the US government for help? There is no way to enforce intellectual property rights in China. Anything made in China becomes a Chinese product.

When I worked for a large US manufacturer, they decided to start making product in China for sale in China. We built several plants there. The Chinese came to the plant where I worked and they learned every job from the US employees. Then the US employees were laid off and manufacturing was moved to China. And this is the story with every US manufacturer who tried to sell things to China. China will happily copy your product and manufacturing equipment and put you out of business. When my large US-company went bankrupt, Chinese people came to the liquidation and bought most of the remaining equipment. We had the only government-approved industrial incinerator in our state. The Chinese even bought that; they took it apart brick by brick and shipped it to China.

My last visit to China was in 2017. I only went to a conference in Beijing, but in general, Beijing was nothing like the sleepy village of 9 million that I visited in 1983. I landed at the airport about 10 the morning and from the air, the city looked like a giant porcupine. It was bristling with 20-story buildings like needles standing proud. There were not many taller buildings among the needles, but there were so many of these 20-story buildings. It was incredible. Beijing in 2017 had about 20 million residents and two airports. In 1983 only two flights a day came in from outside. We landed in total darkness; no city lights were visible. The runway lights switched on when we were about 100 m in altitude. The runway lights were switched off as soon as we landed. Then lights were switched on in the terminal. We were greeted by two uniformed people with machine guns as we exited the plane. We got our luggage, and our Chinese hosts lead us to a bus for a ride to our hotel. The drive-in was unbelievable. It was against the law at that time to use your headlights at night because they could blind bikers. We were guided to the city by roadside willow trees with their trunks painted white. Our hotel was a friendship hotel, a walled compound of one-story buildings built by the Russians when China was friendly with Russian. There were guards with machine guns at the gate. Our (my wife was with me) room was large and spooky. The ceilings were more than 4 meters high and looked like they had never been painted since built. The city was like what the city of London might have looked like in 1820 minus nice buildings. It was very foreboding.

In summer 2017, the airport was landing international flights every 30 seconds. The departure signs showed flights to cities in every country in the world. The drive into the city was on one of the nicest expressways I have ever seen. My Chinese hotel was the lesser of a group of about 20 hotels near the convention center. It was 22 stories with hundreds of rooms. The convention center was fancier than any I have ever seen. Everything was electronic. All people spoke English, or they carried a phone that translated English to Chinese when necessary. The transformation from a sleepy village to modern miracle was complete.
I believe that this transformation was attributable to the fact that China now makes everything that everybody else in the world needs. Everything that I am able to buy is made in

China. Much of what I can buy to eat is made in China, even my blueberries for my cereal. China bought most of the pork production USA. The pork is not raised in China; China just owns the production and processing capabilities. In 2020, China rules the world economically. Is this bad? I think so, but I still can only buy made in China things. The loss of manufacturing to other countries is the loss of the technology and tools to make things that we need. China can cut our supply of essential goods at any time or increase the price to the point where things that people need are unaffordable. They have a manufacturing monopoly. The United States let the lawyers shut down a century-old gun manufacturer in the US; they came up with a scheme whereby victims of crimes where guns are involved can sue the gun manufacturers. America's litigious society pretty much disallows manufacturing of anything in this country. As mentioned previously USA has one lawyer for every 11 people. China has one lawyer for every 400,000 people. The USA on paper has two political parties. However, the one that controls the country at present (2020) is significantly funded by the trial lawyers of America. Lawyers live very well, suing everybody and every company who makes anything or who provides any service. As an example of America's litigious society, the largest percentage of pandemic deaths in my state, were in its nursing homes. If the pandemic ever subsides, most nursing homes will be sued out of existence. The lawyers have a slam-dunk situation. If the nursing home was closed to visitors, the only way that residents get Covid-19 is from the staff and their suppliers. The nursing home residents have no other contact with the outside world.

One US political party tried to make laws to curtail the legal onslaught to businesses and manufacturers brought on by the pandemic, but the party with the trial-lawyer backing stopped all legislation of this nature. Post pandemic USA will be Lawsuit land. It will be the gold rush of the 1850s for lawyers. The only thing that might save the USA from its pandemic liability is a virus mutation that affects only trial lawyers. Reason on the part of elected officials could prevent "lawsuit land", but that is unlikely.

How does China's economy work? How can they make everything for almost free? The simple answer is: an authoritarian government can order to people to do anything that the government wants. As an example, in my 1983 economic mission to China, I gave a lecture at the University at about 3 PM one afternoon. Our university hosts asked if he could he have copies of my 100 slides. I said yes, but our group was leaving at 6 o'clock in the morning for another city. He said: no problem. He returned my slides at 5:30 AM. 1983 you had to use wet chemistry and optical methods to copy slides. It was very time-consuming. University officials probably ordered 40 students to work through the night to make these copies. Even the CEO of Kodak could not do what the Chinese did that night. Authoritarian governments can get things done. This is one aspect of China's economic edge.

Another incredible advantage that China is over United States is work ethic. It may not be innate, but for thousands of years, Chinese civilization has been characterized by an elite class and a working class. So even in the 21st century, it is natural for all Chinese to work. The elite class is now the members of the communist party (6% of the population) and the highly educated; the workers are the millions making products cheap for the world. A very significant portion of

373

the working age population USA opts not to work. A few years ago, a presidential candidate stated on TV that about 40 percent of the working-age US population chooses not to work. He lost the election

In my 1983 tour of China, every person worked. Married couples delivered their one baby on a bicycle to a government-run and free childcare facility before work and they picked up their child after their government jobs which were often the assigned based on a person's abilities. Everybody worked, but not always in the field that they want. As an example, one of our translators wanted to be an engineer, but his English was so good that he was made an interpreter for special foreign visitors like us. He only saw his family in Mongolia two weeks out of the year.

Education is sacred in China; public education is mandated and those with learning ability are encouraged to higher and higher education.   China has a great brainpower advantage over the US. They have the educated people, the equipment, the financial support, and they perform research not possible in free-market economies.

In summary, the global economy means purchasing most everything from China. They have become the manufacturer for the world's durable goods. All of the countries in the world have to fall in-line and buy from China, because nobody has maintained their own manufacturing capability. The biggest companies in market capitalization, all US corporations, now manufacture nothing completely in USA with few exceptions. How should ordinary people deal with the global economy? The short answer is go with the flow, but be aware of the consequences of the loss of the capability to make things that are critical for a civilization to exist.

I still remember my first time that I was allowed to go to the candy/stuff store around the corner. I was about five years old, and I earned 25 cents doing jobs for neighbors. I wanted to buy something rather than save this money. I went to the candy store around the corner and bought a toy. I do not remember what it was that remember my mother made me take you back and get something else. The toy that I had bought home carried a label: made in Japan. We were still at war with Japan. However, in the 1940s to the 1970s in the USA, almost all cheap toys and commodity items were made in Japan. This was for the same reasons that everything is now made in China.

Mindless capitalization dictates make or do everything as cheap as possible. There will always be a low-cost labor country. However, the Covid-19 pandemic has shown the world the folly of letting others make things that you need. A year into the pandemic there is still not a source of surgical masks other than China. The United States was out of toilet tissue, facial tissue, paper towels, and drinking water in the spring of 2020. This is thanks to the global economy. Worldwide survival from emergencies like pandemics, earthquakes, hurricanes, war, etc., requires that each country have the capability to produce what it needs for survival. Somehow this message must be communicated to country leadership. Trade between the city/states is a basic part of human existence as civilizations. It has been documented to be happening for about 10,000 years. There never was or ever will be any effective limit on who a person buys from or sells to, but reason tells us that society needs to be able to supply its own needs or face extinction. .

The business case for diversity

It eludes me. In 2021, the United States is in a frenzy to get people that the federal government considers deprived or disadvantage into power. This year the deprived and disadvantaged are women in jobs traditionally held by men, like President of the United States, also people with skin hue below six (see Chapter 2 for scale). Twenty years ago, it was below-six skin hue people plus any person with the last name that sounded Spanish. The rationale on the part of the US government is that politicians believe that these categorized people are voting blocs; all women vote for candidates who want women to hold elected office. All people with six or lower skin hue only vote for people with similar skin hue or for politicians who claim minority status or leanings. These things appear to be a common belief of politicians.

In the 1990s, in the USA, the rationale for hiring people of preferred physical appearance was that it was good for business and economy. In 2020, the state of California established mandatory quotas for preferred physical appearance people on every corporate board of companies incorporated in California. They (US elected officials) made diversity, inclusion, and equality initiatives into laws. I first encountered the diversity initiative when I worked at a large international corporation. We had to attend weekly diversity talks. Outside experts lectured us on how having diversity in every group, every department, every function, will greatly increase the company's profits and long-range success. We also had to attend company diversity testimonials on how diversity is improving our operations. I'll never forget at one of these sessions the moderator asked the department diversity person to show that he was accepted by his coworkers. He said I really like working with Mary; I get really tired in the overnight trick; Mary does my job when I need to take a nap.

After about three years and diversity training the company brought in a preferred person to head our division, the companies largest. We were about 20,000 strong at the time. His major project was to move a smaller division with about 10,000 employees into our division. After about two years past the merger date, and 250 million over budget, the diversity person just mysteriously disappeared. The same thing happened when the company acquired a diversity person as CEO. She mysteriously disappeared after about two years. The net result of my employer's 20-year diversity initiative was bankruptcy and the disappearance of the 110-year-old corporation. The same fate came to two of my company's major competitors. Both were hundred-year-old household name companies, and they also went into bankruptcy.

As mentioned in Chapter 2, decisions of any sort based on birth circumstance are absurd. People are products of their brain. What they do, what they know, how they behave, how they interface with others defines an individual, not skin hue. Skin hue, heritage, gender, and proclivities do not determine a person's business talent. People themselves determine their ability in all matters and people are controlled by their brain not by skin hue, heritage, gender, or proclivities.

My 30+ years of experience with diversity in big and small business suggests hiring based upon the skin hue of a person, because of birth circumstance, a person's heritage, a person's gender, or a person's proclivities is the path to" diversicide". I have personally witnessed the well-intentioned, but not thought-out, processes destroy so many businesses, so many corporations so many government institutions. Professional sports are my most significant argument against diversity initiatives. Sports teams must win to keep the franchise alive. Professional athletes' families and their livelihood depend on performance results. There are no diversity initiatives in winning sports teams. Owners and managers select team members on talent alone. One has only to consider the birth circumstance of members of a winning sports team. They can have any heritage, skin hue, appearance, origin of birth, etc. What matters is competitive results. My favorite professional sport, professional golf has competitions between contestants from all over the world. The sport is open to all countries, all ethnicities, and winners come from all over the world; competitors are as diverse as diversity can be. And none of these athletes were allowed to play in the competitions based on their birth circumstance. They had to earn their place by performance in competition. Businesses that succeed pick the best players and do not participate in the shameful business model called diversity.

The dishonesty business model

Our definition of dishonesty is: not telling the truth, cheating, deception, and anything else that tries to take things from other people without paying. Economic dishonesty is all of these things plus concealing things that pertain to a business transaction that could negatively influence a transaction.

Selling a car with a failed main engine bearing is dishonest; selling a house with a hazardous level of radon gas in the basement is dishonest; using another person's credit card number for your purchases is dishonest, taking cash from a bank at gunpoint is dishonest. Many things are dishonest from the viewpoint of ethics, and many are deemed unlawful by civil authorities. This section will discuss right versus wrong actions in business. Most humans who live in the situations where it is necessary to deal or work with other humans believe that it is wrong to take another's possessions, to speak untruths, to barter with intent to cheat, to try to sell items with known defects or deficiencies, to sell something that belongs to others. Most people believe that these things are dishonesty and should be avoided in all economic transactions. So why do we have business models based upon dishonesty?

I started my work life with a rationalized dishonesty. I got a summer job in a small factory for the interval between high school graduation and college. I liked the job and I was good at it, however I was laid off after three weeks because the shop owner decided to give my job to his niece. I needed money for college, so I applied at a large factory for full-time employment. I did not tell them about my college plans. Withholding pertinent information is dishonesty. I got the job, and I did the job well and I rationalized my lie by saying that I improved the job in my three months there. Many business transactions like insurance policies involve withholding information, which is dishonesty.

Dishonesty has been part of economics since humankind started business transactions in the origins of civilization. However, in 2020, dishonesty in business has reached epic levels. My most recent encounter with business dishonesty was a Covid-19 payment of $600 from the United States government. All adults were supposed to get 600 dollars to pay for Covid-19 related financial losses. The United States treasury sent me a debit card with a $570 balance. If I activated it, I would subject be subject to fees in the like from a private bank in some other country, like Nebraska. I took the card to my bank, and they got me some money out of it, but it was a dishonest act on the part of the United States government. They were trying to get me personally to sign up for a credit card with some foreign bank.

Governments at every level in the USA steal from US citizens. They extract fees and tributes without really giving services or any benefits in return. Here are some of the most flagrant examples of government dishonesty USA:

Arbitrary taxes, excise taxes, supplemental fees, etc.: A government entity did a poor job of budgeting and applied taxes and fees to cover shortfalls.

Income tax audits: auditors have a daily quota to "extort" from citizens; deductions are disallowed knowing that the paperwork necessary to fight a disallowed deduction is cost-prohibitive.

Allowing sale of cigarettes, any cigarette: Smoking causes all sorts of documented medical issues, yet the USA permits tobacco sales because they want the tax revenue they produce; the same thing is true for marijuana, and they are expanding this medical issue nationwide.

Elective wars that are impossible to "win": We have been in many during my life, and all have produced the same result: a loss for both countries. The USA is ending its Afghanistan war as I write this. Again, there are unfavorable results for both countries.

In general, many actions of the USA elected officials are based upon dishonesty rather than the public good.

Digital dishonesty is now the greatest problem to worldwide economic stability. In 2020, the model for digital dishonesty is to make everything a subscription, close retail establishments, and make all transactions of any type online. Yesterday I had lunch at a national chain restaurant. Today I received an email asking me how I like my meal at their number 21613 restaurant. Companies that you thought that you could trust, are selling your personal information to whomever has the money to buy it. Advertisements pop up at any time that one tries to use the Internet. These ads are very costly. I tried to advertise one of my books on the Internet and I was told that I would have to give the social media company a monthly budget to which they would charge $0.75 per user click, not a sale, but a browse. This is how social media companies generate large cash revenues. They make nothing, and unbeknownst to you, sell your social media information. In addition, social media companies steal a significant portion of your time on earth. One TV Internet provider claims that the average user spends seven hours per day online or in front of a screen. You have only 24 hours a day; subtract eight hours for sleep two hours for meals and it leaves only seven hours. If you work 8 hours per day and spend an hour per day commuting that produces a negative 2 hours in a day. Maybe the negative time means that some of your 7 hours a day of TV is on work time. You steal from your employer by distracted time on social media. And thus, your cyber contribution to the economy is loss of productivity anyplace where cell phones are permitted. This dishonest business model has produced a distracted populace who is not innovating or contributing to preservation of our civilization.

However, maybe the winner in the field of economic dishonesty in USA is the gift-card industry. Gift cards are available every place in USA were anything is sold. They can be for almost any amount and for any subject. People buy these cards, but the people who make these cards available know an estimated 50% of the people buying these cards will not be redeeming the card and get whatever the company offered as part of the card. When my wife died, I found $600 in unused gift cards in her purse. I took them to a shopping mall gift card redemption office. I got three dollars for $600 worth of cards. In fine print there are expiration dates on these cards and information that shows that a depreciated value over time. Gift cards is a business based upon dishonesty. They know for certain that a significant percentage of the cards will not be redeemed, and they keep the unredeemed funds.

We could go on about how present-day economies in USA are based mostly on dishonesty and deceit, but the more examples I think of, the angrier I get. Dishonesty is rampant in US economics; dishonesty is the basis for some industries, deceit is the basis for almost all US industries that sell anything related to TV, Internet, phone service, pharmaceuticals, vacation homes, vacations, physical fitness programs, and fast-food meals. So what aspect of USA's economy is honest? Not much. There are some farmers markets where real farmers market their fruits and vegetables. And there are some small businesses that honestly produce services and goods without deceit, however they are few and far between. Most governments and large businesses and morphed into dishonest behavior, apparently on the advice from their marketing people or advisors. The only real way to reduce economic dishonesty is for CEOs of corporations and elected leaders to ponder the value and meaning of their limited time on earth. What have you contributed to the common good with your life? Was your dishonesty worth it?

The best of times

One incredible thing that happened to me in the last 10 years or so, is that at least four of my best friends of my generation commented to me: we came through at the best of times. They did this independently. Of course, I have felt this way myself. I know that my parent's generation was not so good because of the Great Depression. I know that my grandfather's generation was not that good simply because they had to immigrate to another country. I know from studying history that the 1800's where not that nice for ordinary people. In fact, ordinary people had it quite hard ever since civilizations existed. My life and that of my contemporaries has been the halcyon years. I went to the very best grammar school; it was taught by loving, but super strict Notre Dame Nuns. My high school similarly provided me with the very best high school education possible; I attended an all-male school and was taught by near genius Basilian priests. My college was the best engineering school in the planet and it was free to me because I was a co-op student. My graduate school happened in another best engineering school on the planet. It was also free; I had a fellowship from a technical society. When I finished grad school all of my classmates (including me) had multiple job offers and were flown around the country at the expense of candidate employers to view their facilities. We had our choice of jobs

My wife was given to me directly by God when I finished college and by that time I settled into a career and was given the best of family: three sons. We lived happily ever after, until she died. My contemporary friends all had similar halcyon lives. I attended two fifty-year class reunions and all my classmates had similar stories of halcyon lives. We all had meaningful careers, we had enough money, we had good kids, and the USA was largely at peace with the exception of the elective wars. Some of us were drafted and some of us died in the elective wars, but most of us just lived happy lives. We traveled, we ate in restaurants; we acquired many possessions.

However, by my observation, and by the observation of many of my contemporaries, our children are not having halcyon lives. My three sons for example, will never retire from a long-term job with the pension and healthcare benefits for life like I have. I worked for one large corporation for six years and another with benefits for 38 years. One of my sons made the observation that the life span of private sector jobs held by his contemporaries is two years. He started his own company about 23 years ago and I have worked for him for about 20 years since then. Thus the generations that follow my generation, those from about 1960 to 1990 had the best of times. In 2020, quality-of-life will be far from the best of times. The United States in 2020 is under siege by the woke people. There is nightly rioting in many USA's large cities; the country is more divided than at the advent of the Civil War and people have no work. Manufacturing and large corporations that make things no longer exist. For example, electricity in the city where I live in USA comes from Spain. As shown in the following conclusions, USA's, economy is about as fragile as it could be; USA citizens lack one of the key ingredients to a happy life: something meaningful to do.

Conclusions

1. The capitalist economy is fundamentally commensurate with the behavior, motivations, and consciousness of human beings.

   Basis: Most humans are comfortable with working for a livelihood and keeping what they work for, not sharing what they work for with others who do not work as hard – communism.

2. A viable economy requires peace, laws, and an orderly   civilization

   Basis: Countries at war have unstable economies, for example: Iraq, Afghanistan, Syria etc.

3. Trading goods between civilizations as part of having a civilization.

   Basis: Trade goods from ancient cities were discovered hundreds of miles away from their source in other settlements.

4. Communism does not work as a basis for a viable economy.

   Basis: In my lifetime, the countries that attempted communism as a basis for the economy, have failed: Cuba, Belarus, USSR, China pending.

5. Capitalism is a reasonable economic basis for an economy, but it needs control at every level to reduce volatility.

   Basis: In the USA, the stock market can crash from a negative "Tweet" from a government leader or rumor of trouble ahead.

6. Stock markets no longer operate as intended: buy stock, watch it appreciate and split, and sell it after years of growth for a significant profit.

   Basis: Stocks no longer follow traditional growth patterns; they can no longer be safely held for long times and make money. Constant tending and trading is necessary.

7. Monopolies are rampant worldwide and especially in the USA.

   Basis: Most of the retail and the USA has closed as Amazon and the like control every and all aspects of buying life's essentials. A similar situation exists with use of the Internet. Google and Facebook with their advertising control most people's Internet activity. Worldwide monopolization of all commodities seems to be in progress, for example, steel, copper, tungsten, silicon wafers, etc.

8. The United States is accepted duopolies as acceptable business practice.

    Basis: Most United States cities have two home centers that are essentially the same; the situation is the same with pharmacies. There is a prevailing theory in business having at least three in the business ensures no government intervention for monopoly. In the United States this theory has been modified so that two (a duopoly) is sufficient.

9. The USA government is doing nothing to curtail monopolization of everything in 2020.

    Basis: There has not been any antitrust action of US government entities since about 1980. They do not consider monopoly harmful to citizens or to the economy.

10. Government utility//water/service monopolies are just as damaging to people as business monopolies.

    Basis: Government water supply monopolies have lost the ability to produce potable water. People in USA are having to buy drinking water from private sources and only use government supplied water for toilets and lawns.

11. The United States overabundance of lawyers is created a litigious society that precludes any manufacturing, use of chemicals in any form, and just about any other activity.

Basis: Million and billion-dollar settlements are common in USA courts. Any private US entity with deep pockets will be sued out of existence. It is just a matter of time. There are no limits in awards, and this limits hope for survival of any company who does any kind of business that could produce liability.

12. The law of supply and demand is a fundamental of economics. It applies to most things.

Basis: Gasoline is a basic commodity in USA. The price varies daily. There are only a few suppliers in USA, and they can monitor daily demand. Price goes down when demand is down. When demand goes up you can raise price and people will still buy it. When I started driving gas was $0.25 a gallon (1950). The most that it was in the USA in my lifetime was $4.50 per gallon (2000 or so). The 2020 pandemic brought the price down to my original $0.25 a gallon; that is around two dollars a gallon in 2020-dollars. Lockdowns made demand decrease.

13. Inflation, continual price increase, can devastate an economy if wages do not increase at the inflation rate.

Basis: My father paid $4000 for the family's first used house in 1945; we rented in prior years. It was about twice my father's annual salary. I paid $21,500 to build a new house to 1964. It was about two times my annual salary. I built a fancy house in 1990 for $250,000; that was 2.5 times my annual salary. Home costs correlated with my current wage thus rendering inflation not that damaging. It was the best of times in the USA.

14. In USA, the stock market is the measure of the health of the economy. When the market is down, all businesses are down, and when the market is on the upswing, the economy as well.

Basis: In all businesses that I worked for in my lifetime, the health of the business correlated with the condition of USA stock market. When I worked for giant corporations, layoffs correlated with stock market trends. The stock market is frivolous. It bounces around on rumors and is controlled by the wealthy and institutions. However, as faulted as it is, it has been the bellwether of the economy for my lifetime.

15. The USA's out-of-control liability awards and the likelihood of getting sued for anything that happens is driven manufacturing from United States.

Basis: Every person in the United States who gets mesothelioma can sue and receive money from the companies who were put out of business by lawsuits. In post pandemic USA, every nursing home will be sued out of existence for allowing Covid-19 to enter a nursing home and kill tenants. People who miss-use weed killers are awarded billions of dollars. One lawyer for every 11 USA citizens, creates an untenable economic situation for innovation, manufacturing, and business in general; there are many more lawyers than doctors and engineers. USA's litigious society is not sustainable. I developed a Covid-19 protective device for plane travel that works great. I used it for at least 20 airplane flights during the 2020 and 2021 pandemic, but I will not pursue manufacturing it because of liability concerns.

16. Countries that manufacture the things that people want and need will have the wealth of the world.

Basis: 1983 China was as poor as a country could be. They taught themselves how to manufacture using Western technology and in 2020 they are the sole source of almost everything for the world and they know now have many wealthy citizens.

17. The diversity that is mandated by the US government in all aspects of life and business eventually leads to business failure and bankruptcy.

Basis: My last large-company employer went bankrupt after more than 100 years in business when it made diversity its focus. Many other companies had a similar fate. Diversity mandates are just another business-strangling regulation.

18. The dishonesty business model prevails in most large US companies. Deceit/dishonesty in advertising and often in the product is standard.

Basis: US citizens must buy multiple items (like lightbulbs) when only one is needed. We are brainwashed by pharmaceutical companies into believing that we have diseases requiring daily expensive drugs. Lawyers advertise in every media outlet daily that they will get us billions of dollars for any injury that is our fault. Politicians claim anything to get elected. Car dealers advertise great deals in the paper and make them none-great with unreadable print on the bottom of the ad. Even tomato juice is made from concentrate and other ingredients that are not tomatoes.

19. The family as the basic unit of society is dwindling along with the economic shelter that family can provide.

Basis: My parents gave me and my family our economic start in life on our own by selling us their auto at low-cost, by renting an apartment to us are well below market rate, by feeding our family every Sunday, etc. Parents and family can help significantly in the young family's economic stability. In 2020 in USA, each year brings fewer traditional families. Divorce rate is over 50% and a significant percentage of families are a single head of household. Families consisting of a mother father and their children are becoming rare.

20. Mobile devices and the Internet are destroying many fundamental elements of any economy, like retail, and fair-day's work, and buying something that you want .

Basis: Buying online has closed many retail establishments in USA. Empty shopping malls are everywhere; people are spending an average of seven hours a day online; Internet surfing precludes having a person and expecting him or her to give an hour's attention to work; phone distraction is out of control. On-line apps may offer something useful, but you cannot buy it. You have to subscribe at a monthly or annual fee. In 2020, young people aged 25 to 40, carry an average of 17 monthly subscriptions. These are automatically billed to one's bank account and people are often paying a subscription for something they no longer use or remember. Subscription app is economic dishonesty of the lowest of the lowest form.

Prescription for a viable economy

Certain aspects of an economy are natural to humankind. We are all born with a self-preservation tendency. It is in our genetic make-up. All animals have this as a primary instinct. When humans started to live in what we now term civilizations, we started to differentiate from each other by occupation. We were all hunter gatherers until we learned how to grow food. We no longer had to follow the food (game). Then it was learned how to grow more food than was needed for a family and we developed skills other than farming that were needed. For example, a farmer stopped farming and bartered pottery for other farmer's produce.

Others learn how to bake, make shoes, make tools, etc. and an economy was created where people make things and barter them so that not everybody has to work in producing food. Businesses developed. Fundamentally this is the basis for any economy. Businesses are formed to produce the various goods and services that humans need when they live together. When money was invented, it replaced barter.

Disputes among civilizations led to wars and it was learned that some kind of government was needed to form a military and provide protection and roads and services for the civilization. Thus, a layer of people who did not make anything or produce food emerged; they provided for the common good. Government was invented. Government sometimes became very strong and often interfered with businesses, with making things, with family matters and with farmers producing food. Governments learned how to tax their citizens who worked making things and producing food. One of the earliest government regulations impeding the economy was wars. If a king decided to start a war, he took able-bodied people from their businesses and farms and made an army.

Wars played havoc with the economy. If they happened during harvest, it would negatively affect food production. Businesses also suffered because without food there was nobody to buy their goods. The laws of supply and demand developed. Food was scarce so prices went up.

The basic elements of an economy are:

1. People living together as the city, state, nation.
2. A portion of people producing food.
3. A portion of people producing needed goods and services.

393

4.   A government to supply defense/security and community services.

Anything else is extraneous. For example, we now have the arts, but as shown in the 2020 pandemic, they can be the first to be eliminated from the economy. However, a successful economy should contain the top three basic elements with the government portion (No.4) kept to a minimum.

In communism and dictatorships, the government function controls all other functions. Kings and queens were dictatorships. A monarchy can be an effective government if the monarch is good and serves the people. Historically, monarchies created an elite class and the remainder had little and provided the wealth, from taxes, for the elite. The economy had to be somewhat parochial since remote territories may not be too willing to pay a tax for leadership thousands of miles away. This feeling about monarchies was manifested in the American Revolution in 1776. In 2020, monarchies are mostly ceremonial and serve the economy by bringing in tourist revenue.

There is an advantage of an authoritarian government over competing forms of government: ability to get things done. The singular head of government can order a whole city built and it will be done. Governments with multiple states and with powers limited by legislation, usually have a difficult time accomplishing anything because of disagreements between the legislators.

In 2020, China is the economic winner of the world. They control the manufacture of critical machine tools that are needed to make all things. Their dictatorship can decree things to happen, and they will happen. Capitalism, the opponent of state-run manufacturing, depends on money; capital, from many sources, like stocks, bonds loans etc. for funding and marketing to get economies to purchase with the company is to sell. What makes capitalism work better than completing economic systems is that individuals rather than the state run companies. Individuals who run companies get wealthy and they have more possessions if the company is successful. State-run companies often have wealthy leaders, but the wealth comes from the state or graft rather than from product sales.

The Chinese have become the economic leader of the world with their hybrid communism. They had nothing when the state ran all businesses in industries. Government-run anything is inefficient because there are no consequences for poor performance. A leader's salary comes from taxes, not from sales of product. A good example of the output of government operated entities is the output of government functions in USA during the 2020 pandemic. All public-school schools were closed in a country full of students. They were uneducated for that year. The public-school teachers got their usual pay and benefits but did not teach. My local government shut down the public library, the recreation centers etc. anything with direct benefits to the people. All government employees got their usual salary and benefits and did no work. Private sector employees who are paid from company revenues were laid off with no pay.
 Capitalism forces work effort and innovation; government-run functions seldom produce anticipated results. Once a government is elected, they do not have an incentive to

succeed. Thus, a successful economy requires a government that allows free enterprise and capitalism.

Another foundation for a successful economy is law and order. Countries without stable government laws cannot create order and peace within and with others. Their economy will be in shambles. In 2020, the country of Afghanistan is in chaos; Iraq had 70% unemployment; Yemen is starving people. Millions of people had to leave Venezuela because of government chaos. All these countries are without peace and a stable government. All of these countries without peace and a stable government have failed economies. People and businesses are not prospering. The pandemic that started in 2020, destroyed many economies because businesses were forced to shut down. A healthy economy needs businesses that are open for customers. Emergencies like earthquakes and other natural disasters likewise destroy economies.

However, in normal times, governments usually control the success of an economy. Excess regulations and unfettered lawsuits by parasitic lawyers make small businesses nearly impossible in some countries; government legislators can fix both of these problems. In the same vein, government-imposed diversity initiatives and the like, make it impossible for small businesses to exist. They destroyed even the largest corporations.

Monopolies can be added to this list of business killers. Monopolies are driven by greed and dishonesty. When a company buys a competitor, the winner dignifies the purchase by calling it a merger, they know that they can fire many support personnel, reduce R&D, and raise prices because competition is reduced. There are United States government functions that were given the responsibility to control formation of monopolies, but they will take no action until ordered to do so by elected officials. Elected officials often receive campaign contributions from the parties involved in the mergers and the corporations and their silences are essentially bought.

In the best of times in the USA, we had anti-monopoly elected officials. There was honesty in government. Realistically stopping the monopolization of everything in USA will take an act of God. Maybe God will send the strain of Covid-19 down on the USA that goes after the monopolists and their government facilitators. Only honesty can beat monopolies. And dishonesty in economics requires personal reflections on one's purpose in life. Possessions are not transportable to the afterlife anymore. It ended with ancient Egyptian pharaohs. I have no realistic solution to USA's monopoly problem, and I recommend avoiding them as best you can in all of your dealings. I have never bought anything I need on the Internet and never plan on doing so.

Unfortunately, I have not been able to never buy anything made in China; everything is made in China. USA's participation in the global economy made it not possible to just buy things made in America. I just checked the origin of the blueberries today that I bought for my breakfast cereal. They came from China. It is really very hard to find anything made locally. Yet everyone knows that overnight, the USA could be at war with China and all of our essential commodities that are made in China will disappear. As I write this, a 1300 -foot cargo ship is aground in the Suez Canal; it is stopping all made- in-China shipments to Europe at a cost of about $9 billion per day. This is day three. Thus, it is not far-fetched that our absolute dependence on a global economy is absurd. In "My best of times, USA" we had at least three manufacturers of everything that we needed for life.

The US stock market is in substance an absurdity from the standpoint of economic stability. During our 2020 pandemic, the US stock market may be up 300 points one day and down 500 the next. Overall, the market was up 18% for the year, but individuals lost lots of money in downturns. Like US monopolies, I do not have a realistic cure for the legal gambling called "stock market" Since 1960 I have witnessed the correlation of good business with a good stock market. In the best of times, it mostly performed as intended. We bought stock in companies that showed promise; you held the stock long term and sold it at a profit. Long-term in the 2020 stock market may be tomorrow. My current practice is to totally avoid stocks, bonds, funds etc. I put excess funds into equity: my business or real estate. However, I still preach use of the performance of the US stock market as a predictor of health of the economy.

The traditional family has been the backbone of successful economies since the start of civilization: family members helping each other to create a healthy and stable society, economy, and civilization. My best of times saw the family is the most important part of life and economy. USA's dilemma is that this traditional family is dwindling. Marriage is diminishing, parenting a family is diminishing, respect for elders is diminishing, and accordingly, respect of government is diminishing. Attack of the family has taken a heavy toll on the sustainability of the United States as a country.

Everyone knows how the family is supposed to work. My family made my success in my life possible. My parents were always there, whatever the problem. My wife and I bought our first new house when I was 23 years old. We lived with our parents (both sides), to save for the house down payment. When my parents had to sell their inner-city house for almost nothing because of neighborhood deterioration, my wife and I bought them a little house in the suburbs and rented to my parents for $100 a month. This is how families smooth over economic transitions. This is how a stable family is the basis for a stable economy.

We conclude our discussion on economy with what I believe to be the most significant threat to mankind: ceding intelligent thought and cognition to electronic devices. As I write this, the world's economy is on the verge of collapse because of a 220,000 ton- ship is stuck sideways in the Suez Canal. There is no mobile device app that can help. There is no computer or modeling that they can help. Two weeks earlier, the state of Texas was within four minutes of electrical good grid failure because the computer system could not locate and buy enough electricity. In fact, electricity and USA is a great risk because everything is controlled by computers that everyone knows are susceptible to hacking by enemies, criminals, and teenage geeks. Now we will have them driving our cars and flying our airplanes. Total reliance on computers for essentials is sheer lunacy. GPS could disappear in an instant.

What is even worse than total control of our world by computers is total control of human brains by handheld electronic devices. People worldwide walkabout with one in an outstretched hand as if it was leading them to wherever they are going. They pay for food with them; they take countless photos of themselves with them. They cannot put them down. Cognition is now only a fraction of daily life.

Of course, we had electronic slavery in my best of times. I got a calculator in the 1960s, and a personal computer in 1983, and a smart phone in 2018. I still have my college calculator and use it daily; I went through many computer evolutions, and I mostly use my home computer is a typewriter; there is no Internet; and I use my work computer for email, Zoom, and researching. I use electronic devices as tools, and socialize in person, by email, by handwritten letter, and occasional phone call. Life is possible without guidance from a handheld device.

My proposed solution to USA's electronic maelstrom is the worldwide manufacture sale of a cell phone infusion device. It is a fuel-cell powered pump that disintegrates mobile devices into nanometer-sized particles with cemented carbide gear-like grinders and converts the mobile device into a slurry that can be infused into the owner. In that form it will lose control over the individual's brain and make the return to cognition possible. Unfortunately, I am in hospice and this invention may not be completely debugged before my finish. What I offer as a suggestion, is to imagine yourself 50 feet in the air. Look down and see how you are living and make adjustments to recapture your life from electronic device bondage. This can happen, and the economy will do well in spite of government attempts to ruin it.

Chapter 10
Self

This is what God asks of you, only this: to act justly, to love tenderly, and to walk humbly with your God
Prophet Micah 6:8

This chapter addresses a person's inner peace, thoughts about others, thoughts about life, and end of life: finitude. Most of this book, followed the pattern: state the current situation, draw conclusions on issues, and then propose solutions. The basis for everything that has been written, is my life experiences. The first chapter chronicled an environmental problem that I fought for 35 years and continue to fight. Most of my observations and conclusions on education, health, government, diversity, and all issues in this book are the subject of argument. However, this is what I saw in my lifetime. This is what I came to believe from my observations. This is my life experience. The suggestions for improvement that we offer up are for readers since I am at end of life and cannot carry on corrective action from the grave.

The purpose of this final chapter is to discuss issues that have to do with what people believe, their faith, the way that they behave, and their philosophy of life. According to some philosophy experts, what differentiates humans from animals is free will. All animals have brains and everything that they do is implemented by brain action. Allegedly animal brains are mostly controlled by instincts that are embedded in their brains from their DNA. All animals have parts of their brain that are beyond their control, like the functions of the autonomous nervous system: breathing, the heart pumping blood to organs, how the organs interface etc. This part of the brain also controls instincts, like self-preservation. If we touch a too-hot surface, our brain immediately tells our muscles to act to withdraw the affected body part from the too-hot surface. The part of the brain that people control is termed the conscience part of the brain and when using this part of the brain a person has to think about pulling a body part away from a too-hot surface. Animals rely on the non-conscience part of the brain more than humans. And this part of the brain is largely controlled by genetic instincts. At least that is what I gleaned from courses on how the brain works.

Humans have choices in matters of life and the objective of this chapter is to have readers ponder acceptance of the life choices that my lifetime experiences suggest lead to a happy life and better life outcomes. We will touch on the meaning of life. Earth is billions of years old. We get to inhabit it for about 80 years or 700,000 hours. We are here for an instant in time. What has resulted from our instant on Earth?

This chapter starts with a discussion of our gifts, what we are given at birth to deal with life. We discuss the personalities that we form, the challenges that we will face, the spirituality that is possible, our beliefs, dying, the afterlife, and finitude in general and the meaning of life in our finite stay on planet earth. What will be our legacy?

Gifts

Incredibly, the secret to life was discovered during my lifetime. In fact, I had a beer where it was discovered. There was a bronze plaque on the building wall next to the door attesting to the discovery event. I was giving a paper at a conference at Cambridge University in the UK. After the talks, I was walking with a colleague back to our hotel when he suggested that we stop for a beer at the pub at the next corner. This is where I saw the plaque on the wall "Birthplace of the secret of life". Two professors from Cambridge struggled for years to explain the arrangement of protein molecules in dioxyrybonucleic acid or DNA, which is the genetic material that makes the cells in the body reproduce in a particular way. Legend has it that the Eureka moment occurred over beer at this pub. A spiral arrangement was the breakthrough that gave the professors the Nobel Prize.

DNA, RNA and other molecular biology alterations are being employed in the 2020 pandemic vaccine. In any case, the molecules that comprise DNA make us what and who we are. They are found in the nucleus of human cells and human bodies are made up of these tiny cells that are less than 100 μm in diameter. Genes are short segments of DNA, and they encode the proteins in our body so that we have physical personalities and skills and other traits of our parents.

My three sons have a nose like mine and my nose is like my father's and my grandfather's. My grandfather was a carpenter and builder as was my father; my brother and I are engineers as are my three sons. We get our building skills from my grandfather. These genetic traits are the "gifts" that are the subject of this section. Everyone is different because their genetic code is slightly different. Identical twins came from the same egg so their physical traits are the same. However, they may have different personality traits, because of upbringing differences or subtle changes in genetic replication.

What happens at the molecular level when a "person" is created is what we have been calling "birth circumstance" in this book. People have no control over their birth circumstance and birth circumstance cannot be used in civilization to determine life status. People should not be categorized at birth by skin coloration, size, eye shape, country of birth etc.; only two categories are valid: male or female. Only females can bear a child and only males can fertilize an egg to create a child. In 2020, people suffering from mental illness may try to change their gender, but after puberty, it is a medical impossibility.

Another absurdity of this millennium is woman competing with men in all matters. The feminist movement that was started by unmarriageable, troubled, women advocated women seeking jobs traditionally held by men. The State of California in 2020 passed a law that all corporations in that state have a minimum number of women on their Board of Directors. This is another example of using birth circumstance rather than credentials as a basis for hiring for a job. Life is a stochastic process and abilities are similarly stochastic, and it is nothing to do with gender. The human brain controls job results and there are women that can do any job and vice versa. The observation that few men are nurses, and few women are stone masons does not mean that either could not excel in those positions; it has to do with proclivity. Men, by instinct, are builders; women by genetic differences are nurturers. That is why certain jobs are preferred by men and women. Promoting a competition of men versus women for jobs, damages both genders. Women are forced by "ego" and the feminists to seek men's jobs and companies are forced to hire women who would rather be doing something else.

When the women-in-men's job movement started, I was working in an R and D lab at a large international company. To comply with the company's diversity initiative, they shuffled my lab director to some other job and elevated one of the PhD chemists in the lab to director. She was an accomplished chemist and a very nice person, but at my meetings with her it was quite clear that she was not comfortable in her role as lab director. I sensed that she hated meeting one-on-one with me and other employees. She fulfilled the company's diversity initiative, but now she hated her job. She retired about two years after her promotion to director. Force-fitting people into jobs for diversity is not just absurd, but it can severely harm all parties involved. Diversity initiatives are the product of shallow thought.

Besides gender, a person's gifts at birth include intellect, physical traits, personality, athleticism, manual skills, proclivities, and others. Unfortunately, sometimes diseases can be passed on from parents to offspring. However, when it comes to the outcome of a person's life, we start out usually with traits that are in our parents. Our upbringing may cause traits, such as personality, to be modified. This is where free will comes into play, for example, a child can opt not do the things that a parent, charged with nurturing the

405

child, asked the child to do, like go to bed at bedtime or eat your cereal.

A child can be lost as a human being if its free will is not "contained" during developmental years. Some parents ask their three-year-old child: what do you want for breakfast? What do you want to wear? Do you want to go to daycare today? This will result in a lost adult. The child will become self-centered, selfish, and incommensurate with society in other ways. Animals instinctively nurture their young to behave certain ways. This is part of the genetic preservation of a species. If lion cubs are allowed to roam away from their mother, they are likely to end up as some predator's breakfast. Similarly, humans need to nurture their young to not do things as toddlers that will impair them for life, like allow selfish and disruptive behavior. Parents must preserve and nurture an offspring's gifts to the age of reason which might be seven years old. After that, they must be taught as individuals to effectively manage their gifts.

Physical characteristics - Heredity determines what you look like, your skin color, facial features, adult size etc. sometimes even mannerisms. Some babies are chubby at birth, but children are not born obese. Obesity takes concentrated effort, but some obese parents produce eventually obese offspring because of their offspring inherit the low willpower to prevent over-eating.

Happiness in life will be easier if a person is content with their situation. My parents were both short, both around 5 feet tall. I realized when I was five years old that my parents were shorter in height and most other parents; I tried to do something about this situation. Since I went to Catholic school I went to daily Mass, and I prayed that I might be normal height and not short like my parents. I did grow taller than others in my family and got to five feet 10 inches which was sort of my goal. Prayer worked.

Openness- People with a high degree of openness will try new things, new approaches, and new places. The low spectrum means people do not want to take a chance on new ventures, new ideas. My wife must have been on the low spectrum of openness. She never tried new foods. In our 52 years together, I never saw her eat a dead bird (chicken, turkey, goose, etc.). I never saw her eat sausage of any type. In fact, the only meat that she would eat is well-done prime rib end cut. Similarly, she never ate anything that lived in water, any kind of sea food. Of course, I never considered that a fault. She cooked all things for me and the boys. However, she never ate most of the things that she cooked for us. Thus, openness may not be wrong on either extreme, but it is still a personality characteristic and a gift.

Emotional stability - This attribute is self-defining. This can be your most precious gift. Having moods is a typical manifestation of emotional instability, and moods can range from changeable, to hostile, even to psychotic. For about 15 years we had a divorced woman as a next-door neighbor. She was a great neighbor, very friendly and pleasant to talk with, however, about one week out of every month she would disappear in her house and not come out for any reason. She would not answer the door. After her down week, she would be her normal friendly self. She eventually moved away, and I never learned what her problem was, but it was certainly a manifestation of emotional instability.

Emotions are the product of the conscience part of our brain, like most brain functions we can control them with effort. We can train our brain. Road rage is a common form of emotional instability that all who drive encounter from time to time. I drive the speed limit on all roads, and this enrages lots of drivers behind me. Driving the speed limit should not illicit emotional instability in other drivers, but it does. I do not get upset when I see a driver behind me flailing his arms and shaking his head, because I am driving the speed limit; I know that I am obeying the law and his wants to disobey the law.

Conscientiousness -This gift means that you try to do the right thing and complete tasks on schedule. Working in a big department in a large factory gave me the opportunity to observe the spectrum of conscientiousness. When I needed some laboratory work done, I would give it to one if the dozen or so technicians that were available to do my lab work. I soon learned the degree of conscientiousness of each. Some would do the assignment perfect and on time, others, not so much. And the degree appeared to be consistent. The best technician was always conscientious, and the worst always did below–expectation work. This suggested to me that this gift may be influenced by heredity. However, free will allows all to be conscientious. It just takes will power.

Morality- The USA's systemic problem as I write this (2020) is immorality. The federal government and governments at every level promote a life counter to reason and sustainability. For example, honesty is part of morality. As discussed in our chapter on economics, America's economic system in 2021 is based upon dishonesty. Big pharma is misrepresenting drugs on TV; gambling and the use of intoxicants is encouraged by government and infanticide is the foundation of one of the two major political parties. These things are immoral because they do harm to others in every and all instances. To knowingly harm others is immoral.

The USA government promotes immorality because they tax drugs, intoxicants, gambling, and other forms of immorality. Abortion and obtuse sexual proclivities are promoted to quell the part of their citizenry that are devoid of reason and concern for others. Morality becomes ingrained when children are raised without religion or philosophical concepts for life standards. Self does not suffice. Living a moral life usually requires outside help.

Health - Some people are born with good health; some people are born with health issues. Myself and my siblings fortunately were born healthy and we had had no health issues until we approached end of life. My sister died 10 years ago. My brother and I are pending. To those of us with spirituality, good health is a gift from God. To secularists, good health is in your genes and how you treat your physical and mental gifts. I recently attended a memorial service for my old boss's wife. She died of a unique form of brain cancer even though she was a health nut and in great physical shape. At the memorial service I was surprised to learn that the form of brain cancer that killed her also killed her son when he was six years old some 40 years earlier. To me this is clear evidence that something was amiss in her DNA, and she passed it on to her son. Eventually it caught her. Some health problems are genetic in origin, but I believe that many are self-induced.

Every time I go to the supermarket to buy food, I see obese people on scooters filling shopping baskets to the hilt to further increase their obesity and health deterioration. Body mass can be controlled by Self and should be. Activity to sustain health can be controlled by Self, and so it should be. Use of medical professionals can be controlled by Self, and so it should be.

Love - Almost all babies are loved at birth by family and all who marvel at new life. Babies learn to love activities, things, people etc., very early. By age three, a person's capacity for love starts to show. One of my sons, adopted a stuffed elephant that he received for a present. He was never seen without "Eldo" in tow. When he was about 7 years old, his brother's teasing finally made him assassinate Eldo. The three boys did in Eldo in with their air rifles. However, my son never lost his love of stuffed elephants.

A low capacity for love can produce an adult that mostly cares for him or herself. We all know people who refrain from getting involved with others and not being close with family. Love is wanting good for others. The opposite is usually not hatred of others, but love of self, selfishness. People who find it difficult to love to do not, as they say, put themselves out for occasions or events. They avoid anything that distracts from their own pleasure. To those of us with spirituality, God will deal appropriately with the lost life of selfish people.

One of the main reasons for my acceptance of my Catholic faith is that its founder, Jesus Christ, preached love of others, as a tenet of the faith. Certainly, this cannot be wrong. Everybody loves being loved. Love of others is a requirement for a society with peace and order. Love is fundamental for life, for happiness, and for the preservation of the human species. Love should never have finitude.

Empathy - The United States is currently (2021) in chaos and declining in all areas of civility in part because of faux empathy. Empathy is understanding or concern for those who have lesser situations. The political party of faux empathy is currently in power, and they want to end poverty by taking the wealth earned by the working-class and giving it to the poor. Giving your possessions to the poor is empathy. Giving the possessions of others to the poor is stealing renamed.

Empathy is a personality trait that is probably acquired by life experiences. When I was in Catholic grammar school, our class would donate money to support an orphan in some faraway country. I used to bring in my $.25 on Mission Friday and it would be coupled with my classmate's offerings and sent away. In high school, the biggest sports event of the year was the Mission Bouts. These were boxing matches among students and the proceeds of the money raised by attendance at the bouts was sent to missions that the priests running the school maintained in South America. Of course, there were quite-close weight categories to keep skinny kids from getting clobbered by bigger kids. I sparred once with the light heavy-weight champ. That is when I decide that this was not my sport of choice.

Some people have a high degree of empathy, like my mother. She sent money from the little that she had, to just about any cause that asked. Some people are not so good at empathy, like me. I stopped donating to most causes in high school. Jesus said" you will always have the poor". I remembered that from religion class and I interpreted it to mean that you cannot eradicate the poor by giving your possessions away. You only diminish your ability to do things in life to help people by ways other than giving them your earnings. Empathy requires caution in administration, lest you become part of the not-thought-out giveaway culture of the USA government.

Summary- Our gifts at birth are a substantial part of Self. Learning to be satisfied with what we were given is key to a happy life. This satisfaction can be considered to be your self-esteem. Self-esteem is an assessment of ourselves. If we do not like what we see, others may also not like what they see. People who do not take good care of themselves physically and mentally have low self-esteem and this can have a negative effect on one's entire life. High self-esteem leads to confidence in whatever you undertake. It is a good thing.

Challenges

A person's personality is based upon a person's gifts and how he or she deals with personality challenges. Every person will have life challenges to deal with. We will address some of these challenges.

Mental health- My only granddaughter died at 19 years old by her own hand because of gender dysphonia. Her public high school, like so many in the USA taught her that she does not have to be a male or female but can ignore gender at birth and take on whatever one felt like at the time. So, she tried being a male and it troubled her mind to the point

412

where she took her own life. I had a cousin who got addicted to drugs in the US military service. He took his life at age 21. I had a nephew who got involved with selling drugs. He blew his head off in the woods at age 19.

Mental health is controlled by Self. What we call mental health is really brain function. One mental health concept that has changed in my lifetime is the disappearance of institutions to separate and treat people with mental illness. The city where I live built a gorgeous 20-story building to house people with mental health problems to help them recover. The government of the country and state shut the building down maybe 20 years ago. It used to have probably 1000 beds. Where did this people with mental illness go? What about the people with issues that pertain to hurting others? I assume that government mental health officials decided that psychotic people will cure themselves. However, I remember vividly a murder of an innocent woman about a year ago by a deranged woman. The murdered woman was on a lunch break from her job. The deranged woman did not know this woman she just walked up and shot her. This is just like some of the mass murders that have plagued the USA in recent years. Mental health officials in the USA are simply not doing anything as far as I can see to protect the public from crazies.

In 2020 in the USA, mental health issues must be handled by Self. Every person needs a mental wellness plan since the government has decided that it does not want to get involved. Meditation and mindfulness training can be tools for maintaining mental health, but spirituality is the tried-and-true technique that has worked for thousands of years.

Many of the homeless people in the USA are homeless because of mental health issues. Institutionalization used to be employed for people who could not live normal lives and now governments at every level allows people with mental health issues to live on the streets and wander aimlessly about city centers begging for food and money. They really need the help that used to be given by institutionalization. There is a general problem in the USA, and it will not go away with the present government strategy: doing nothing. Unfortunately, doing nothing has a negative effect on the entire USA population.

Sickness- In 2020, health care was the largest industry in the United States. A significant part of the industry, patent medicines, as pedaled on TV, are dishonest in intent. I asked my primary care physician if any of these TV medicines were any good. His reply was that none were any good. In the USA, all medicines have to be approved by regulators. However, what they are approved for is usually kept a secret. It may be in the fine print on the bottom of the screen, and this cannot be read without special equipment. For example, one drug that is supposed to let you live longer with metastatic cancer, shows in fine print that the study that produced approval of the drug showed that the drug increased life from an average of 15 months to an average of 17 months or some such insignificant amount of time. And the drug may cost $10,000 per month to use. I recently inquired about a chemotherapy drug for one of my cancers. I was told that I would need six infusions of about one teaspoon of the drug (with a catheter) and that each would cost $22,000. And my health insurance would not pay for it. It was only approved for mild cancer and my cancer is high grade.

My niece has epilepsy and the drugs that she takes to suppress seizures cost about $3000 per month. She cannot work or drive a car because of the seizure risk. Medical costs are the USA can be prohibitive. Nursing homes typically cost over $100,000 per year per patient. My insurance company sends me periodic updates on their coverage cost for the year to date for my treatments. For the first 6 months of 2021 they paid out $66,000. My costs were about $3000.

What is a person to do? The short answer is: avoid getting sick. Daily exercise and healthy habits are your best defense for sickness; the next line of defense is family support (caregivers from family), then friends. Over and above these is prayer and spirituality.

It has been 23 years since my first cancer diagnosis. My response to this fist cancer was medical treatment and daily Mass. I used to pray for suppression of my cancer, but now daily Mass is part of my life and I believe that it is still keeping me alive even that I know have 4 types of cancer active and in treatment. I suspect that this is my last year and that is why I am rushing to get this book done. I hope that my lifetime observations can help others.

Dementia- Loss of one's cognition in the form of mental illness is different from the physical deterioration of the body that we all see with age. Healthy people, young people, can become public problems because of the way that their brain processes data. There can be electrical faults in their hard drive. Dementia occurs when your hard drive deteriorates. Alzheimer's is characterized by shrinking of the brain – less data storage capacity. A best friend of mine recently went into "memory care" which is a nice term to say that he was locked up in an institution because his cognition is not sufficient for him to make his own decisions. He said that he has vascular dementia, which means that the blood supply is not reaching certain parts of the brain for various reasons and when is happens parts of the brain that store data no longer work.

There are many things that scientists have learned about the brain over the centuries. It has been studied by our best brains. However, brain researchers have yet to understand how the brain stores and retrieves data. I can remember an event in the corner candy store 77 years ago. However, I have trouble remembering today's date. Then there are words that I know very well, and they will disappear from my memory. I have to write them down in my Day-Timer. Research continues on how the brain functions, but the reality of it is that function usually diminishes with age. The brain's electrochemical reactions (neuron transmitters) that produce memory and thought decline. Mental activity is said to reduce the decline. My father's sisters lived longer that the boys in his family and none ever suffered from dementia. One of my aunts lived alone and worked daily in her church office as a bookkeeper until age 99. She died at 100. I visited my father's aunt that I had not seen in 70 years, and she remembered me and questioned the source of the curls in my hair. She was 101 at the time. She had all of her mental faculties, but her physical body was frail. This deterioration of the brain is part of life, but the Self can help minimize this deterioration with proper nourishment.

Free will -I have come to believe that that a person must carve consciousness from one's brain. Some philosopher stated this in one of the philosophy journals that I read, and I now believe it to be true; another statement that I recall from one on my DVD courses on the function of the brain: an average person has 30,000 thoughts per day. I also accept this is fact. For example, on driving to work in the morning I bet that I have a hundred thoughts on what I want to accomplish this workday. It is really tough to have a quite mind. Where do these spurious thoughts come from? They come from the non-conscious part of your brain. This is the part of the brain that would take over your brain completely if allowed to. You need to really carve out your part.

This dithering of thoughts suggests that the free will that humans believe that we have may not be that free. For my entire lifetime, I have seen cartoons and magazines and movies showing a miniature angel talking into one ear of a person and a devil talking into the other ear. There are "god" thoughts from the angel, and bad thoughts from the devil. I had a good example today on how the brain completes from within. I sat down to eat dinner and my house started to vibrate and be filled with the noise of a 747 at takeoff. I looked out the window and sure enough it was the person across the street running his 200-horsepower riding mower on his 3 acres of lawn. I repeatedly asked this person (in writing) to not mow at dinner hour, from 4 to 7 each day. He took issue at my request so now each day he cuts his grass only during those hours. He does not work and can cut his grass anytime. I am not home until 4 PM each day and I leave the house at 8 AM.

My brain immediately brought up thoughts of placing a large steel casting covertly in his travel path to wipe out his mower blade. Another thought was to use the rifle in the upstairs workshop to wipe out the mower motor. Fortunately, the part of my brain that I control said to go up to the soundproof room off of the workshop and take a nap until his two hours and 25-minute cutting episode is over. I firmly believe that people's brains offer good and bad option in most matters. This observation pertains to free will. We humans believe that we have free will to do whatever we want, but something in our brain is always questioning our "free will" Do we really have free will? We definitely do not use free will when we touch a too-hot surface. Our non-conscience brain takes over and jerks our hand away before our conscience brain could conjure up a plan of action.

The "is there free will" argument cannot be won. I have read books on this subject written by famous philosophers; they simply offered different arguments and theories. I think that the statement that one must carve cognition from one's brain applies. Our carved-out cognition is our only "free will".

Addiction is incontrovertible evidence that a person's brain can end a person's free will and cognition. It is well documented that there is a medical basis for addiction. Drugs, alcohol, marijuana, and the like chemically alter the electrochemistry of the neural transmitting fluid that controls neuron firings that are necessary to thought and memory and the like. The more alcohol one drinks, the lower the performance of the neural transmitter and the brain calls for more alcohol.

People become addicted to electronic devices because for example, a favorable response to a video posting produces a shot of melatonin, the pleasure chemical, in the brain. That is why people spend countless hours on devices: to get another shot. The same thing happens when phone addicts cross check every statement that you make on their device. One of my acquaintances does this to me. Whatever I say, she fact checks on the Internet. Every time that she corrects an imprecise statement, she gets some melatonin or some such thing in her brain.

Addiction is free will and cognition ceded to one's non-conscience brain. The "bad" component of everybody's brain is likely related to the self-preservation part of our genetic code. It is the same protein molecule that pulls your hand away from hot surface at work. Free will is just a term that people use. There may be no such thing as free will. A limited time of controlled cognition may be the best that a person can hope for.

Dementia, psychoses, gender dysphoria, obtuse sexual proclivities, are probably what the ancient's called possession by the devil; are all manifestations of the non-conscience part of our brain. Neural scientists probably have theories about this, but only God really knows.

Attachment- My philosophy school teaches that "attachment" is a major challenge to a happy life. Indian holy men often possess nothing but the swath of cloth covering their private parts. Buddhist monks beg for food every day. Acquiring possessions is not a path to happiness. As I write this, two of the richest men on the planet lost their long-time partners. They have every possession imaginable, but they do not have the inner peace of a mate.

I have many possessions, and I love them all, but they are not wealth by any standards. Because of medical issues, I

419

believe that I am at end of life, and I am trying to decrease my attachments by giving them to my three sons. I was a lifetime shopper as was my wife. I continually buy new clothes and I like to drive a car that is less than three years old. I live in a custom-built (I made it myself) house and I have a bespoke pied-a-terre in Florida. I feel that I have as much treasure as any person can accommodate and my attachment to my "things" is high. I am not a good example of what I have been taught in my philosophy school. However, my philosophy tutor drives a very expensive car and lives in a very expensive neighborhood. Maybe she leases both and thus is not that attached.

It is easy to get attached to one's stuff, but finitude dictates that we only will be able to use our stuff for an instant in time. Thus, it is not advisable to get attached to one's stuff. People are still pilfering the stuff accumulated by the Egyptian pharaohs.

Ego- Ego, like attachments, is to be suppressed. I suspect that ego is a principal of the non-conscious or bad component of our brain. It may also stem from the heredity gene that is responsible for self-preservation. Egotistical may be the worst thing that a person can be called by another. Ego means "I" in Latin. Nobody likes an egotist; nobody likes self-aggrandizement. The 2020 presidential election in the USA was proof positive of this. Many Americans became "no-Trumpers" to the point where nothing in their lives matter but seeing President Trump disemboweled publicly or worse. Never have I witnessed such hatred from people that I have known for many years. These no-Trumpers believe that President Trump was an egotist and nothing else mattered even if he was doing a great job of running the country. Thus, humans tend to not like egotists and this is an important reason for one to suppress ego.

However, some ego is warranted. Self–esteem and winning in competition require a bit of ego. However, bragging about a win in competition and denigrating opponents may turn off some people. The current trend in American's professional and school football is to beat your chest and stomp on a tackled ball carrier. When a player makes a touchdown, he dances a jig and makes all sorts of gestures to denigrate opposing players. This kind of ego-centered celebration makes watching football on TV or in the stands something to avoid. It is poor sportsmanship on display; it is everything bad and evil in a person's brain on public display for all to see. I opt out. I cannot stand to watch mental breakdown on the part of a ball carrier making a tackle or touchdown. Displays of ego out of control have made many spectator sports not worth spectating.

Some healthy people try to satisfy their ego by donating money to colleges and hospitals. If you give enough, you can get your name on what you bought; that is, until somebody gives more. In my city, some wealthy people gave lots of money to our two major hospitals. They got lobbies and wings named for them. However, somehow those two hospitals are now just big businesses that make a huge profit. Gifts from deceased donors were simply incorporated into the hospital buyout by some large medical conglomerate. The Walker Cancer center is now just building A. Leaving a fortune to institutions or foundations does not guarantee lasting name recognition for your ego.

I recently updated my curriculum vitae. I do this once a year even though I have no plans to send this information to anybody or to seek a job. It is 26 pages long and cites all of my published papers, my presentations, my work history, my books, my awards, and my college degrees. I started my CV as I was moving upward in my technical field. However, after 56 years of doing tribology research I suspect that I may never progress above my current position: technical director at my son's tribotesting company. However, that is OK. My now–departed wife coaxed all of my remaining ego out of me years ago.

Sickness/disability- Sickness or disability can be a huge challenge to a person's opinion of their Self. However, it does not have to be a limiting factor for self-esteem self-worth. I will never forget a customer that I had on my newspaper route. His family was like my other 174 customers. There was a husband and a wife and a bunch of kids in a single-family house in a working-person neighborhood. A car came every morning at 6:30 to pick up the head of household at this particular house. He was blind. I did not know where he worked or what he did for a living; all that I knew was that he was a good father, a good provider, and a fair tipper. When I started working in an auto factory as a cooperative engineering student, I saw where my former newspaper customer worked. He was a tubing bender in the short-run parts department of the tubing mill. They bent short lengths of tubing to carry fluids in fuel pumps, carburetors, transmissions, and brake systems. They made the parts that did not have sufficient quantity to build an automatic bending machine. Bending was done on wooden fixtures with rollers and levers that were hand actuated. About 6 blind men ran the entire department. This department was deep within the plant and fellow employees guided the blind employees to the workplace and to lunch and to breaks. My newspaper customer lived a well-off life with huge self-esteem in spite of being dealt with blindness at birth.

My father-in-law was about as disabled as could be and still be able to live a "normal" life. He was paralyzed from the neck down, a quadriplegic, from a spinal anesthetic at a government hospital during the war. Of course, he was bound to a wheelchair or to his lounge chair in the family living room, but his demeanor was such that he participated in running the family and household of six children. My mother-in-law had to work full time to support the family and the federal government paid for my father-in-law's medical expenses.

He interfaced with neighbors on the street regularly. In nice weather, the kids would take him out on the porch or front lawn, and he would talk with passers-by and the neighbors. Every morning he had coffee with the mailman, and his physical therapist came most afternoons to throw him around on the living room floor, to keep his muscles from atrophying. When I became a member of the family, we went someplace every weekend. The government provided him with a van with a wheelchair lift and we did all sorts of things and went all sorts of places. Eventually my in-laws bought a cottage on a lake and my wife and family went their every weekend. The boys helped with taking care of grandpa. I did the heavy lifting and building maintenance. It was a happy time. My father-in-law was never distraught, never did he complain about what he was given. He accepted his situation and made the best of it. Thus, sickness or disability can make your life difficult, but your attitude and acceptance can make it "normal" for you and your caregivers.

Sin - Sin is a challenge for Self to control. In 2020 in the USA, sins identified by the Christian Bible's 10 commandments are considered to be quaint examples of pre-modernity. Bearing false witness against a teacher from your childhood will bring $300,000 from a child abuse lawsuit. There is no need to prove guilt. Guilt is assumed by the courts. Women who do not like their boss can allege that he made me "feel uncomfortable". He will get fired and sued by the woman, even though there is no evidence that anything ever occurred. Babies are murdered every day of the week under the pretext that they are not people yet, since they are unborn. Dishonesty is standard practice in business, especially in anything having to do with on-line transactions. For example, after I booked a flight for $306 dollars I learned when I went to get boarding passes that I had to pay another $90 for a seat each way. Looting and destruction of city-center businesses and institutions is rampant in all USA cities, as are murders that nobody knows anything about. In my city at least one murder happens each week; these are termed "peaceful protests" in the local print "news". A body is found on the sidewalk, and nobody saw anything or knew the person. Deceit in government operations is standard. They offer all sorts of programs in the media. Anyone trying to use these programs soon finds out that they are a ruse. Sin does not seem to exist in the USA and it sure shows in citizen behavior.

I was brought up to abhor sin; when it happened by accident, we got rid it in to a priest in the confessional on Saturday afternoon. Both (confession and priests) have mostly disappeared in 2020. Americans do not seem to believe that anything is wrong; nothing is a sin that affects one's afterlife situation. Most young Americans do not believe in religion or an afterlife. Life is only about pleasure and instant gratification. Sin was something believed by past generations.

The 10 commandments and their designated sins are the basis for the peace and order laws that are necessary for civilization to exist. As sin disappears, so does civilization. People should ponder the merits of sin. People need to make morality and ethics part of Self. My lifetime observations support this. The happiest people that I have known in my lifetime have been the people of impeccable moral and ethical behavior, the people who recognized good from evil, and the people who believed in sin. Sin is a needed metric for human behavior.

Personality disorders -There are many opportunities for the non-conscience part of one's brain to mess with your behavior. Paranoia can be manifested in the distrust of others. Schizoid people tend to have no need for other people. Some people obsess over certain things like being hyper about germs or being a neat freak. Some personality disorders get to the point where professional mental health intervention may be needed. A personality disorder that, to me, appears to be growing exponentially in the USA is animal dysphoria. Everyone seems to have 1 or more dogs and they use animals as mental health adjuvants. Many people who harbor pets make them human. I went to dinner this evening at a nearby restaurant and the couple at the table next to ours seemed normal. However, when they finished their meal and got up to leave, the woman was pushing a baby carriage and a white dog was sitting in the baby carriage. Airport and airplanes are full of animals. Once nice apartment buildings now accept animals, and the entire facility becomes a urine and feces dog park. A large something dog is at church every Sunday bringing his owner up to Communion.

However, the worst part of this personality disorder is not even the ceding of cognition to an animal; it is animal cruelty. My dead wife always said that keeping an animal is slavery revisited. People are buying a living creature to do their bidding. Kept animals suffer greatly from their incarceration. These animals are kept against their will 24/7. They are incarcerated. The women in the restaurant today did not even let her enslaved animal walk. Animals suffer greatly from their incarceration in owner's homes

All dogs evolved from wild animals that hunted for survival. Ancient peoples domesticated dogs to perform certain jobs. They did not domesticate them to be incarcerated to lick their owner when he or she returns home from work or to be dressed up for Halloween and laughed at by all. Domesticated animals originally had jobs; they had dignity, they had self-worth. They were not enslaved.

Beliefs

The famous American comedian W. C. Field one said: "Everyone need to believe in something. I believe that I will have another beer." Beliefs are thoughts emanating in your brain that alter your actions. People who believe that natural water resources like rivers, lakes, and oceans, must be kept free of contamination are not likely to throw a soda bottle in a river. People who believe in extraterrestrial life, will support space programs. People who believe in communism want government edicts to be the basis for their life. They believe that the state's interests supersede all others.

Our lives are steered by our beliefs, and we acquire these beliefs often with little due diligence. For example, I believe that the current Covid-19 pandemic will rage for three years. I base this belief on what my niece, the medical doctor, told me about the pandemic and because the 1918 pandemic lasted three years and my grandmother died in it. Some people base beliefs on their life experiences. Some of my life-experience-based beliefs are:

- Belief – All people are the same in wanting a peaceful living environment and enough for needs.

  Basis – I traveled all over the world and found people at my level (ordinary) to be just like the neighborhood people that I live with, just with different traditions and sometimes clothing.

- Belief – Every country must strive to be self-sufficient in manufacturing necessities and in building infrastructure.

Basis - In the USA, we no longer manufacture essential materials of construction, drugs, and many food supplies. In 2020, in the stores that I visit, there is no plywood; there are no drywall screws; there is no titanium; there are many essential materials that we do not have a USA source for. We rely on shipping essential across oceans. Any interruption in shipping leaves the country without needed essentials.

- Belief – Any reference to a person's skin coloration is racist and needs to stop.

   Basis – US media and the US government are fanatic about a person's skin coloration. They make your skin coloration a significant factor on legal documents and in all discussion on TV and in print.

- Belief – The 2021 global warming crisis is mostly caused by vehicle emissions and that these emissions can immediately be reduced to half of current value by taxing gasoline and diesel fuel so much that people will be forced to reduce vehicle size. All vehicles must get at least 50 miles per gallon. The gas tax revenue will be mandated to support research in energy production. It will not be blown by the government as is the current case.

   Basis_ Fuel economy of 55 miles per gallons was possible in the 1957 Nash Metropolitan (my girlfriend had one). With fuel injection and computer-controlled ignition etc., we should be getting 60 to 70 miles to a gallon, but we are not because people are buying more massive vehicles each year in the USA.

I have hundreds of beliefs, but these are some typical ones that pertain to issues in this discussion. Beliefs are an integral part of Self.

Spirituality

My cousin wrote a book about spirituality, and I asked her for her definition of spirituality. She replied"authenticity". I did not understand her definition. I thought that authenticity meant "real". But I did not question her further. I use the term to mean having to do with things that cannot be identified as real by our five senses. You cannot smell, touch, taste, see, hear or feel a thought, admiration, love, and many such things. But they exist.

Spirituality is the product of accumulated beliefs, faith, feelings, thoughts, and other such parts of life that are not physical in nature. All humans with reason and cognition have some type of spiritualty. Humans who have never been exposed to group spirituality like an organized religion, develop their own spirituality. Atheism is a form of spirituality. It is a strong, common belief. It gives mental comfort to followers in the same way that organized religion gives mental comfort to those who participate.

Native Americans often have used terms like "great spirit" and "sacred grounds" in referring to tribal customs, lands, and traditions. The spirit of a movement, mean-spirited, and other sayings associated with thoughts or beliefs that are not physical in nature are part of spirituality. Prayer is part of spirituality, as is love, compassion, empathy, reverence, worship, sacrifice, praise, etc.

Religions are organized spirituality. Meditation is self-directed spirituality. Atheism is a special form of spirituality. Atheists have firm beliefs, such as, only things supported by science are real. Nothing else exists. You are born, you live and die, and that is all that there is. Spirituality can be the foundation for life, and it can be a path to a happy life. It can make life issues more bearable.

Spirituality probably has its origin in inherited genes. The archaeology course that I recently completed, showed videos and photos of very early civilizations and most cities/states had a temple or pyramid or some other evidence that the people that lived there had spirituality. They worshiped something or some person. Civilizations started when humans learned to farm. A family could produce enough food so that all people did not have to spend most of their day searching for game or food complaints. Successful farm yields depend on favorable weather; maybe people developed the practice of offering sacrifices for favorable growing weather. Or maybe they invoked guidance to help them overpower their enemies. In any case, by about 2000 BC there are many religions. Civilizations emerged and spirituality usually followed. Thus, spirituality, very likely has its root cause in some protein molecule in a DNA string, it may be genetic. It is natural to human existence. In 2020, maybe 4 billion of the planet's 6 to 8 billion people claim to participate in some religion. Some believe in one God: Christian, Judaism, Islam; some believe in many gods: Hindu; some do not believe in God or God's: Buddhism, secular humanists. The common denominator of most religions is belief in the supernatural things that are not physical substances. You have spirituality when you have beliefs that are beyond this world.

A significant fraction of the humans that have a "religion" were born into their respective religions. The word "religion" is derived from the Latin word "relegate", which means "to bind". Many people are exposed to the beliefs of their parents even before they can speak. I was baptized into the Catholic Church when I was six weeks old. I do not remember any religion activities before first grade. I went to the grammar school associated with my parents' church. It was staffed by Notre Dame Nuns. They taught us about an hour of catechism each day, and we went to Mass every day. We learned the 10 Commandments and all the traditions and church songs. My life was centered on the Holy Family church and school. My friends were my classmates, I played on the school baseball team, I banked at the church credit union, I bowled at the church bowling alley, my family and I attended plays and performances in the church school auditorium. The church-centered life was simple and comfortable.

I attended an all-boys Catholic high school, as did my brother. My sister attended an all-girls Catholic high school it was near the boy's Catholic high school. Grammar school was only two blocks from our house. Our high schools were about 3 miles away. My sister was three years older, so she drove us to school until my brother and I bought cars at 16 years old with our paper route money. High school transitioned me from my grammar school neighborhood nest to the secular world. Challenges mostly centered on spirituality; my girlfriend was non-Catholic. I never discussed my religion with her, but it seemed like the only arguments that we had we about religion differences. We parted company when I went to college out of state. I used my Catholic faith in the form of Mass before exams and silent prayer to make it through vector and tensor analysis and applied differential equations.

In my senior year in college, I met my wife to be at a church sponsored ski trip. We were married in the Catholic Church and that was the start of my happy life. I learned that a compatible mate can be key lifetime happiness. Our combined spirituality was typical of traditional married Catholics; we had three children; we had them baptized and took them to Mass every Sunday. We sent them to Catholic grammar and high school and spirituality was part of our life. We celebrated Easter, Christmas, and various Catholic "holy days".

Our spirituality was typical "Catholic" until at age 59 I was diagnosed with prostate cancer. I had many career goals yet to complete. I did not want to leave the planet just yet. I decided to solve this dilemma by prayer I started going to daily Mass and asked God to let me live a while longer. I had a medical treatment and hoped for the best. It has now been 23 years since my first cancer and I have three more, but I believe that my spirituality was responsible for my extra 20 years of life. It has also given me the attitude that death is the completion of life is not to be feared if you made the most of your birth gifts. Also, it helps if you try to make the planet and its inhabitants better because of your stay.

Prayer

Prayer has been banned by the US government at all public entities. I guess that elected officials thought that they would lose their jobs if the prayers of American citizens were heard by God. Prayer is part spirituality and the beauty of it is: if done in private, it is free of government interference. There is no sales tax or excise tax, no regulations, no paperwork, no approvals, no masks. Where do prayers go? Is there a God? Do people have souls? Where is a person's mind? How can one believe in his or heart?

Philosophers have been arguing over these questions for centuries, probably back to Socrates and Plato. There are no verifiable correct answers to any of these questions, but I offer mine. Is there a God? I believe in one; he created the universe and all that is in it. Where do prayers go? They go to the supernatural person that you direct them to. Prayer can be spoken aloud or spoken in the brain/ mind. Where is a person's mind? The mind is in a person's brain. The human brain is like what we now call "a computer". It can compute, but mostly is used for other things. Our mind is like an operating system in a PC. People, like computers, have different operating systems. It is one method of operation.

Every person has a soul. It is a repository in one's brain for life experiences, thoughts, deeds, memories. It is like a PC's hard drive. It stays with the person forever and it is what is contacted in prayer on the part of the living. I communicate with thought prayer and spoken commands with my dead wife. The commands however do not work well. She communicates to me through my falsetto voice and through miracles. Miracles have been a little sparse these days. I get her verbal commands throughout my day, every day.

Miracles are part of spirituality. They are happenings that defy the sciences and possibly laws of nature. I mentioned this miracle previously, but here it is again: My sister was in the hospital like she had been many times for a variety of medical issues. One Friday I was scheduled to play golf in the afternoon, and I also did not know why, but I decided to visit my sister in the hospital instead. I did not know why she was in the hospital. In any case, when I go to her room, she was surrounded by her family and was nonresponsive and breathing heavily. Her husband got close to her and said:

your brother is here. She died a few minutes later. A miracle made me go to the hospital. I had no idea that she was even that sick. I have had many miracles in my life and this is why I have the spirituality path that I have.

Prayer and meditation allow a person to quell one's brain, to have inner peace. Peace is a person's most important possession. People can have all of the fame, power, and possessions that the world can offer and be unhappy, depressed, anxious, and even suicidal, if she or he does not have inner peace. I suspect that the richest man in the world does not have inner peace. He just lost his life mate to divorce. A famous billionaire entrepreneur recently committed suicide; he was 48 years old.

The philosophy school that I have attended for about 10 years stresses meditation and all sorts of ancient sacred writings/ traditions as the way to quell one's mind. Prayer, meditation, and words of wisdom can bring a brain under control. A fully realized yoga has learned how to do this. Everyone can pray and meditate to work on control of emotions and thoughts.

Summary - Every person can have spirituality, it makes life's issues easier to handle. Nature is a visible form of spirituality; terrorism can be a product of wrongful spirituality. Religion is organized spirituality. Most religions promote practice of good deeds, self-control, and love. Some religions increase their numbers by evangelism and good example. Some ideologies claim spiritual basis and impose their ideologies on others by force. This is not a religion. It is not spirituality.

I accept and practice my Catholic faith as my personal spirituality. I rationalized this choice by saying that the tenets of Christianity, love of God, Self and others, cannot be wrong. There are physical symbols, many specific practices, beliefs, rituals, traditions, etc. in Catholicism, but the basis of all of these is love. The world would be at peace and we would have global order, trust, and freedom if the world accepted Christ message: love one another, love your enemies, love God.

End-of-life

I am there. As I write this, my cancer treatment options are more frightening than anything I've ever experienced. I viewed a YouTube video of one of the operations that I am supposed to get using a robot and it is incredible what must be done to take out a kidney and ureter. They have to cut many veins and arteries and plug them; they have to cut away lots of flesh; they have to move organs around to get at things. All of this is for treatment of just one of the four cancers that I am being treated for. This is why I believe that I am in end-of-life. Incredibly, I am not fearful. If I apply the teachings of my Catholic faith, when I die, I will be judged by life's decisions. If I die in mortal sin, I go to hell forever; if I die with only minor sins, I go to purgatory for a time of cleansing. We have the sacrament of confession, to absolve sins. So, we only need confession, or another sacrament called the" last rites" to wash away sins before death. This sacrament is a blessing performed by a priest before death. One of the miracles in my life, was Father Bush showing up at my house one Sunday afternoon, to give my wife the "Last Rites". She died two hours after receiving this sacrament.

I am reasonably sure that she did not sin in those two hours; I believe that she made it into at least purgatory. I think that religious rituals regard death and dying helps the affected family greatly. This is one of the reasons for my strong belief in my Catholic faith; its teachings and traditions have evolved over some 20 centuries to ease and accommodate life issues. It makes life easier. In the remainder of this section, we will address end-of-life possibilities, responsibilities in dying, afterlife, and the meaning of life.

End-of-life responsibilities- Since my wife died nine years ago, I started the tradition on my part to send a Christmas message, a one-page letter, to all the people in my wife's address book. There are about 80 families. Two years ago, I facetiously announced that I was entering into self- hospice because I had reached the maximum age for all males of my family, my father's side, and my mother's side. Now my prediction has come become reality. It does not appear that I will last six months from this writing. People with limited life expectancy have certain responsibilities to themselves and to their families. An up to date will is a prime responsibility. A lawyer is recommended for this task. My will turned out to be the longest that my lawyer ever wrote; so, he told me. It was long because I included a letter of intent to dispose of my nonmonetary and non-real estate possessions: my stuff. I also read someplace about bequeathing digital assets. So, I wrote a section to cover my book copyrights and book royalties. I also wrote a living will to tell doctors when to stop treatment. This is an important document, and a copy should be in the hands of your primary care physician.
If you have multiple children, you must write your will to produce equal shares to each. Anything else will destroy your family. I observed this in my wife's family. My mother-in-

law did not leave an equal share to each of her five living children, because one daughter was a millionaire and did not need any money. Well, the millionaire daughter and her large family found out about this before my mother-in-law died. My sister-in-law was staying at my mother-in-law's condo when she was in hospital and came across her will. She found out that she was not getting a share of the $300,000 that was her life savings: about $60,000. As the result of being left out of any inheritance, she and her large family boycotted my mother-in-law's funeral. The millionaire daughter's explanation was that she was well aware that she did not need more money, but she wanted to disperse her share of any inheritance to her sisters and brothers herself.

My daughter-in-law gave me a 500-page book written by a tax lawyer. The book was full of examples of family breakups caused by not equal shares to children. When my mother died, my sister was taking care of her finances since my father died. All that she had was $30,000 in the bank account and furniture that nobody wanted. My sister gave my brother and I each $10,000 and she divided the family photos. I also got my mother's mattress, which I still sleep on 15 years later. There were no equity squabbles.

I'm using my last ability to do manual work to get my real estate properties ready to sell. I'm fixing leaks in the commercial building roof; I cut down six trees on my lakefront building lots; I trimmed the trees at the house where I live, and I arranged for a realtor to sell my Florida pied-a-terre. My most valuable personal possessions: my bicycle, my grandfather's mason trowel and my down comforter will likely be of no interest to my three sons. My memories are in the form of hundreds of framed photos on three floors and most walls of our commercial building. They will probably go to a landfill when the building is torn down to build a chain restaurant. As a Catholic, I am required to die with no ill will towards my" brother". I will write letters to my elected government representatives asking them to forgive me for all the ill will that I brought upon them in my writings. I will try in some way to resolve the ill will that I have for the public TV station that regularly takes off the only show that I watch on TV, whenever they do a "begathon". However, I am certain that my redress will fall short of leaving them any money.

One final responsibility that I have assumed is to try and say goodbye to my many best friends. I just visited my brother, my only immediate family left. I will keep emailing my lunch ladies and female confidants. They have made my widowerhood bearable. They have been great. Thank you, ladies.

Dying - Finitude requires a start (birth) and a finish (death). No human has avoided this part of finitude. Everybody sort of fears a suffering death; most would like to go to sleep and not wake up. My parents both died pain-free; they did not have any long in-bed terminal illnesses. None of my immediate family ended up in a nursing home, and none had dementia. My ski partner is currently in a memory care unit affiliated with a hospital and he is cared for and treated nice and seems happy, but his physical condition is deteriorating. Once your mental function declines, so may your physical function decline. He did a 2 mile walk each day before the going in, and after two years in memory care he walks very slow and really needs a walker. Old people homes seem to make people older. This is my life observation.

My wife's death was like a second honeymoon for me in ways. We had such busy lives most days we were only seeing each other at dinner and when it was time for bed. She was asleep when I went to work; we always had dinner together, but after dinner we always went our separate ways. She liked to work in the garden and after dinner I sailed, or I rode my bike. After dark she liked TV laying on her favorite couch, and I went into my office to write or do research. At 10 o'clock, I kissed her good night and went to bed. She followed after I was asleep. We took vacations together, but that was only a few times a year. So, once she got sick, I ended up taking care of her 24/7. It was like being on our original honeymoon. We were together all day every day. She had multiple strokes and was not able to cook or to walk. I never cooked in my life before. Somehow, I managed to cobble together meals for the two of us for the six months that she was incapacitated. We were so close. I took her to work with me. I set her up in one of our conference rooms with the TV and she went to lunch with my son and I in a restaurant in her wheelchair every Wednesday. I took her to all of the doctor appointments, hospitals, and visits even to her hairdresser. We were really together, and I thank God daily for letting me say goodbye for six months. She died at home on her favorite pink couch with me feeding her a gin and tonic with a large eyedropper.

Of course, the funeral was horrible, but I thank God that she did not have to deal with the financial and social issues that would have occurred because of our many business interests. We had a lot of earthly stuff that she would have had to deal with. It is better for me to deal with these issues. The widows that I know seem to have more stress and security issues than I do. It may be that widowhood is more stressful than widowerhood.

Overall, dying is something to anticipate and possibly fear if you did not grow your allotted talents. This is in reference to the Christian Bible story of a king giving talents or money to servants than going away for a long time and calling them back for an accounting of what they did with their talents in his absence. The king did not look kindly on the servant who buried his talents and did not grow them. The other two servants were congratulated for doing what they did. They grew their talents. If you live life in a manner to please the king, you have nothing to fear and death. This is where Self plays a principal role. What you did with your gifts, your beliefs, your physical body, your intellect, your attitude, your friendship, your knowledge, your wisdom, determines your contribution to the species. The person in my life who contributed the most with her life was my aunt Agnes. She worked many ordinary jobs during the USA's manufacturing area, but basically, she was just a housewife with six children and husband with a decent factory job. What made her stand out among all other men and women that I have known in my life was her empathy for others and the dedication of her life to performing acts of kindness to others. Her children called on her for help for everything from dog sitting, to holding a measuring stick at a construction site. She went to Mass daily it was helpful in maintaining the church. In her role as church custodian, she met countless strangers and immediately started doing acts of kindness for them. She baked banana bread for me when my wife died. She was a confidant to my brother's wife, who disliked most people. She was forever driving neighbors who could not drive to doctor's appointments. And she did these acts of kindness right up until she died at age 97.

My technical mentor was a college professor with two PhD's. I was not one of his students, but we met through technical committee work and technical societies. He directed my research and taught me my trade. He did this with countless students and associates. When he died, his students arranged an international symposium in his honor. All speakers parroted how they were guided and helped in their research careers by all that he did for them.

Death is part of life, and there is no need to fear it if your life was meaningful. – At least that is what we Catholics believe.

The afterlife

My original philosophy school tutor was very concerned about what happens after death. He probably read every book ever written on the subject. He did not belong to a religion and was sort of an avowed atheist. Philosophy was his religion, but he was completely objective about an afterlife. Is there one? Is there not one? I never learned the conclusion of all of his study and all his book reading. He developed Alzheimer's and eventually was unable to ponder such matters.

I believe in what the Catholic Church teaches: you have an immortal soul that lives on after the death of your mortal body. Earlier in this book, I talked about thoughts memories, spirit, heart, feelings, soul, work ethic, and other human traits and properties that reside in the brain. So when you die your brain ceases to function all these things stop forever, but your essence, your life in the memory of others' lives on. This is your soul. Your soul is who you were during life.

This is not speculation on my part. I have direct evidence of the afterlife of a person's essence in my wife. When we got married, she made a slip of the tongue as she repeated her wedding vows. Instead of saying: I take this jerk until death do us part, she slipped and said: I'll take this jerk forever. So even though it has been almost 10 years since she went to her afterlife, she still is taking care of me. She gives me minor miracles now and then, but she is with me every day for my daily guidance, and sometimes punishment.

I say "Bonjour" daily in my brain, to about 250 relatives, friends and coworkers who were part of my life. I believe that they hear my daily Bonjour. Without a doubt, afterlife exists in people's beliefs. Dealing with my dead wife is like storing computer data in the cloud. My wife lives on in the cloud and she usually responds to my request for additional data or guidance. The afterlife is real and busy for those who believe.

Finitude

Everything has limits; that is finitude. This book started as a critique on an environmental issue and on America's democracy. We addressed what's wrong and what needs to be fixed. However, when I stumbled upon the extinction of the human species in researching this book, I decide that finitude is probably the most important message of this book. When I was a fresh out of school and working as an engineer in one of the largest manufacturing factories in the world, I befriended a manager in the engineering division where I work. He was very high up, maybe three levels above the boss that hired me. He first introduced himself to me at a random visit to my cubicle and said he likes to meet new engineers. We exchanged pleasantries and he left.

However, he came back to see me in my cubicle every few months and we would chat about how my company career is going, and this continued for several years. Early on, I realized what he was up to. He wanted input on the how I was acclimating to the corporate climate. What were bosses doing right? What were the issues of young engineers? Was I starting to contribute?

I enjoyed our unsolicited discussions and acquired the opinion that this manager knows how to manage. He takes the time to find out how his management is working on the people that he manages. When I gave him my "complaints" he told me something that became the basis of my whole life:

You cannot criticize something unless you have a better idea

This book is full of criticism, mostly of government, but I tried to conclude each chapter with a better idea. Every individual at every level should make this a philosophy of life.

This section on finitude includes finitude of Self, finitude of the USA, and finitude of the human species. Our objective is to have readers ponder the nature of their lives, our civilization, and our human species. We can do some things to try to minimize our situation, but we are in real crisis in all three areas: Self, in perpetuation of the United States, and extinction of the human race. The latter could be addressed with some solutions like doubling the country's fertility rate but that requires extra effort on the part of fertile women: more babies. As individuals, we can do some things about finitude of Self and finitude of the United States

Finitude of Self –There is a Broadway play in USA about the cycle of life of a lion. Many animals have a definite lifecycle and often they are relatively short. A typical human life contains distinct stages:

1. Birth
2. Development of cognition, communication, and physical abilities
3. Learning how to survive, school, skill training, athletics etc.
4. Develop skills and strengths to deal with the competition
5. Nutrue strengths and aguie possessions-your work life
6. Decline: reduce fighting the competition; defer to those younger
7. Death

This is the finitude of human life, of Self. We can make these phases of life unequal. For example, we can extend the schooling or the work life phase, but in the end, statistics on the human race states that there is a life limit of 78 years for men and 83 years for women in the United States. How does Self interface with the cycle of life? What can an individual do to address finitude of the USA and finitude of the human species?

Self in the form of personality, work ethic, attitude, and other characteristics of an individual, determines the outcome of all phases of the cycle of life. A disruptive baby will not learn as easy as a happy curious baby. Attitude is important for success in formal education; personality or mental health

444

challenges affect an individual's competitiveness in the job market. Personal characteristics, which are controlled by Self often are critical and determine success in life and career. An individual's work life success and financial success depends on self-esteem, self-confidence, compassion, cooperation, cognition, all relate to how one does it work life. Humans accumulate wealth or possessions during the work life phase of life, and Self determines how one interfaces with wealth and possessions. Self is important in life's declining phase. Lots of friends and socializing can make the transition from work life to retirement easy and retired life can be the most wonderful life phase of the life cycle. It can also be lonely not so wonderful phase of life.

The evils in life: dishonesty, murder, rape, gluttony, deceit, false witness, anger, hate, adultery, arrogance, licentiousness, envy, assault, lust, fraud, etc. are the product of Self. They are often produced by the non-conscious part of our brains, that part that is associated with self-preservation.

Self also produces all goodness in humans: honesty, empathy, work ethic, attention, love, compassion, goodwill, caring, nurturing, knowledge, wisdom, etc., the human characteristics that are products of our consciousness, the cognitive brain the part of the brain that we control.

The last phase of life, death, interfaces with Self in many ways. If you had significant spirituality throughout your life, death need not be fearsome. My mother was very spiritual; she went to the funerals for all relatives, all friends, all work colleagues, all neighbors, just about everybody that she knew and even relatives of people she knew. To her, a funeral was a final visit with the one that died; it was a final statement of friendship. To her, death was like another completed phase of spiritual life, like Baptism, First Holy Communion, Confirmation, and Marriage. It was a definite phase in the cycle of life. Self in the form of attitude, prepares an individual for dealing with the last phase in life. Thus, the cycle of life is the finitude of Self, human life. It is the beginning and the end of human life; Self controls the quality and contribution of our finitude

Finitude of the United States - Finitude of the United States is a function of our fragile, fractionated, democracy. The ancient Greeks who invented democracy recognized right away that it was a flawed concept; how do you get a civilization to all agree on anything? As mentioned earlier, the USA is really a republic not a democracy. Individuals do not participate in running a civilization is in a case with a true democracy. Instead, we elect representatives to make decisions about governing. America's democracy is now reliant on voting on leaders at every level and on some laws. We do not get to vote on laws like how we are taxed, how we are regulated, and how we are educated. And that is a problem for the continuation of our democracy. Most of my life I voted with a mechanical counting machine. You showed up at the place where the voting occurred. You went into a shrouded booth pulled down little levers for the people and propositions that you wanted to vote for, and machine recorded the votes. There were election inspectors present to count the votes and additional inspectors to supervise counting the votes for the larger area. I trusted this system. I wife was an election inspector for many years, and she told me how rigorous vote counting was. Maybe five years ago

446

our mechanical machines disappeared, and we went to filling in spots on a paper ballot and scanning the ballot into a machine that allegedly counted every vote. However, the only person who knew what was being counted was the person who designed the software that operated the scanning machine. In the 2020 presidential election, for the first time in my life, significant voting could be done without proof that there was a person behind the vote. Voting by mail was widely allowed and I have no idea how the number of ballots mailed out was controlled. Did the printers print 250 million ballots for the 150 million people who normally vote in the presidential election?   I did a statistical analysis of the percent of registered voters in presidential election in the USA for the past 100 years (with the help of Google). The average turnout of voters for the past 100 years was less than 60 percent. The voter turnout for the 2020 presidential election was between 68 to 72 percent. (Google vacillated on the final percentage). In manufacturing, we used to use statistical process control on all of the widgets that we made. When measured quality parameter did something out of the ordinary, we had to investigate and identify an assignable cause. Something was incontrovertibly amiss in the 2020 elections and no government entity has offered an assignable cause. Essentially many Americans, including myself, now have complete distrust of our voting system.

Another major flaw in USA's democracy is the petitioning system required to get candidates' names on the ballot. This system, which is secret to most Americans, keeps candidates for office at every level restricted to political party cronies. Our candidates for elected office do not come from our best and brightest citizens; mostly they come from the least of our numbers. Political parties should be forced by

US law to accept applications for elected office from the general public, not just from party cronies. Applicants should present their curriculum vitae and their platform in print to the media. Public forums should be held for candidates to present their ideas prior to a primary vote for any elected office. The present system is incest. Candidates for elected office only come from the ranks of the political parties and mostly they are public employees already.

Another key reason for the finitude of American democracy is the loss of the Free Press. As I write this, the USA is involved in another elective war; this is one against a foreign country and it was initiated in retaliation for a terrorist assault on the USA, but not by the country that we are at war with. American politicians want to impose their ideology on other cultures and other countries and this is the root cause of the elective wars that have occurred in my lifetime. Our elective wars were not initiated in response to a physical attack on the United States. In any case, Americans are watching TV, the Internet, and some are actually reading newspapers, however every American knows that the so-called "news" that we are getting is tempered by the owners of the news monopolies. News monopolies are not regular monopolies; there are lots of newspapers, but the only ones that are still standing after the newspaper decimation of the past two decades, are owned by a handful of billionaires who buy newspapers and TV stations and other media outlets to aggrandize their public appearance. If the billionaire has a delusional bent, the output of his newspapers and media will similarly be delusional. The local newspaper in my area one that I get daily is one of 50 or so newspapers owned by a corporation that is controlled by one person. I do not know who controls the corporation, but the editor of my local newspaper announced when he took over the job that the paper will be dedicated to voicing opinions of designated minority factions. He stated unapologetically that he will distort reporting any news to favor his designated factions.

He has kept his promise. During our current war crisis, front page news on the local paper is about eviction of people for not paying their rent for 18 months. There was no mention about 12 Americans killed in the war that day. The TV and Internet behave in similar fashion. What is an American to do? I subscribe to three newspapers and watch three TV news presentations each day and try to pick elements of truth from each. This is a very difficult task.

A democracy can only exist if citizens make rational decisions when they allowed by voting to make such decisions; mostly this means election of people to public office. The biased media censor's news to promote their candidates and causes. The most powerful woman in America, has a curriculum vitae that includes jobs in retail, as a bartender OAC a big-city beer joint. She was promoted to a position of leadership in USA government by delusional media. The solution to media bias in US is complicated by our free will and a US government that allows billionaires to control the media. They buy what were originally real news-reporting newspapers and TV stations and transform them into entities to promote the proclivities of the billionaire owner. The solution may be to establish a law in USA, that all news media must report upfront the identification of their owner or biggest corporate shareholder. Just like mandated "made in China" labels that appear on all of our things. We should have: "owned by XXX" labels on every printed newspaper and stated at the beginning of every TV show or

Internet broadcast. America's civilization needs to know who is tempering the news. America needs the return of free press.

The demise of the United States of America is imminent because of these critical flaws; this is my opinion based upon my life observations. In 2021. Its finitude is only a short time away.

Finitude of the human species-The human species is incontrovertibly on its way to extinction, because too many humans use their cognition to overpower the nonconscious self-preservation instincts that we were born with. Like all living creatures, there is a genetic code in every living cell that makes each cell reproduce, and each animal to reproduce. This tendency for self-preservation is in every living creature. It may be the strongest urge produced by our non-conscience brain. It is manifested in the urge for nourishment, avoiding sensed dangers and in competing. Newborn babies cry when they want nourishment. There are genetic reasons for a baby's brain to do this. Similarly, pain makes us take action without thought. The self-defense urge is similar. Animals want to mate when their instincts tell them that it is time. Large wild animals may travel huge distances to satisfy their urge to mate. Animals continue to survive if they follow their genetic instincts. The human race is ignoring genetic instincts. They are not reproducing at a sufficient level to maintain the species.

Meaning of life – I completed at least three DVD courses on the meaning of life and each course ended with a lecture in double-speak. None of the distinguished philosophy teachers had a concise statement on the meaning of life.

They offered too many possibilities. What do I think the meaning of life to be? I pondered this deeply and I keep coming up with: The meaning of life is to follow our genetic instincts, to do what nature intended. We Catholics substitute "God" for nature. The meaning of life is acceptance of responsibilities: to God, to Self, to family, to society, to the environment, to sustainability. Life is a treasure; life is a joy; life is bliss; it has been a hoot.

Thus, I also have failed to come up with a simple concise statement, something that young people can use as a screen saver on their device. I am at the end of life and I have enjoyed it so much that I hate to leave it. It is like when you have a great vacation someplace and it is time to go home; you wish that you could stay longer. It is like attending a great concert by a philharmonic orchestra and you want to hear another great musical piece.

I loved every minute of my life (except maybe for a term of vector and tensor analysis in engineering school). The darkest event in my life was the death of my beloved wife of 50 years. However, as I mentioned previously, our last six months of complete togetherness was beyond description. God allowed me to care for her mostly at home. Because of my spirituality, I believe that she is still with me every day; she got a gig as my guardian angel. I have trained my conscious brain to accept this as one of my beliefs. Maybe the meaning of life is:

Life is what you make it.

I love life; my physical body is decaying and my current cancers will likely end my life, but:

451

It doesn't matter.

I have done everything; I have everything (that I need); I have been everyplace (that I cared to go to) and I have spirituality that transcends all. My beliefs, right or wrong, make my life meaningful no matter what happens and no matter what others may think. Countless Catholic martyrs forgave their executioners and died joyfully. Maybe the meaning of life is getting to know, to love and to control your conscious brain and cognition.

Maybe the meaning of life is to be constantly happy. You always have the big three: something to do, something to love, something to look forward to. I have all, even with my finitude pending. I am currently scheduled for six weeks of chemo and my fifth operation of the year, but I am working on a hot project at work; I have lots to do. I have lots to love: my family, my work, my friends, my colleagues. Finally I have something to look forward to: a good outcome on my research project, getting this book published and finishing the building of my lake breakwall.

How bad can death be? How bad will it be to never pay taxes again? How bad can it be to never hear lawnmowers, jet skis, leaf blowers, and vroom cars? How bad can it be to never be surrounded by inconsiderate people blathering in public on cell phones? How bad can it be to never have a too-soft tire on your bicycle when you go to use it? Thus I perceive some benefits in death. Plus, somehow, I will hopefully reconnect with the 250 departed people that I say"bonjour" to every day. Some of us who are big into spirituality believe that we live on as an eternal soul with

452

God. Nobody has ever risen from the dead to give out the details of afterlife except Christ and he is not telling.

Life does not have to be difficult in meaning.

Epilogue

This book is a call to arms. It started as a book about a dam at the outlet of the Great Lakes and northern USA. The dam is half owned by Canada, have by the USA, and the problem that I wanted to address was that the dam and its related ship canals and locks have destroyed all natural beaches on Lake Ontario and the ocean-going ships have brought in more than 150 invasive marine species that are destroying all of the Great Lakes. And the Great Lakes are 20% of the planet's freshwater. This is a significant environmental problem. I have been petitioning the government agencies that created the problem or 31 years to no avail. This book was intended to publicize the problem to the green-leaning world.

However, because I have many other causes, I decided to include other issues and make it a book about the most important life issues. The lake environmental problem would be just one of many environmental issues that our planet is facing. Then I learned about our extinction problem. It never occurred to me, that the human species is going extinct. I learned that it definitely is the path to extinction based upon what I learned in a molecular biology course that I took on DVD. Thus, the title of this book is now "Finitude" and it deals with finitude of oneself, the United States as a country, and the extinction of the human species. As we pointed out in this book, are some things that can be done by individuals to extend personal life, the life of the United States' democracy, and extinction of the human race. However, the latter requires cooperation on the part of many.

The purpose of this epilogue is to try and summarize and rank world issues to make them easier to address by those who will be around for a while. I am leaving but, but not by my will.

I tried to prioritize all of the issues that need to address, but the list was simply too long for this section, so we shortened the list to three action categories:

1. Environmental

2. Economic

3. Societal

We will conclude with a bit more on the meaning of life.

Environmental

The worldwide media has painted a doomsday picture regarding global warming: melting polar ice, rising seas, more powerful storms, etc. I have lived most of my life in the United States' northern Rust Belt, the area surrounding the Great Lakes. In my lifetime of 7+ decades, I admit to seeing less snow, but not less cold or unusual rain or wind. I am a skier and snow has been on the skimpy side for the past 10 years or so. I spent part of my life in Central Florida and the weather seems to be the same to me over my 36 years as a partial Florida resident. The incontrovertible evidence of warming in my opinion, is melting of glaciers and polar ice. It is also incontrovertible that the 2 to 3 billion vehicles in the world negatively affect the environment with their toxic exhaust.

I believe that vehicle emissions are the most significant factor that needs immediate attention. The world could reduce vehicle emissions by one third easily by mandating 50 miles per gallon minimum automobiles and 30 miles per gallon minimum small trucks, and banning gas hogs and unnecessary vehicles, like four-wheel play toys and cigarette boats. Thus, remedial action on clean air could start immediately. In the USA, a five dollar per gallon environmental tax on gasoline may do the job.

The burning of fossil fuels to produce energy is a significant source of greenhouse gas; so we are told by many experts. However, I believe that the world is going down the wrong path on reducing air toxins by replacing generator plants that burn fossil fuels with wind turbines, solar panels, and hydro energy production. None of these are available to meet our 24/7 electricity needs. Solar, wind, and hydro all depend on the vagaries of nature. The sun does not always shine everywhere; the wind does not regularly blow between 9 and 29 mph, and flowing water for hydropower depends on rainfall in the watershed of a body of water. Almost all rivers and the like that can supply energy to turn turbines are strong in the spring and run lower from then on. This energy source is not consistent.

What should happen to address the clean electricity issue is an international research program to evaluate potential solutions, like carbon capture,(piping effluent from natural gas-fired power plants to deep underground storage), geothermal heating steam (conventional steam turbines using the 10,000°F core of the earth to make steam), gas from biomass, (pets for power programs etc.), adiabatic buildings (no heat in or out), and none-waste nuclear power plants. The USA did a save-the-planet project during World War II. It was called and the Manhattan Project. The project team, which included a personal friend of mine, came up with the atomic bomb. This project result in turn ended all world wars since its demonstration near the end of World War II. It did the job. The Manhattan Project team took the best talent from all over the USA. The same could be done for clean energy.

In my opinion, the most grievous sin of mankind has been to strip the world's forests for lumber and fuel without replanting. We really need trees to supply the oxygen that we humans have evolved to depend on for life. Clearcutting of timber-quality trees has produced commercially useless scrub forests over most the United States. For example, the Upper Peninsula of Michigan is 30,000 square miles of scrub forest. Most of the forests in New York and Pennsylvania are useless scrub. The logging frenzy of the 1800s which built our cities destroyed most productive forests. This happened in many other countries. The world's forests need to be replenished and managed. This can be done by requiring that the 4 billion able-bodied adults in the world plant at least 100 trees each year in designated spots. I witnessed China do this with its 900 million people in my 1983 visit there. Proper forest management could possibly be done in USA by the 40 million people who are paid by the US government not to work. Planting trees can be done with less-than-perfect bodies.

Human and animal waste also needs to be addressed worldwide. Animal waste is not treated in the USA. We US citizens allow it in our potable water. This world needs another international research project to find better ways to detoxify our body and animal wastes. In USA, we settle solids, bubble air, and add poisons to our wastewater then pump it into our drinking water. Municipal and animal waste could go into a biomass gas generator that produces methane to burn in our power plants and the methane exhaust gas could be pumped to deep carbon capture. This is a project for the world's chemical engineering community.

I believe that there are viable solutions available to solve the world environmental issues. We do not have the project teams to do the work. The United Nations would be a candidate for the parent organization for the work. Participating countries would supply the talent and funding. I belong to an international standardization organization. We produce worldwide consensus standards. The organizational framework of standards organizations could be duplicated for our proposed clean energy and sewage-treatment projects.

Economics

This book or any book will never solve the economic theory dilemma: communism, socialism, free enterprise, capitalism, etc.-which one to use? There will never be agreement on a right answer. However, we can propose solutions on: jobs, the global economy, and monopolies that are achievable in short order.

The history of human life has demonstrated in every case that monopolies are bad for all parties except the instigators of a monopoly. They kill jobs and innovation and do nothing but create billionaires who often use their wealth to create other societal problems.

How can monopolization be stopped? In my lifetime, a witnessed monopolies form and grow because they bought the consent of elected leaders with direct payments or with disguised payments, such as campaign contributions and by funding candidate events such as $10,000 per plate dinners, paying for inauguration events, use of private jets for campaigning, and the like. I have a simple fix for influencing politicians to support monopolies.

1. Make paid government lobbyists illegal at all levels.

2. No campaign contributions or paid advertising from individuals or any entity over $100 per candidate. Also, individual candidates for elected offices cannot spend more than $10,000 of their personal wealth in a single campaign.

3. Establish a Covid-19-like advisory board with at least one member from every state that must vote on any and all mergers affecting companies with over $1 billion in annual sales. Board members must be 50% from the private sector and 50 % from the public sector.

4. The evils of monopolies must be taught in every school's civics class.

5. Outlaw acquisition companies: buying companies is not a legitimate business.

6. A 70% income tax on profits and companies with over 1 billion in sales when there are no more than two companies in the United States in a particular

market (like home centers, pharmacies, search engines, international social media, business software etc.).

What is even worse for the world's economy than monopolies is the so-called global economy. As mentioned in several chapters the term "global economy" is a euphemism for "made in China". This economic theory started as a way to make cheap products available in wealthy countries using the lowest-cost labor in the world to manufacture products. China and other countries mostly supplied to the lowest-cost labor. The absurd requirement of this economic model is that there will always be cheap transoceanic shipping to deliver the cheap products all over the world. Container ships are as seaworthy as a football stadium. They are also sitting ducks in any war. Crews of container ships can be terrorists or people carrying incurable contagions from around the world. The world has no control on who owns ships, who pilots ships, what is hidden in the holds of ships, and what horrible diseases and alien species the ships carry in their discharged bilge water. The entire concept is an absurdity, but the most significant harm that is done to the world's countries is their loss of any and all manufacturing capability. The USA in 2020, cannot defend itself in a war without Chinese-made armaments, ammunition, metals, electronics, chemicals, medical supplies, clothing, footwear, headgear, underwear etc. A war with China would last a fortnight.

Every country on the planet needs to develop their own manufacturing capability in critical areas so that their home technology and equipment capabilities are not lost. For example, the country that cannot make machine tools can never make anything; any building, any machine, any forming tools, anything, requires engineering materials and machine tools to shape parts. In 2020, certain critical engineering materials like some metals are not available in the United States.

I believe the solution to this existential problem is for all countries to have laws to make government entities only buy made-in-their-country goods. Every military could only buy within-country made armaments, vehicles, uniforms etc. This will give countries core essential technology and manufacturing capability.

The countries of the world also must develop job strategies for its citizens. The USA has none. China has one. In contrast, the USA federal government keeps expanding its pay for no work program to buy elections. This anti-job scam may be the reason why 40 million people in the United States have opted out of the workforce. Why work? If you know the system, you can get free money without working. Unfortunately, this system denies millions of people the happiness of something to do. It is cruelty and dishonesty beyond comprehension, but some people in elected office will do anything to any person to sustain the power and wealth of their elected office.

The free money, no work, issue could be easily solved by elected officials pondering the effects of what they are doing. Maybe the solution is a single term limit on all elected offices. Morality does not seem to work. Common sense does not seem to work. In 2020, every private sector business has help-wanted signs posted; yet the federal government keeps handing out federal funds to buy the votes of those who opt not to work. Many of the 40 million opt-out Americans have made obtaining free money from the government their job; it is now their life's work.

A wise country, and one that will survive, will have a strategy to provide meaningful work, jobs to all citizens. We had the Works Progress Administration (WPA) before World War II and they built incredible infrastructure and environmental projects. My father worked for the WPA during the US depression. It was meaningful work for all involved.

Societal issues

America's number one societal issue is the complete and absolute breakdown of public education of our youth. America's grammar and high schools fail in every international education metric. We discussed the details of this in the chapter on knowledge and learning, but the common denominator for America's existential education and governing failure is caused by not teaching and governing to the mean of a normal Gaussian distribution of intellects. US schools give special attention to the extremes of the intellect distribution; they cater to those with special needs, and to our geniuses and ignore the mean and both sides in the mean, the largest percentage of the population.

US schools also teach trite, like critical race theory, and ignore the essentials like reading, writing and math. America's woke movement is currently (2020) working on banning free speech, thought, and social behavior. This government-supported movement is producing a country of troubled people, uncomfortable people.

There is no discipline or order in public schools. I drove by a high school at dismissal time yesterday and it was like witnessing a Halloween costume contest. Teenage girls wore shredded jeans with bare midriff tops. Young boys dressed like I often dressed for Halloween trick-or-treat when I was 12 or 13, like a hobo. I read in today's evening news that the superintendent of a very large school system in my city publicly apologized to 700 high school students who walked out of class in protest of something that was posted on Facebook. He was subservient to the students; he is supposed to lead and be a model for students and a leader and model; he does not have to cave in to 12 and 13-year-old students.

The civilized and successful education systems of the world have students in uniforms that respect their leaders, teachers, and administrators. Responsible leaders and teachers teach and nurture students in life essentials. They do not embolden sophomoric actions and teach trite.

I believe that the only thing that can save America's young people from a life of inadequate knowledge is to change the system to allow the return to private schools who can meet international learning metrics. Public preschool, grammar, high school, and even vocational programs are a failed American experiment. They fail because they became controlled by local entities like school boards and labor unions often comprised of people with intentions other than the education of our youth. Also, interscholastic sports must be banned countrywide and replaced with intramural sports where all students can participate. Interscholastic sports aggrandize sports as more important than knowledge.

Another key requirement of a successful education system is vocational testing and guidance for each and every student. It was a must when I was growing up. It also got lost in America's public school system chaos.

Similar to America's failing education system is the failure of the public sector. Accountability is nonexistent in almost every elected position and in almost every public sector endeavor; legislators only come out at election time. In 60 years of petitioning elected officials at every level on all sorts of problems, I only had one town leader, one county manager, one state senator, one US senator, and one US President respond to my written letters for help in governmental matters. I sent countless letters and emails to countless elected officials. One time, I even mailed the same letter to one US senator from every state. I received zero replies.

Elected leaders at every level in USA seem to recuse themselves from accountability to the citizens that voted for them for public office. Why do they do this? Most of them are in their position for the power and wealth rather than to represent their electorate and meet their constituent's needs.

Hopefully, America's elected leaders will repent and start to communicate with their constituents after reading this book. They will stop giving public sector jobs to family and friends; they will govern to the mean of the normal distribution of constituents; they will stop taking money and gifts from organizations seeking unequal treatment under the law; judges who know that they are no good will resign. Police officers will acknowledge that the speeder that they stopped pays their salary and thus should be treated with a modicum of respect. Hopefully, this book will instill innate accountability in all of America's public sector employees and in all of America's elected officials; this is our vision.

Finally, a comment in the most existential problem that I have witnessed in my lifetime: social media. This term is a euphemism for ceding human cognition, civility, peace, order, and intellect, to a dry cell battery-operated device. What started as a college prank by a troubled student, has morphed into a pandemic-like brain disease. Addicted humans have no idea who they are, where they live or what they should be doing. Their brains tell them to hold their device in one hand and poke and swipe at it throughout the day and force-feed your non-conscious brain constant trite. As they claim on USA TV, for up to 7 hours per day.

Mindless dithering and meaningless posting have produced extinction of intellect in 2 billion or so former humans worldwide. They are enslaved to the so-called tech companies who make lines of code on a computer screen a product. An app is a group of code that can be sold by subscription so that people pay monthly to have cognition sucked from their brain. The 2 billion addicts no longer contribute to the production of food and durable goods because their full attention to a task has been ceded to their battery-operated device. In other words, participation in social media is a mental illness that has produced in situ extinction of civility and work ethic within the human species. Survival of the human species is not possible with the loss of so many intellects.

One more final comment on societal matters: An aid for men in preventing human extinction is to always cede the best of everything to your wife. This is one of the vicissitudes of life. Women rule the nest. It is in the nature of the cosmos.

The meaning of life

Those who still live, should take it upon themselves to each do their part in continuing the availability of life for future humans. My best data on declining fertility rate is my observation of declining families and children in the public spaces that I use. My observations convinced me that the current path of USA's civilization and other civilizations in our world is incontrovertibly extinction. I do not see enough babies today to give me confidence that the human species can survive.

The meaning of life unfortunately has become pleasures and possessions for many individuals. Having babies is not on their agenda for too many. However, if humans do not regain their 2.1 offspring per female, the human species will become extinct and it will not take all that long.

This book has followed the path of famous philosophers and sort of sidestepped the meaning of life issue. One philosophy professor summarized the meaning of life as responsibility: responsibility to Self, to family, to country, to the planet. A good friend summarized the meaning of life to be "accountability" to the same list as given for responsibility. A concept that I firmly believe in is that the meaning of life includes growing your talents. Using you birth gifts to help others.

All of my life's observations incontrovertibly show that possessions is definitely not the meaning of life. As I write

467

this, three of the richest billionaires on the planet are trying to outdo each other in rockets to outer space. They cannot get enough toys, enough possessions, enough publicity, and enough ego. How pathetic they are.

Consideration of others certainly is part of the meaning of life. Christ told us so. Love others: do unto other as you would have them do unto you.

Care of the planet, our environment, is certainly part of the meaning of life. Have we left the planet better off from our brief visit, or have we taken more than we added?

Overall, the meaning of life is what you make it. You control Self; you control your usable consciousness. Have you subdued "Self" sufficiently and given God a significant return on investment?
It's been a hoot; Thank you Lord.

My grave marker epithet